# HIT M[illegible]

**Brian Hughes MBE**

Brian Hughes has been the chief coach at the Collyhurst and Moston Lads Club in north Manchester for over forty-five years. He has produced boxers who have won British, Commonwealth, European and world championships. He has also coached a string of national champions at schoolboy, junior and senior levels, as well as Olympic representatives.

A Manchester United fan, he has written books about some of their greatest figures, including Tommy Taylor, Dennis Violet, Jimmy Murphy and Denis Law, as well as biographies of boxers Sugar Ray Robinson, Willie Pep, Howard Winstone, Jackie Brown, Johnny King and Jock McAvoy. Details of these books are available at www.brianhughesbooks.bravehost.com.

Awarded an MBE in 2000 for his services to boxing and the community, Brian lives in Manchester with his wife Rosemarie. He has three sons, a daughter and two grandsons, Joseph and George.

**Damian Hughes**

Damian Hughes, Brian's son, is the founder of change management consultancy LiquidThinker Ltd, helping individuals, teams and industries to achieve success. He is the author of four books: *Liquid Thinking*, *Liquid Leadership*, *The Survival Guide to Change* and *The Change Catalyst*.

He is a former England schoolboy footballer and Manchester United coach and works as a consultant and sports psychologist for the England and Great Britain rugby league teams and a number of professional sporting clubs. His innovative approach has been praised by Sir Richard Branson, Muhammad Ali, Sir Terry Leahy, Tiger Woods, Jonny Wilkinson and Sir Alex Ferguson.

He lives in Manchester with his wife Geraldine and son George. More information about Damian can be found at www.liquidthinker.com.

# HIT MAN

## The Thomas Hearns Story

*Brian & Damian Hughes*

MILO BOOKS

Published in December 2009 by Milo Books



ISBN: 9781903854907

Printed in Great Britain by CPI Mackays, Chatham ME5 8TD

MILO BOOKS LTD
The Old Weighbridge
Station Road
Wrea Green
Lancs PR4 2PH
United Kingdom
www.milobooks.com

# CONTENTS

# FOREWORD

by Jackie Kallen

I AM DELIGHTED to write the foreword for this fascinating book on the boxing career of the charismatic, dynamic and multi-talented Thomas Hearns. As a boxing manager, promoter, and former publicist, I owe my success to the wonderfully hot, smelly, crowded gym in Detroit, Michigan called Kronk which was originally opened in 1920. As a sports writer for a daily newspaper, I first walked into the basement gym in 1978 to write a story on a young Tommy Hearns and I quickly fell in love with the sport and signed on as the Kronk gym publicist. It was a unique experience because during this period, we witnessed the most exciting times in Detroit's sporting history and Tommy Hearns and Emanuel Steward were at the epicentre.

I cannot recommend a better guide to take you on this journey than Brian Hughes. I first met him in the late 1970s, when he visited the Kronk with a couple of his own English boxers. His appetite to learn about the coaching methods was voracious and prompted Emanuel Steward to offer him a coaching position at Kronk. Instead, he has taken on board all he could about our training methods, techniques and psychology and adapted it to his own stable of champions in England. I trust that you will be equally absorbed by the story of the Kronk gym's greatest student, Thomas "The Hitman" Hearns.

# INTRODUCTION

AS A SCHOOLBOY growing up in Manchester, England, in the 1940s and early 1950s, I loved to devour American boxing magazines. I would read them from cover to cover and immerse myself in the world of such wonderful craftsmen as Willie Pep, Sugar Ray Robinson and Archie Moore. I attempted to carry the lessons I learned from them into the ring and started to box in tournaments at the nearby American Air Force Base situated at Burtonwood, Warrington. After my own contests, I would sit at ringside and watch the other fighters. I became fascinated with the way that the American servicemen fought. They were so smooth, loose and relaxed, and delivered what I later learned were called "combination punches."

One boxer that caught my eye, and left an indelible impression on me, was Sergeant William Cherry. The beautiful way in which he dipped to the sides of his opponents and made them miss was something I had never seen British fighters do. He would punish their carelessness by delivering left hooks to both head and body. He was breathtaking. I put American coaches on a pedestal, and determined that I would learn their secrets.

In 1961, I started coaching youngsters at Collyhurst Lads Club, located a mile outside Manchester's city centre. I wanted to learn as much as I could about the noble art and started to correspond with several world-renowned trainers, writing hundreds of letters. I put their advice to good use. I also vowed to myself that if I ever got the opportunity, I would pay a visit to America to learn all I could about how they taught their fighters to be so successful in the ring.

In the mid 1970s, I read about a Detroit gym and a dynamic boxing coach named Emanuel Steward who was rearing two outstanding young prospects named Mickey Goodwin and Thomas Hearns. I contacted Emanuel to ask about the techniques and systems he was employing and within days he replied and sent me information about Kronk. This started a long-distance friendship which continued for many years. He was obviously very busy, but in 1980, I finally managed to take two of my young protégés, Ensley Bingham and Lance Williams, to Detroit, where we spent three weeks working alongside Emanuel and his team. We were the first British group to go there.

On a sweltering day, we made our way to the Kronk Gym. It was a huge building that had seen better times. The gym was in the bowels of the building. What hit you straight away was the humidity and the heat coming from overhead pipes despite the summer conditions outside. Just sitting was torture, with sweat coming from one's body like a running tap. The gym was spartan, with a ring in the middle of the room, one speedball and one heavy punchbag. Yet it was packed solid. We found out that each boxer had his own speedball, and when it was his turn he would retrieve the ball from his training bag and screw it to the overhead stand, then remove it when he had finished. On the four sides of the ring, four coaches supervised the sparring, shouting instructions. It was very intimidating. New members, or visitors like us from England, were greeted with shouts from the coaches of "New meat, new meat." We later found out that it meant, give them a welcome they wouldn't forget.

What I saw there simply amazed me. Most major gyms may have perhaps one or two world class stars within their team, but Emanuel Steward had, without any doubt, at least ten or twelve world class fighters and a seeming conveyor belt of youngsters being groomed to reach similar levels. I was privileged to witness some of the finest boxing talent in the world. I saw different styles, different movements and different punches delivered in combinations with lightning speed and accuracy. I also learned very quickly the American method of coaches using fight psychology on their aspiring boxers. There was a huge difference between a trainer and a coach (or teacher.) The trainer got the boxer prepared physically while the coach taught skills and technique. It was a fascinating and enlightening experience.

I made a number of visits to the Kronk, taking my own boxers there to gain experience and knowledge in this unique atmosphere, while all the time learning myself. During one trip, I was watching the sparring when the tall, stick-thin figure of Thomas Hearns appeared. After a brief bit of stretching he put on his sparring gloves and got in the ring to spar against a light-welterweight named Dujuan Johnson, who was known by the nickname "Mr Excitement." I watched with total absorption as they boxed four rounds of extraordinary ferocity and skill. It was better than any fight I had ever seen.

Hearns would go on to prove himself as one of the most loved and respected world champions and an all-time great. His story – and that of one of the best trainers in the world and his unique gym – has been a real pleasure to recount.

*Brian Hughes, M.B.E.*

# 1 THE DEFINING MOMENT

THERE IS A defining moment in every boxer's career. A moment when he faces a choice, both mentally and physically, about the direction in which his career is going to travel. Thomas Hearns's moment arrived on the steamy summer night of 18 August 1980. His actions would change his life and the boxing landscape for ever.

For a fleeting moment, the 11,500 crowd in Detroit's Joe Louis Arena were silenced as the lights dimmed and shrouded the arena in darkness. From what seemed a distance, the thudding bass of Survivor's "Eye of the Tiger" began to rise up, shaking the foundations and reigniting the carnival atmosphere that had infected the night air. Standing in the dark entrance to this gladiatorial bearpit, Thomas Hearns made his decision.

The spotlight searched and then bathed him in its glare. When the Detroit fans saw their idol, the decibel level rose to a crescendo as Hearns, wearing an all-white ensemble of shorts, shoes and dressing gown, quietly mouthed the words he had insisted be stitched into the back of his gown: "Let's Get It On." He looked ready to go. At the first sight of their man, the spectators erupted and, as he danced and shadowboxed his way towards the ring, the waves of emotion reached a stifling intensity. Lindy Lindell, a local boxing historian who was at the ringside, described the atmosphere as "a cauldron of undiluted throbbing noise. The noise shook the arena to its very foundations."

Waiting for him, like a hawk watching its prey move into range, was the impassive welterweight champion of the world: Jose "Pipino" Cuevas. The Mexican, wearing a simple green dressing gown, was a son of a butcher and assumed the same detached, clinical – and brutal – manner to his work as his father. He had made his way towards his workplace with a minimum of fuss or ceremony. He, too, appeared eager to dispense with the hype and keen to get down to business.

Indeed both fighters looked irritated by the extended formalities conducted by an immaculately-dressed Master of Ceremonies, Jimmy Lennon, Senior, who theatrically announced the contest between the Hit Man and the Butcher. Lennon summarised both fighters' backgrounds and pedigrees in some detail. Cuevas was twenty-three years old, Hearns two years his junior. Both men had enjoyed long winning streaks. The champion had lost only once in his last twenty-one fights and had held the world crown for over four years. A thunderous puncher, he had made eleven successful defences and just one of those fights had gone the full distance. Hearns had the perfect record of twenty-eight straight victories, with twenty-six opponents failing to hear the final bell. No-one expected this bout to go the distance.

When the referee, South Africa's Stanley Christodoulou, called the two men to the centre of the ring to issue his final instructions, they both strained at the leash. Hearns glared straight through Cuevas, who studiously ignored him and chose to study the canvas instead. By the time they momentarily retreated back to their corners to await the clang of the bell, there was a palpable buzz of excitement all around the arena.

Hearns came out quickly, eager to stamp his mark first. He adopted a side-on stance and his initial punches carried authority and accuracy. His left jab was thrown with speed and with a technique straight from the pages of a boxing textbook. His battle plan, honed over long months in the gym, was a secret no longer. His world title was going to be captured from long range; he didn't intend to win it in the trenches.

Cuevas's poker face, the blank, emotionless expression he had adopted throughout his reign, for once betrayed him. He appeared surprised by the tactics he faced. His plans had been accurately gauged by the boxing press who assumed that he would assume the role of aggressor, storming forward and forcing his challenger back, where he could unload his heavy artillery at the lithe body in front of him. For a fleeting moment his eyes registered confusion and Hearns saw it. He had made his decision. He knew what to do. The wily boxing veteran, Angelo Dundee, who was commentating for television also spotted it and counselled viewers, "This will be one heck of a fight. Don't take your eyes off the action for a second."

The first round passed in a blur as Hearns's footwork had kept the champion off-balance and unable to unleash his much vaunted power, especially his fearsome left hook. When the second round began, Hearns moved quickly and continued to carry the aggression. His eagerness contained some unnecessary anxiety and caused him to miss with a left jab and right cross. He recovered his poise and followed through with two powerful left jabs which drove Cuevas even further back into his corner. Cuevas summoned up an animal instinct and threw a right cross to the jaw of the onrushing challenger. The surge of adrenalin coursing through his veins ensured that Hearns showed no effects. Instead he offered a lethal left hook in response. Cuevas acknowledged this blunt-edged riposte with a grimace.

Hearns pawed a left jab at his opponent's left eye. It didn't contain any venom. Instead it was merely a decoy. Cuevas moved to catch the punch and missed the straight right cross which followed and fizzed with power and accuracy directly onto his unguarded cheekbone. The impact seemed to shake Pipino right down to his toe-nails. With his momentum carrying him forward, Hearns positioned his feet and delivered a second right cross. The fog which enveloped Cuevas slowed his reactions and although he saw it coming and attempted to protect himself by bringing his guard up toward his chin his body refused to move at the speed he willed it to. The snaking right whipped from the right shoulder and smashed directly into Cuevas' face and the courageous world champion pitched violently head first straight towards the canvas, his impressive reign as world champion coming to a brutal and final conclusion.

It seemed like the perfect finish. As referee Christodoulou went through the count, the Mexican warrior drew on his reserves of courage and strength and amazingly staggered to his feet before the South African official reached "nine." He looked dazed and disorientated, the surprise having as devastating an effect as the speed and brutality of Hearns's assault. Yet despite his legs looking like they were crafted from rubber, his fighting instincts remained intact and he nodded his assent to continue.

Hearns had watched this and his focus was as intense as a laser beam. He stepped forward with an increased menace when Lupe Sanchez, Cuevas's manager, trainer and a father figure to the Mexican dynamo, sensed the risk to his charge's welfare and rushed to the ring with the white towel of surrender. Christodoulou intervened between the two men and waved his arms to signal exactly that, after five minutes and thirty-nine seconds of a chilling and calculated attack. Detroit had a new world champion. Hilmer Kenty, Hearns's stablemate and himself a world champion, was first through the ropes to embrace him, and he held his hand aloft.

Ringside press observers were stunned. They reported to their sports desks that they had witnessed one of the most compressive victories ever recorded in a world championship contest. They said, with little exaggeration, that Hearns's total annihilation of the fearsome Mexican champion would send vibrations rippling throughout the boxing world. Purists marvelled at the manner in which he achieved his task, showing textbook boxing skills allied with devastatingly accurate punching. They all agreed that they had witnessed the arrival of a new superstar.

# 2 DETROIT

GRAND JUNCTION IS an American crossroads, a speck on the map in what is traditionally cattle and cotton country. Named after the intersection of two major rail lines, the Memphis and Charleston and the Mississippi and Ohio, it sits in rural Tennessee, an hour east of Memphis, on the edge of the land of the Delta Blues. For a brief period, during the American Civil War, it was of vital strategic importance in the bloody conflict between North and South. Those days are long forgotten. Travellers now barely notice as they pass through this tiny settlement of 300 souls. For most, it is not even a brief stop on the long road to somewhere else.

A baby christened Thomas was born poor and black in Grand Junction on 18 October 1958, the first son to Thomas and Lois Jackson. The couple already had two young girls. Despite being named after his father, Thomas would later say that he had no memories of the man, as his parents separated not long after his arrival. Lois married again and her turbulent relationship with John Hearns, whose surname young Thomas adopted, produced six children in successive years before Lois was, once again, forced to face a future as a single mother when John Hearns walked out on the family. The experience had a traumatic effect on Thomas, who watched the violent disagreements between his parents often spiral out of control. His mother's subsequent decision to relocate her young brood to Detroit, Michigan, in search of better prospects of employment would have an equally significant impact.

It was the wrong time to move to the Motor City. Once the engine of America's auto industry, the home of Chrysler, Ford and General Motors, Detroit was in near-terminal decline. In the words of *TIME* magazine, "In the auto boom after World War II, Detroit put the U.S. on wheels as it had never been before. Prosperity seemed bound to go on forever – but it didn't ..." Car production peaked in 1955, to be followed three years later by a recession that saw twenty per cent of the workforce unemployed. Automation and consolidation by the carmakers meant fewer jobs and major firms like Packard, Hudson and Studebaker closed down. The middle classes packed and headed for the suburbs, taking their taxes with them and so depleting the city coffers, while at the same time poor black migrants still arrived from the South, seeking work that was no longer there. Never pretty, large sections of the city began to take on the appearance of warzones. One of the few bright spots was Berry Gordy's Motown Record Corporation, whose production line brought soul music to the world and put the city on the map for more than urban decay and crime.

Lois Hearns settled on Helen Street, one of the most deprived areas of the notorious east side, where she had to raise nine children alone. The area was, she admitted, "pretty bad," and the move exacerbated the feelings of isolation which the timid Thomas felt. He retreated to the safety of his bedroom and chose to lose himself in the emerging world of television, spending hours watching cartoons and films. Lois soon noticed that there was one particular sport that her oldest son showed a great deal of interest in. She would watch with wry amusement as he sat entranced before the grainy images of boxing matches on their black and white set, before insisting that his younger brothers shadow box with him. His hero was Muhammad Ali, then in his incomparable prime and the reigning heavyweight champion, before his refusal to accept the draft to serve in the Armed Forces led to him being stripped of his title. Like many a young Detroit blood, Thomas dreamed of being the next Ali.

Lois was a worker. She held down two jobs, working as a beautician and a store clerk to support her brood. "I'd come home and I'd sit down and say, 'Lord, I'm so *tired*,' and little Tommy would come up to me and hug me and kiss me and say, 'I'm sorry, mama,'" she told *Sports Illustrated*. "He said some day he'd buy me all the things I never had – a house of my own and nice clothes. 'I'm going to fill your lap up with money,' he told me."

That was unlikely. The American Dream seemed to have passed by inner-city Detroit, where black unemployment stood at around sixteen per cent. In the summer of 1967, the city erupted in five days of bloody rioting, sparked by a police raid on an illegal drinking dive on the west side. At the end of the carnage, forty-three people were dead, 467 were injured and more than 2,000 buildings had been burned to the ground. The "white flight" from Detroit became a stampede, businessmen and investors turned away in terror and the city slumped further into economic decline.

One of the few options open to black youths was to join a neighbourhood street gang, which at least offered some solidarity amid the menace of the ghetto. The most infamous in young Thomas Hearns's area were the Errol Flynns and the Latin Dogs, but eventually he joined a smaller clique who called themselves the Helen Hoods, after Helen Street. Strict local codes dictated that gang members could not encroach on another's patch. Hearns struggled to understand this logic and, after a number of near misses when chased by rivals for trespassing, gang membership quickly lost its appeal.

Some of his friends had already taken up boxing. So one day after school, ten-year-old Hearns came home and asked Lois for her permission to join the King Solomon Recreation Center's boxing gymnasium, which was near their home. Her heart sank. Boxing summoned up nightmare visions of broken noses, swollen eyes and slurred speech. But Thomas went along with his friends Elijah and Phil Hannah and Ricky and Lester Hill and was instantly hooked. "When I walked in the gym on that first night," he later reflected, "I fell in love with boxing." Hearns' nascent love affair blossomed for the next three years and he became part of the gym furniture. The confidence which the sport gave him surged into all parts of his life and helped him to settle into the city environment.

"Mom told me not to be a fighter," Hearns later told an interviewer. "But I was the oldest boy and I would holler and carry on something awful. And when that didn't work, I'd just stand around looking all sad-eyed until I got my way. But the thing is, man, what my mama didn't realise, what nobody felt but me, was that I always *knew* I would make it to the top. I knew it. It came to me in a dream while I was sitting on a playground swing." His education fizzled out and he never completed school. But boxing drew his full attention. "I worked and studied it. If I got beat up or did something sloppy in the gym, I'd go home and work on it until I got it right. Man, it was hard work. It's got to become – um, something you do without thinking about it – instinct."

If Detroit was a gang town, it was also a boxing town. Two of the greatest champions the sport had ever produced – some would say *the* greatest – had perfected their trade there. First came Joe Louis, the great "Brown Bomber," like Hearns a country boy whose family fled north to escape rural poverty. His flashing fists cut a swathe to the heavyweight title, which he went on to defend twenty-five times, a record that may never be surpassed. Louis was succeeded, perhaps even superseded, by Sugar Ray Robinson, whose name became a byword for boxing brilliance. Robinson had it all: grace, courage, power, speed, and the looks of a movie star. Any young boxer had only to ask, and his elders would bore him for hours with stories of the prowess of these two legends of the ring.

After a couple of years, however, Frank Hill, the trainer at King Solomon and a man young Thomas liked and respected, retired, and so Hearns was forced to look for a new home. The Kronk Recreation Center was located on a barren corner of McGraw Street on the west side of Detroit, in one of the city's poorest districts. The area had once housed a large Polish community, and the two-storey brick building took its name from a local politician of Polish heritage, John F. Kronk. Now most of its clientele was black. Presiding over the young charges that fought in its basement gym was Emanuel Steward, a dynamic young coach who had been one of America's top amateur boxers before becoming a trainer at the Kronk in 1970.

A year after arriving there, Steward was distinctly unimpressed when a stick-thin thirteen-year-old came asking for membership. "First time I saw this kid was in 1970," Steward later told *Boxing Illustrated*. "He was just eleven years old and he'd already been fighting for a year. He was so scrawny it was awful; he weighted fifty-five pounds and his little old boxing pants were falling right off." Instead, it was Walter Smith, the gym's sixty-four-year-old veteran trainer, who saw beyond the initial impression. "Even as a beginner, Hearns had fortitude," Smith said. "Thomas listened attentively. He respected his elders. That made a difference."

Smith spoke up for the young man and Steward knew better than to ignore his sage counsel. He began to take notice of the quiet youngster who never seemed to miss training. Steward observed that despite his reticence, Thomas was frightened of nobody. "I'd never seen anybody, ever, who had no fear of nobody," Steward would recount. "But Tommy didn't." He would box whoever his trainer suggested and never questioned advice. He was also inordinately determined. He had to take two buses to reach the gym from his east side home yet would never miss a training session. After gym training, he enjoyed playing basketball with his close group of friends but avoided trouble with the police. He seemed to live and breathe boxing. Steward discovered that Hearns had a steely resolution. He wanted to win championships, as this was the route to the fame and riches that would allow him to look after his mother and siblings. He idolised his mother and recognised the sacrifices she had made for her young family. He told the Kronk trainer that he was determined to achieve these goals and would do whatever it took. Steward smiled at the youngster's fierce determination and agreed to help him make it a reality.

In 1974, Hearns took his first steps to future glory by winning both the Midwest Regional Junior Olympics and the Michigan Golden Gloves. Two years later, aged seventeen, he lost a points decision to the stylish amateur star Howard Davis, who went on to represent the USA at the 1976 Montreal Olympics and to take the lightweight gold medal and the trophy for Most Outstanding Boxer. To his great disappointment, it meant that Hearns missed out on Olympic selection, though he garnished his reputation further by reaching the National Golden Gloves final, which he lost to future world light-welterweight champion Aaron "The Hawk" Pryor. A year later, at the National Amateur Tournament, held at the Ohio State Fair in Columbus, Hearns finally earned the country's number one ranking at light-welterweight. He went on to represent the USA on twelve occasions, his only defeat coming with a debatable 3-2 points decision to hometown favourite Syamsul Anwar in the President's Cup tournament of champions in Jakarta, Indonesia. He won both the National AAU and Golden Gloves championships in the 139lb class, in the AAU final outpointing Ohio's Bobby Joe Young, a top amateur who would later become a well-respected professional.

Touring with the US team took Hearns not only to Asia but to Europe, and broadened his limited horizons. But success inside the ring came at the expense of failure outside. After repeating eleventh grade and beginning his senior year at North-eastern High School, Hearns finally dropped out. "I was nearly eighteen years old and had to make a decision. It was either boxing or high school. Although I had no problem with school, I knew that I must become completely focused on my boxing career." In later years, however, Hearns attempted to make up for his decision and privately picked up his studies again by employing a tutor in English, speech and maths. He later reflected, "Although I was only a C student and may not have been able to pass every test, what I learned in school, on the streets and in the gym, I think I can handle almost anything that comes up."

# 3 THE KRONK

IT WOULD NOT be glib to suggest that Emanuel Steward was the father figure Tommy Hearns never had. It was a role he fulfilled for many youngsters who shuffled through the doors of his sweatbox gymnasium in one of the roughest areas of one of the roughest cities in the USA, and Hearns himself would say Steward was "like a daddy." Their partnership would become one of the most successful in boxing.

Emanuel Steward was born on the 7 July 1944, in Welch, West Virginia, the first child to coal miner Manuel Steward and his wife Catherine. He would later be joined by his sisters Diana and Lavern. He was a small child but robust and energetic, and enjoyed a happy, outdoorsy childhood, picking strawberries in the hills and fishing in the creek. At the age of eight, Emanuel was given boxing gloves as a Christmas present and fell in love with the sport. His dad taught him the basics and he soon spent every spare moment throwing punches.

At the age of eleven, however, little Manny's happy youth was marred when his parents divorced. In a journey that would be repeated by Lois Hearns ten years later, his mother took him and his sisters from West Virginia to Detroit to begin a new life in the Motor City. "I'll never forget that long, lonely ride," said Steward of their train journey. "We left on Friday and it rained the whole trip. We got to Detroit on a Saturday evening. I thought it was the end of the world – not knowing that it was the beginning of a new life."

Catherine found employment in a small factory. Eager to assume the mantle of the family's senior male and to help with the finances, Emanuel also worked in a variety of odd jobs. He delivered newspapers and groceries before school and used his holidays to work as a garden landscaper and ice-cream salesman. In 1958, at the age of fourteen, he also joined the Brewster Recreation Center, where the great Joe Louis had learned to box. The stalwart coaches, Jimmy Myland and Festus Trice, taught Steward the fundamentals of the sport, and everything about the gym, from the smell of liniment to the rat-a-tat of the speedballs, fascinated him. He approached boxing with the same dedication he had shown to his family finances and, fighting as Little Sonny Steward and later as Sonny Boy Steward, he quickly won consecutive Detroit Parks and Recreation Junior Tournament championships in 1959 and 1960. A smooth, sharp counter-hitter, he set his long-term sights on turning professional in order to support his family, and moved to the Lasky Recreation Center, where he came under the tutelage of Bill O'Brien. This precipitated further success and in 1961 he won the Detroit Golden Gloves title.

A year later, he travelled to Chicago to represent his city in the National Tournament of Champions. This was his first trip outside of Michigan and his first experience of staying in a hotel and dining in a restaurant. When he returned to Detroit, he viewed his neighbourhood through different eyes and felt that there was a better world for him and his family. His determination was further strengthened that he would work hard to give them a better standard of living. When he graduated as an honour student in the springtime of 1962, a local politician named Coleman Young, later to become the first black mayor of Detroit, helped the budding boxing star get a full-time job in a small plant which supplied motor parts.

During this time, when combining his familial duties with boxing, Steward was unexpectedly bitten by the coaching bug, which would come to shape his whole life and define the future success which he dreamed about. He had started to date local beauty Marie Steele and, eager to please her, had agreed to take her younger brother, Elbert, along to the gym. He began coaching Elbert and some of his friends and found that he enjoyed it. When he entered Elbert and three other young members into a local amateur tournament, he was thrilled that all four won. When he repeated this feat again the following year, he began to consider his potential as a coach.

The boxers that Steward most admired were the great stylists, the men who moved with poise and rhythm, who made the Noble Art a thing of beauty and grace. Men like Willie Pep, the little defensive genius, and the peerless Ray Robinson. He learned from watching them, and in turn began to pass that knowledge on. His own boxing career still continued on its upward trajectory and when he returned again to Chicago, he scored four consecutive victories before upsetting the heavy favourite to win the 1963 National Golden Gloves Tournament of Champions in the bantamweight division. He was the only Detroit boxer to win an individual championship and, due to the overall team performance, he was a member of the squad which won Detroit the team title, the first in twenty years.

Nineteen sixty-four was a seminal year in the life of Emanuel Steward. He married Marie and changed jobs to work for the Detroit Edison Company, first as a construction labourer and later as a journeyman electrician and then a special projects director. He was still keen to box as a pro but failed to find "a good, honest professional manager who I can trust to look after my interests. I looked everywhere around the professional scene for the kind of manager who I could blend with and trust," he said. "I wasn't satisfied so I decided to stay as an amateur." The reality, however, was that his family and new employment took precedence over the sport, and he took a sabbatical from boxing from 1966 until 1969. Instead he committed his energies to his job at Edison and to night classes in electrical engineering at the Henry Ford Community College. He was determined to rise up the ladder from labouring to more technical jobs.

During the summer of 1969, his fifteen-year-old half brother, James, arrived from West Virginia to live in Detroit with Emanuel's young family, which included two new daughters, Sylvia and Sylvette, in their little brick bungalow in a quiet subdivision on the city's west side. Soon after his arrival, James asked his older brother if he would teach him to box. This request seemed to reignite the passion for the sport he had enjoyed with Elbert, and after five months of dedicated training at the nearby John F. Kronk Recreation Center, Emanuel proudly watched James win the 1970 subnovice Detroit Golden Gloves. His ideas about training young fighters, which had lain dormant for three years, re-emerged, and he began to think seriously about his potential as a trainer. Should he commit?

A year later, he accepted the position as a part-time coach at the Kronk. He took training sessions starting at five o'clock every evening and was paid $35 a week. The new commitment towards developing young boxers had a profound impact on Steward. He brimmed with enthusiasm and knowledge and ideas about how to approach the sport. This paid an immediate – and spectacular – dividend. He entered James and six other young novices – Wilson Bell, James Stokes, Robert Johnson, Desmond Hickman, Jerry Cook and Louis Holland – into the 1971 Golden Gloves tournament. Amazingly the team scored twenty-one consecutive victories and won the team title. Soon after this success, however, most of the team were obliged to join the armed services to fight in Vietnam. When Wilson Bell, who had joined the Marines, came home on leave, he called to see his coach and presented him with the Marines' red and gold dressing gown. Although the Kronk colours at this time were traditionally blue and gold, Steward introduced a further change by deciding that the boxing team would adopt the red, gold and blue colours from now on.

Emanuel's career within the corporate world of Detroit Edison also continued to rise. By now a master electrician, he was offered a lucrative promotion to special projects director, a job created specifically for him by company chiefs and paying a healthy $500 a week. However, after a great deal of soul searching – and after overcoming the protests of his wife – he resigned from Detroit Edison in March 1972. Although he was risking the security and salary he had worked so hard to attain, boxing offered something that the daily nine-to-five couldn't: unlimited possibility. "I decided to see how far I could go in this," he later said. "My dream was to take an amateur team and make it nationally famous." Professional boxing, at that time, was a long way from his thoughts.

His first task was to search for fresh faces in the wake of the break-up of his successful Golden Gloves squad. He soon unearthed a prodigy down at the Kronk. "I stopped by the area between the swimming pool and the locker room and I saw [Bernard] Mays sitting there waiting to go swimming like the other kids," recalled Steward. "I remembered him because he was a friend of Louis Holland ... and I asked him if he wanted to learn to box. I wanted to teach somebody to box and I started picking him up every day."

Even as a schoolboy, Bernard Mays was something special. Indeed a number of Detroit boxing fans still maintain that Mays remains Steward's greatest work. "We spent hours and hours in the gym and I taught him every little trick I knew. I developed a tremendous fighting machine. When he had his first amateur fight, everybody was shocked at how good he was." Mays was so exceptional that he enjoyed the rare status of headlining amateur tournaments at just twelve years old. By the time he was fourteen,

Mays had won National AAU Junior Olympic championships and was being tipped for the very top. His blend of speed and power earned him the nickname "Superbad." Because of the publicity Mays generated, Steward found that he was inundated by hundreds of young men applying to attend the Kronk boxing sessions. "He was a twelve-year-old that was knocking out sixteen-year-olds. Every kid in the city and their parents were coming to Kronk because of this one kid I taught."

Steward always considered Mays to be the most talented boxer he ever coached. "He was a combination of Joe Louis and Ray Robinson; he could box and punch and didn't waste motion," said the trainer. "He could slip a punch by half an inch on either side and then nail you."As an amateur he won two National Junior Olympic championships and reportedly lost only once in over two hundred amateur contests. "Whenever he fought," Steward later recalled, "the first two or three rows would be packed with managers and trainers from all over America. Some would bring their boxers to watch Superbad perform."

Robert Tyus, one of the original Kronk members and winner of two national titles, confirmed Steward's assessment of his gym mate. "It gave me chills just to talk about him. Mays was like Sugar Ray Robinson reborn. He had it all." Another early Kronk member, John Johnson, recalled his prowess: "Superbad Mays was the most awesome fighter I ever saw. He could devour you with his speed and power, which were something special. Bernard had a wicked left hook that would take the breath from your body." Mays also left an indelible impression on Hearns, who later told *Detroit News*'s Fred Girard that he almost quit boxing rather than face the prospect of sparring with his stellar gym mate every day. "Bernard Mays was the king," said Hearns. "I dreaded going into the gym every day because I knew I'd have to get in the ring with Bernard and it was going to be a brawl."

However, by the time he was all of sixteen, Steward's multi-talented star was no longer showing up for training. He smoked dope and had secretly become addicted to malt liquor. Yet for a time he continued to shine in the ring, destroying every opponent. Having been too young to try out for the 1976 Olympic team, he decided not to wait for the 1980 Moscow Games but to turn pro. In 1978, he left the familiar environment of the Kronk, where Steward had nagged him about his lifestyle, and eventually signed up with Elbert Hatchett, an Oakland County attorney. Hatchett acknowledged the grooming Steward had provided and recalled that "Mays fought like Joe Louis but at middleweight. He was a beautiful classic boxer." Superbad turned pro and, in twenty-eight professional bouts, would lose only once, but his alcoholism meant he never fulfilled his seemingly limitless potential. At the age of just thirty-three, he died from a combination of diabetes and chronic pancreatitis. He was buried in an unmarked grave in Mount Hazel, a small cemetery on Detroit's far west side in March 1994.

THE DETERMINATION AND focus with which Steward approached his new boxing career was typical of his nature. His was not, however, a path without pitfalls. On one particularly difficult occasion, when his revenue streams trickled to a halt, he invested his life's savings of $26,000 into a range of cosmetics which he began to sell into Detroit businesses. Steward's charming patter and work ethic ensured that he enjoyed a decent return on his investment until the company that produced the products went bankrupt. Without missing a beat, he turned his attention to selling life and health insurance instead. He was determined that his wife and young children would not suffer while he chased his dreams.

In the evenings, he worked on his growing squad of boxers in his own unique way. The boys were expected to behave well, to dress neatly when representing the club and to cheer for each other at every tournament, but at the same time the competition within the gym was ferocious. Sparring could be brutal and no-one was spared, while the heating was kept turned up to more than ninety degrees to produce an airless, sweltering, survival-of-the-fittest atmosphere. The Kronk, noted *Sports Illustrated* writer Will Nack "became a kind of paradox: a Boy Scout troop set in a Darwinian laboratory." Or as Steward himself said, "Those guys at Kronk, they're not fighting just to get better. They're fighting for their very lives."

And fight they could. The team began to dominate the local boxing scene and soon won several amateur titles. Despite his workload, Steward took on electrical jobs during his spare time to pay for trips to tournaments outside Detroit. Impressed by his efforts, Mayor Coleman A. Young appointed a team to help find funding, while wealthy benefactors including Sam LaFata, Doctor Richard Rasmussen and his wife Patricia, along with Harvey Moore, who became Emanuel's best friend, also came forward to offer support. In 1977, this allowed Steward to become the full-time boxing coach at the Kronk. Soon the Kronk was brimmed with an array of young talent never seen in Detroit – or perhaps any other American city – before. Anywhere between sixty and ninety young men would be under his supervision at any one time and the Kronk Boxing Team soon became the envy of other coaches and managers. But Steward was reluctant to relinquish any of his power, which he feared could be diluted by jealous rivals. He therefore did most of the coaching single-handedly and still did electrical jobs at weekends in order to pay for trips to tournaments outside of Detroit.

Around this time, Steward encountered another young man who would play an important role in his later life. He had established a friendship with Dave Jacobs, who laid claim to discovering a prodigy named Ray Leonard. Jacobs escorted his young charge to the Kronk for a few weeks' sparring while Leonard tried to win a berth on the Olympic team. Steward soon saw that in ability he rivalled even Superbad Mays.

"Ray Leonard was one of those once-in-a-lifetime boxers," recalled Steward. "When he trained at Kronk, he was brilliant. He had plenty of sparring partners and everyone liked him." Indeed, Steward later called him "the most naturally gifted kid I've seen," more gifted even than the wondrous Mays. He would go on to win the Olympic gold – and to haunt Steward and Thomas Hearns in the future. For all his ability, young Hearns was not yet the star even in his own gym.

Mickey "Sneaky Pea" Goodwin, a hard-punching and popular young white fighter, was another Kronk stalwart and would play an important part in persuading Steward that it was time to invade the professional ranks. Goodwin quickly learned the rudiments of the sport and this, allied with his fierce determination, meant he enjoyed a gilded amateur career, reportedly scoring twenty-one first-round knockouts in his first twenty-one contests. His all-action, slam-bang style made him a huge attraction on the circuit and he ended his amateur career with seventy-five victories against just ten defeats, scoring fifty-four knockouts. When he entered the trials for the 1976 Olympic team, he battled his way through to the Midwest Regionals but received a badly cut eye which ended his dream. Steward knew that Goodwin would not wait another four years for the next Games and so elected to turn him professional. Thomas Hearns, too, was ready, so on 25 November 1977, Sneaky Pea and Hearns made their professional debuts at the Olympia Stadium in downtown Detroit, for Steward's new management vehicle, Escot Boxing Enterprises.

Professional boxing is a different beast to the amateur game, and to help make the transition, Steward recruited Don Thibodeaux, a heavily built, no-nonsense character who sported long hair and an untamed red beard and was the only white trainer at the Kronk. He joined the team when Hearns was an amateur; Steward had seen him at a boxing tournament and invited him to the Kronk. "We really have some great kids developing," Steward enthused. "We have a great team." He told Thibodeaux to come down and witness it for himself. "The Kronk had a great boxing team and were winning all kinds of tournaments," Thibodeaux recalled. "When Goodwin, Hearns and Hilmer Kenty all turned professional, Emanuel wanted me to help with their training. Stuart Kirshenbaum [a podiatrist and a Michigan State Boxing Commissioner] taught me a lot about stopping cuts and so I also became the cut man for the Kronk team."

Besides Thibodeaux, there were lesser-known trainers helping out, men such as Floyd Logan, John Brown, Taylor Smith, Luther Burgess, Walter Smith and Bill Miller. All were understated figures and not often seen on television but they were ever-present in the gym, working on the production line of young talent that continued to emerge. Thibodeaux was charged with coaching Hearns, especially when Steward was away. He was a quietly effective coach, especially skilled on boxing technique. He was instrumental in polishing Hearns's right-hand punching. "I had him throw punches from the ball of his foot, twisting it so it would go straight," he explained. "I would shout that Thomas should throw his punch from the ball of his foot to his knee, through to his hips, through to his shoulder and twist his fist and reach forward and land it." Thibodeaux emphasised that Hearns should use his punches like a whip, a weapon that would prove invaluable within the paid ranks.

Steward and Thibodeaux planned to sell Hearns's debut to network television. Olympians Ray Leonard and Howard Davis had signed TV deals on turning pro and were already making a lot of money. Armed with a scrapbook of Hearns's amateur exploits, the Detroit pair drove to New York to approach the network moguls. It was a long day. "CBS told me not to bother," Steward later told *Sports Illustrated*. "NBC let me talk to them, but they weren't interested in getting involved in a fighter. With

ABC I got into the lobby. I talked by phone with someone upstairs, and he told me to leave the scrapbook. I never did. I wanted to cry. Don and I said the hell with it and went back home."

# 4 THE MOTOR CITY COBRA

AMONG BOXING AFICIONADOS, there is a school of thought that suggests that the truly big punchers are born with the inherent gift known as knockout power. Joe Louis, one of the great knockout artists, belonged within this camp but advocated regular practice. "Even a pianist has to work on his technique," reasoned the Brown Bomber. When he was first starting out his amateur career, there were few who would have put Thomas Hearns in this bracket. Hearns was firmly classed as a hit-and-run merchant and this reputation preceded him.

Two thousand of Detroit's more ardent boxing followers watched with interest and surprise on the rain-swept evening of 25 November 1977 when Hearns, the latest member of the Kronk production line of amateur champions, made his professional start in the Olympia Stadium. It was a "no-name" card, showcasing aspiring youngsters and debutants. Hearns faced Cincinnati veteran Jerome Hill and despatched him with ease inside two rounds. Although Hill was regarded as a suitable journeyman opponent who would not extend Hearns too much, the manner of victory was impressive. From being perceived as a fleet-footed boxer who relied upon pure boxing skill and finesse, he appeared to have added another string to his bow by developing his two-fisted punching power. Emanuel Steward would later say that he used $2,000 life savings, took a second mortgage on his house to get another $2,300 and borrowed more from his grandfather and some friends in order to stage this first promotion. It would turn out to be a very wise investment.

Hearns's second contest took place shortly before Christmas at a $50 dinner-boxing tournament at the Hillcrest Country Club in Mount Clemens, Michigan. He had little trouble disposing of Jerry Strickland, who had a decidedly modest record of seven wins, one draw and twenty-four losses. Hearns made it twenty-five by finishing the hapless Strickland in three rounds. Nine days later he added another win by stopping three-fight novice Willie Wren, from Toledo, inside three rounds.

In January of 1978, Hearns travelled to Knoxville, in his birth state of Tennessee, where he was matched against Anthony House from Winston-Salem, North Carolina. House had fought in the ill-fated, scandal-ridden United States Boxing Championship Tournament which had been promoted by Don King. He had boxed professionally fourteen times and had lost three of his last four bouts inside three rounds. It was no surprise when Hearns flattened the gun-shy House in two rounds.

Steward was eager to keep his latest protégé active, and less than two weeks later, 2,058 fans turned out in Detroit to witness his burgeoning punching power. He didn't disappoint, achieving another third round stoppage against Philadelphia's Robert Adams, who had a record of five wins in ten fights. For Hearns' next outing, Steward personally selected Milwaukee's Billy Goodwin. Goodwin had an unspectacular win-lose-draw record of 13-20-2 but, standing at six feet two inches, with a long, ranging jab, he represented a new challenge for Hearns to master. Two thousand eight hundred fans saw the eager pupil settle to his task and solve the puzzle in two rounds. Steward was impressed by the adaptability of his charge. Another bonus was that the Michigan boxing fans were beginning to get right behind Hearns and his Kronk teammates.

The fights kept coming at a dizzying pace. In Detroit's Cobo Arena, Ray Fields was stopped in two rounds – and afterwards declared that he would never fight again. Philadelphia's tough 'Skinny' Jimmy Rothwell, the Pennsylvania area welterweight champion, was next up and the local boxing press mused that he would offer a tougher assignment on the learning curve. Rothwell had even been chosen as Prospect of the Month by *Ring* magazine but Hearns breezed past him with nonchalance, ending the contest within one minute and forty-nine seconds of the opening bell.

Hearns was quickly acquiring admirers and the clamour to see his fights grew. Raul Aguirre, a tough, seasoned Mexican with a respectable record of nineteen wins in thirty-five, was brought in as a warm-up before Hearns faced Trinidad's Eddie Marcelle two weeks later. Aguirre was routinely dismantled in three rounds. Marcelle watched the fight with interest.

Eddie Marcelle was a fighter who had mixed in world class. Although he had lost to the highly rated Jo Kimpuani and the hot prospect Scott Clark, he had beaten Johnny Gant, who was ranked number eight by the World Boxing Association. In the days preceding the Hearns fight, the Trinidadian told the Detroit newspapers that he was planning "to severely punish" the local hero and cautioned Emanuel Steward "for selecting him as a sacrificial lamb." His talk certainly did the trick amongst the public as 6,125 fans came to see if he could live up to his hype. Thomas Hearns, however, simply would not allow it. After outboxing Marcelle for the first couple of rounds, he opened up in the third with a dazzling three-punch combination to the body, followed by a searing right cross to the side of the head which put Marcelle on the canvas for the full count. This was an impressive victory and what was more pleasing for Emanuel Steward was the way Hearns was developing his right cross.

ON 1 SEPTEMBER 1978, the secret of Thomas Hearns was revealed to a wider world. *Boxing News* was a British magazine, but as the only weekly boxing publication in the world, and also the most authoritative, it was avidly read among the international fight fraternity. On page seventeen, Eric Armit, who wrote a regular page highlighting the fight scene around the globe, led his column with the story of the new sensation:

### HOTSHOT HEARNS IS CHASING SUGAR RAY

Thomas Hearns is really setting Detroit alight. The 6ft 2in welterweight is now 11-0 with all 11 opponents stopped within the first three rounds.

His recent victory over Eddie Marcelle drew a full house of over 6,000 for Ron Moore at the Olympic Stadium and Tommy was mobbed by excited fans when he knocked Marcelle out in round two.

The Detroit press has also taken to Hearns and he gets plenty of coverage which is helping to stoke the fires.

Hearns' manager Ed [sic] Stewart will now take his boy on the road for a couple of bouts and the aim will be to take on a few of Sugar Ray Leonard's victims to try and better the ex-Olympian's effort. Not that Tommy needs to follow in Leonard's footsteps: the kid from Detroit looks to be a class fighter in his own right, and rates as good a chance as Leonard, Howard Davis or Aaron Pryor.

It was accompanied by a posed photograph of Hearns stripped to the waist, with his impossibly long arms, a youthful yet vaguely menacing half-smile, and the makings of what would become his trademark laser-beam stare.

It was around this period that one of boxing's fabled encounters was nearly prematurely delivered. Thomas Hearns was scheduled to meet Sugar Ray Leonard. Leonard's attorney, Mike Trainer, agreed to the bout and a press conference was arranged to witness the penning of contracts. The purse had already been settled:

Leonard, who had fought about the same number of pro bouts as Hearns, was to receive $100,000 and Hearns a meagre $12,500. The venue would be the Providence Civic Center and the date would be September 1978. Although Hearns had never been seen on national television, golden boy Leonard had secured a million dollar deal with the ABC television network, who were eager to broadcast. Before it could be announced, however, Angelo Dundee stepped in to stop the match. The wise old trainer told Leonard and his advisers to be patient and wait for a couple of years. He presciently declared that when these two did eventually meet in the ring, they would earn millions.

Hearns turned his attentions elsewhere. Four weeks after his victory over Marcelle, he was matched with the experienced Bruce Finch of Ohio. The craggy-faced Finch had a record of 14-1-2, which enticed 5,718 Detroit fight fans to the city's Olympia venue, where they screamed themselves hoarse in support of Hearns. He responded by hammering Finch to defeat inside three rounds. (Finch would prove his pedigree four years later when he fought Sugar Ray Leonard for the undisputed world welterweight championship.) In its next rankings, *Boxing News* had Hearns as number six welterweight contender to the two champions, Carlos Palomino and Jose Cuevas, based on his "run of quick wins". Wilfred Benitez was the top contender, while Ray Leonard was number twelve.

A month after the Finch fight, and a week before his twentieth birthday, Hearns was paired against Venezuela's Pedro Rojas. The South American was the Central American welterweight champion and had been ranked just one place behind Hearns in the *Boxing News* ratings. Burly and square-jawed, he claimed a record of twenty-four wins in twenty-five fights and was a rugged hombre: one pre-bout training session with a Detroit sparring partner had to be halted after it exploded into a furious exchange of fouls. "Since nobody seemed to know if the Detroiter could take a punch," reported Eddie Cool in *Boxing News*, "the South

American speculated that he would find out for himself by launching a two-handed assault as soon as the first bell sounded."

It was a big mistake. Within twenty seconds, Hearns had jarred the Venezuelan with a left hook followed by his trademark overhand right. A thundering follow-up volley saw the referee step in to give the beleaguered Rojas a standing eight count. This was followed by another volley, and another standing count, before the referee wisely waved it over. The "fight" had lasted just sixty-nine seconds. "We want Leonard, we want Leonard," chanted the crowd of 8,547, as Sugar Ray and his famous trainer, Angelo Dundee, watched from first-row seats. "Hearns was devastating," conceded Dundee, "but it was over too quick." Others speculated that Dundee had learned plenty – not least to keep his fighter a million miles from the Detroit bomber. Promoter Bob Arum, also there as a spectator, lavished praise on Hearns. "Nobody, not even heavyweights, hit that fast and that hard," he said.

"Twenty years from now," said Hearns afterwards, "I want people to compare the fighters of today to Tommy Hearns."

Within a couple of days, Hearns's backers were in Arum's New York office, asking for fights against a series of opponents, including Carlos Palomino, Pipino Cuevas and even middleweight champion Hugo Corro. Present at the meeting was the twenty-eight-year-old promoter Don Majeski, who had booked Rojas for the Detroit bout. Majeski was later asked how good Hearns really was. Could he take a punch? Did he have heart? Could he stand up under rough going?

"How can you tell," replied Majeski, "about a guy who knocks out his opponents in less than three rounds?"

HEARNS WAS SETTING the division on fire, but he faced a series of formidable hurdles if he was to realise his dream of a world title. Indeed the welterweights at this time constituted the fiercest division in boxing, with an array of competitive talent not seen for decades. As in most weight classes, there were two "world" champions: Pipino Cuevas for the World Boxing Association, and Carlos Palomino for the World Boxing Council. Both were Mexican, though Palomino had lived most of his life in California, and both were redoubtable. Cuevas, the younger of the two, was a puncher of terrifying power who had put several opponents in hospital. His defence was porous but his opponents were usually so busy trying to protect themselves that it didn't matter. Palomino was a more considered fighter, a cool, experienced body puncher with a sold chin and excellent stamina.

The leading contenders for their titles were, if anything, even more daunting. Wilfred Benitez, a young Puerto Rican of preternatural wizardry, had already won a version of the light-welterweight title and was now on the warpath for more honours. Roberto "Hands of Stone" Duran, the undisputed lightweight champion who had lost only once in almost seventy contests, was also moving up the divisions and had his dark eyes set on the welterweight crown. And TV darling Sugar Ray Leonard was matching Hearns step for step in his inexorable march up the rankings.

Certainly there was no time to take the foot off the pedal, and Steward arranged for Rudy Barro, a California-based Filipino, to give Hearns another test in his boxing education. He had fought in fifty contests before facing the Motor City sensation at the Cobo Arena and his confidence was high after winning his last four bouts. His record included an impressive array of opponents including Seansak Mauangsurin, Alfonzo Frazer, Esteban DeJesus, Andy Price, Bruce Curry, Monroe Brooks and Pete Ranzany, all highly regarded world operators or champions.

Nearly eight thousand spectators watched as Hearns had to box past the third round for the first time in his career. He remained composed throughout the fight and watched for a glimpse of an opening. It came after fifty-one seconds of the fourth round when he unloaded a powerful right cross-left hook combination, followed up by another devastating right cross, which duly ended matters.

This was his final contest of 1978 and his fourteenth consecutive inside-the-distance victory. He was declared *Boxing Illustrated's* number five welterweight and number six by the World Boxing Council. *Boxing Illustrated* also afforded him their "progress of the year" honour. Someone had also coined a nickname for him that seemed to fit his sinewy frame and his deadly striking ability: the Motor City Cobra.

WHEN CLYDE GRAY climbed into the ring on 13 January 1979, he was nearing the twilight of a long career. Gray, from Toronto, Canada, was a throwback to the skilled craftsmen of yesteryear. The reigning Commonwealth welterweight champion, he had fought, and lost, three times for the world title. He had first taken the great champion Jose Napoles the full fifteen rounds and had then lost another fifteen-round war to Angel Espada when tilting for his World Boxing Association title. Finally, he had succumbed within two rounds in his third challenge, against the murderous Pipino Cuevas. His record on the night he met the twenty-year-old Hearns was sixty victories from sixty-seven bouts, and he was riding a wave of seven consecutive victories.

A crowd of 11,115 paid the largest indoor gate in Michigan boxing history – $149,909 – to see Hearns prove himself to be a genuine contender in one of the best bouts seen at the Olympic in years. Gray looked to be in serious trouble in rounds five and seven, taking heavy punches on the ropes and bleeding heavily from the nose, but employed all of his vast experience to hang around until the second minute of the tenth round, when Hearns managed to connect with a lightning fast, crunching right cross which dropped him to the canvas. Displaying the courage which had become his trademark, Gray beat the count but referee Arthur Mercante showed him mercy by sensibly waving his arms to save the brave Canadian from a certain knockout.

The performance had a significant impact on a number of different levels. The win was a big psychological fillip for Hearns, who acknowledged that it was his toughest fight to date. "Going ten rounds was the best thing that could have happened. It proved to all the doubters who said I could only go for four or five rounds," said a jubilant Hearns, even as he stuffed his right hand in an ice bucket, the result of an injury suffered in the early rounds. "Although Gray never hurt me, I've never been as tired in a fight." At the end of nine rounds, referee Mercante and Judge Ken Offert had Hearns winning every round. The Canadian judge, Chuck Williams scored the bout 6-2-1 in favour of Hearns. This victory also made the promoters outside of Detroit really sit up and pay attention to the figures which were being generated by the Detroit youngster. Finally, the trade press also felt that the victory was a watershed and started to seriously tout Hearns to fight for a world title. One reporter remarked that he had "the cold eyes, under the ring arc lights, of a professional assassin," and someone had coined another nickname for him, "the Detroit Hit Man."

Gray, who claimed he had wrenched a muscle in his back when he stumbled in the fourth round, was effusive in his praise for his opponent but his words were laced with realism. He acknowledged, "He's a very good boxer and a really tremendous puncher. I believe he's good enough to become a world champion, but his people should take their time with him. His left hand gave me a lot of trouble; it stopped me from getting inside and punching to his body. I never saw the punch that put me down, he was so fast and precise." Gray cautioned Hearns against meeting Jose "Pipino" Cuevas, the WBA champion, who he felt would be too strong for him. "Cuevas is a heavier puncher than I am and Hearns wouldn't be able to push him off like he did to me. Hearns needs room to punch, Cuevas doesn't."

Emanuel Steward shared Gray's sense of caution and believed that his charge needed further schooling. Hearns, however, possessed that impetuousness of youth and thought that he was ready to box for a title straight away. He told reporters that he had a preference for a fight against Wilfred Benitez, who six days after the Gray fight dethroned WBC welter champ Carlos Palomino by decision in Puerto Rico. Steward played down this championship talk both privately and publicly and urged Hearns to concentrate on his next foe, "Slithering" Sammy Ruckard. He had thirty-nine professional fights on his record although he had emerged victorious on just nineteen occasions. Clyde Gray had beaten Ruckard in three rounds but he had extended a number of class fighters like Johnny Gant and Floyd Mayweather, the father of the future world welterweight champion of the same name. Hearns took heed of his trainer's warnings and stopped his South Carolina-based opponent in eight one-sided rounds.

Five weeks later, CBS television screened highlights of Hearns' next bout against the Continental American welterweight champion, Segundo Murillo. Murillo was ranked eighth by the WBC and had never been stopped, but all his contests had been in his native Ecuador and it was difficult to assess his true quality. Hearns was announced as the "Motor City Cobra," partly out of sensitivity about the "Hit Man" tag in a city with the highest murder rate in the USA. Hearns himself was uncomfortable with the Hit Man tag. "I don't try to kill nobody," he protested. He could have fooled Murillo, who was decked five times and stopped in eight rounds. The delayed highlights of the fight, at the Olympic, were broadcast nationally, bringing Hearns to a nationwide audience.

The media was now buzzing about him, and the New York Boxing Writers' Association named him Fighter of the Year and Emanuel Steward, Manager of the Year. Argentina's Daniel

Gonzalez was offered $15,000 to face Hearns, while Harold Weston was offered $40,000, Pete Ranzany $35,000. Former champion Carlos Palomino was reportedly tempted by the $100,000 being cited and his successor, Wilfred Benitez, was even more so by the reported $500,000. Despite this, however, the eventual answer from each one was an emphatic refusal. It was a testimony to Hearns's rising confidence that he was not intimidated by the prospect of facing any of these fighters. In one interview, he was asked about the possible outcome of a match against the WBA welterweight king, Pipino Cuevas. Hearns said he had watched Cuevas on quite a few occasions and declared, "I can knock him out." He explained that "he's a converted southpaw and he stands square on, making him easy to hit. I'm too big and fast for him, and would outbox him until I saw an opening for my straight right to the chin, which would finish him."

Before he could deliver on this boast, he had to resume the business of building his reputation. His next bout, on 20 April, was against the tough Philadelphian brawler Alfonso Hayman. Hayman, a thirty-year-old veteran, had fought thirty-six times and had knocked out the respectable Johnny Gant and had also fought the likes of Clyde Gray and Maurice Hope, the world's best light-middleweight. He entered the ring buoyed by victories in his previous two fights. Hearns's burgeoning reputation meant that CBS decided that this was the appropriate time to broadcast the young star for his live television debut.

Unfortunately, Hearns was suffering from a bout of flu and his fists were troubling him, although he kept this quiet. It turned out to be a competitive contest, with Hayman exceeding himself while Hearns seemed content to box beautifully and avoid looking for a spectacular finish. In round six, Hearns again hurt his right hand and it bothered him for the rest of the contest. The fight went the full ten rounds and Hearns took a lopsided decision, while the spectators gave both fighters a standing ovation at the final bell.

Even though it was the first time Hearns had failed to finish a professional opponent, the feedback from CBS and its viewers was also encouraging. The gutsy Hayman finished with his left eye swollen tight shut, his right badly marked and his lips puffy and bloodied; one report said he "looked like he had been run over by a train." But he had taken the Hit Man the distance for the first time in his pro career.

Of his injured hand, Hearns said, "It's happened a few times before, a couple of times in the amateurs and once since turning pro. But never this bad. I was thinking about my knockout streak going into the last round but I wasn't about to break my hand going for it."

JUST THIRTY-THREE days later, Hearns and Steward travelled to Las Vegas to prepare for a twelve-rounder against the classy New York boxer Harold Weston, who had reconsidered the $40,000 offer he had been made earlier in the year. Their 20 May fight, in the Dunes Hotel, was advertised in neon lights on the Strip. Hearns accepted this honour in laconic manner. Asked if he was excited at seeing his name in lights on the huge marquees outside the hotel, he told reporters, "It makes no difference to me. I'm here to fight."

He seemed more animated when he was taken to the home of Joe Louis, the former all-time-great heavyweight champion. Louis had been reared in the same Detroit neighbourhood as Thomas forty-five years earlier and, though Hearns was much too young to have seen him box, he often listened to the wheelchair-bound champion reminisce. When he was asked about his thoughts, Hearns said, "Louis wasn't really my hero but I look up to him for what he has achieved throughout his life."

The Weston bout, transmitted live by NBC, was dubbed as Hearns's baptism of fire, as Weston was perceived as a considerable step up in class from his previous opponents. He was coming off a fifteen-round points loss to Wilfred Benitez, the WBC welterweight champion, with whom he had previously fought a hotly disputed draw. He had also challenged WBC champ Pipino Cuevas but had been stopped in round nine after suffering a broken jaw. Weston was more of a boxer than a puncher but he had stopped the concrete-jawed middleweight Vito Antuofermo with a cut eye. Apart from his considerable boxing talent, twenty-seven-year-old Weston was a qualified accountant and a fashion model.

The New Yorker was dismissive about his opponent. "I saw Hearns in Philadelphia against a ham-and-egg fighter called Alfonso Hayman and I walked out after five rounds suffering from boredom," he said, provocatively. "Hearns will try and knock me out, but after he finds out who I am, then his whole plan will have to change. He will then get discouraged when there is nothing he will be able to do to counter me. There will be no alternative. I will beat him and give him a lesson in boxing."

The boxing gods, however, were with the younger man. On the morning of the fight, Hearns bet $15 on a keno card at the Dunes and won $1,900. And when he stepped into the ring, he soon made Weston's boasts look hollow. Instead of looking straight for the knockout, he defied Weston's predictions by boxing behind his left jab. Then, towards the end of round one, he caught Weston with his trademark right and followed up with a wicked barrage of punches to have his man in trouble on the ropes. Weston tried slipping and countering but was repeatedly beaten to the punch and his left eyebrow began to puff up. Another inside-the-distance win seemed imminent.

But Weston could take a punch, and he had heart as well as skill. By the middle rounds he was getting through with hooks to the body and even making the six-inch taller Hearns give ground. Hearns seemed to be suffering in the desert heat and things were getting interesting. But at the end of six absorbing rounds, it was clear that Weston had a serious problem with his right eye. His cornerman, Howie Albert, held his hand up in front of Weston's bruised face as he sat on his stool.

"How many?" he asked.

"How many what?" said Weston.

"Fingers."

"Howie, I can't even see your hand."

The ringside doctor insisted that the fight be stopped and Albert concurred, saying he wasn't prepared to let his fighter suffer possible serious injury. Weston was diagnosed as suffering a detached retina.

Weston's injury meant he would never box again. The New Yorker was bitter about this decision, claiming he had been thumbed in his right eye, albeit accidentally, even as his left eye was swelling shut. "I think the Good Lord wants Thomas Hearns to win the world championship and it was He who took my vision away for a moment," he said. "Tommy Hearns is nothing. He is not in the same punching bracket as Pipino Cuevas."

The bout had raised the first serious question marks about Hearns. Did he have the stamina? Did he have a Plan B when his opponent failed to fall over early? Then there were the unavoidable, and not always flattering, comparisons with the other rising star of the division: On the same night Hearns scored his nineteenth straight win, Ray Leonard had made it twenty-two wins in a row against rugged Mexican middleweight Marcos Geraldo in Baton Rouge, Louisiana. And the Sugarman was already lined up for a title fight, against Benitez in November. He had beaten Hearns to the punch. But in June, Hearns made the cover of *Boxing Illustrated*, under the mischievous headline "Sweeter Than 'Sugar.'" A rivalry was building.

Emanuel Steward refused to ease up on Hearns's education process, and five weeks after the Weston fight he faced another solid opponent. Bruce Curry, from Marlin, Texas, was the reigning North American Boxing Federation light-welterweight champion.

The older brother of Don Curry, who would achieve boxing fame in the 1980s, he had enjoyed an impressive amateur career, winning four Fort Worth Golden Gloves championships, two Golden Gloves State titles, winning the Western Olympic Trials at light-welterweight and coming runner-up to Ray Leonard in the 1976 Olympic boxing trials. Since turning professional he had fought twenty-four times and had stopped the well-regarded Monroe Brooks to win the NABF title. His most famous contest had been a ten-rounder against Puerto Rican wonder boy Wilfred Benitez: Curry had lost a split decision but had knocked down the normally untouchable Benitez three times. He had also beaten England's capable Clinton McKenzie and was certainly no pushover.

In an action-packed battle, Hearns suffered a cut over his left eye but had too much power and too many ideas for Curry, beating him comprehensively in three rounds. The finish was reminiscent of a young Ray Robinson, with Hearns lashing in a frightening barrage of hooks to leave his opponent semi-conscious on the canvas. The victory would look even better after Curry went on to win the WBC light-welterweight championship four years later. "He butted me," said Hearns afterwards, "and when I felt blood running down my face I knew it was do-or-die, and I did."

HEARNS WAS IN demand. His victories were publicised across America and the powerful promotional organizations wanted him to appear on their tournaments. The success he had achieved was all the more creditable because Hearns had not started his career with a big build-up or an Olympic medal, like Sugar Ray Leonard or Howard Davis. He did not possess their natural charm or charisma either. Hearns was only too happy to put a great deal of his success down to Emanuel Steward. Although Steward was also new to the professional ranks, he had studied the boxing business and done a magnificent job in guiding Hearns to top ten contender status without the power of Don King or Bob Arum. King, for one, would later go through his patented turn-your-head routine by trying to woo Hearns's mother Lois with promises of limousines, hotel suites and mink coats, in an attempt to sign the boxer away from Steward, without success.

It was around this time that many fans who were taking an interest in Hearns began asking why a stylish boxer who had scored only twelve stoppages in an amateur career of 155 wins in 163 bouts was suddenly knocking out his opponents. Steward was happy to answer. "As an amateur, Thomas was a super boxer. He would be up on his toes and he would jab, jab, jab, throw his right occasionally and dance away. I don't think he ever threw a left hook." Detroit-based reporters supported this viewpoint. As an amateur boxer, he had been compared to a young Cassius Clay, before his three-and-a-half-year exile. It was during the countless hours spent in the gym, under the tutelage of Steward, that he learned how to throw a left hook and use its leverage. Steward suggested that the power had always been there but he simply didn't know how to use it. With Steward's guidance an astonishing transformation was taking place. Thomas Hearns turned into one of the most chilling knockout punchers in the history of boxing.

Four weeks after his blowout of Bruce Curry, Hearns returned to action again and demonstrated his increasing awareness of how to utilise his punching power by stopping a trial-horse named Mao De La Rosa within a couple of rounds in Detroit. It was clear he was ready to step to the highest level.

# 5 THE CONMAN

THE WORLD OF professional boxing has always been dominated and controlled by a small number of rich, powerful promoters. The rules of the game are brutally simple. The power brokers want to tie up the outstanding fighters to long-term contracts under their promotional banner. Then they use these boxers as pawns in their negotiations with the television moguls, who pay the big money which maintains the status quo of rich, powerful promoters. Their *modus operandi* therefore tends to be consistent. They flatter and seduce young fighters, whispering in their ears and promising the moon. They persuade and cajole managers to sign exclusive agreements to their promotional banner and, once they have these, they are then in a position of strength to offer the fighter whatever they deem acceptable without having to compete on the open-market. Like bookmakers, it is rare to see a poor promoter.

When Thomas Hearns was climbing to the summit of the boxing mountain, the richest, most powerful promoters were Don King, Bob Arum and, in later years, the Duva family. Emanuel Steward knew how boxing politics worked and didn't want Hearns to be tied down like the majority of the world champions and contenders. Ray Leonard, who maintained his own independence under the canny guidance of his lawyer, Mike Trainer, had proved that there could be exceptions to the rule, and Steward was keen to buck the trend too. The tournaments in which Hearns and the other Kronk fighters had appeared early in their careers were promoted by Steward's friends. Although they offered great experience, the pay was meagre because they didn't have television networks backing the shows.

However, as Hearns's reputation continued to grow, Steward knew that he had to think bigger. He looked around to find the right promoter or organization for his team. In the late 1970s, one new company was blowing through the boxing scene like a breath of fresh air. Muhammad Ali Professional Sports (MAPS) bore the name of the great champion though he had little do with it, merely lending his name for a fee. The use of his name brought crucial credibility both with athletes and, more importantly, with the big TV network officials. MAPS was actually run by a flash, fast-living, thirty-seven-year-old entrepreneur named Harold Smith. Smith – whose real name was Ross Fields but who had used a number of aliases during his life – was an imposing character, a former track athlete who stood over six feet tall and wore a bushy beard. His customary attire was blue jeans, cotton workshirt, cowboy boots, a wide Stetson hat and gold-rimmed sunglasses.

When he first set up MAPS, Smith's past was regarded as something of a mystery. In the 1960s, he had worked alongside Stokely Carmichael in the Civil Rights movement. In the 1970s, he emerged as a Las Vegas promoter. His association with Muhammad Ali began in 1977 when he sponsored some amateur athletic meetings and forged a friendship with the heavyweight legend. In 1979, he announced that he was intending to join the professional side of the boxing business. He flaunted large amounts of money as if to prove his intent.

Smith enjoyed the trappings of wealth and lived a lifestyle which was the envy of Hollywood movie stars, owning homes in fashionable sections of southern California such as Pacific Palisades, where President Reagan had lived, and Marina del Rey. He possessed an $84,000 cabin cruiser, a fleet of top-of-the-range cars, including a brown Cadillac and custom-made Cadillac convertible, a stable of thoroughbred racehorses and even a private Beechcraft jet. Smith was also a high stakes gambler. It was not unusual for him to bet $10,000 on a single horse race or $25,000 on a roll of a roulette wheel in Vegas. When he was asked where his money came from, Smith would offer two stock responses: "My wife is very wealthy," or, "I make money the old-fashioned way: I earn it."

Smith's entry into big-time boxing promotion was not subtle. He used money – and lots of it. Stories soon began to emerge of his extravagance. He carried flight bags full of cash around and offered boxers over four or five times as much money as the other promoters. Incredibly, Smith seemed able to outbid both Don King and Bob Arum, and they were worried. On one occasion, Smith flew to Las Vegas, which was rapidly emerging as the new capital of top-class boxing, to watch the Ray Leonard–Wilfred Benitez welterweight title fight. There he arranged a meeting with Larry Holmes in his suite, where Smith attempted to lure the world heavyweight champion away from Don King. Holmes recounted how Smith offered him $1.5 million to sign an exclusive contract with MAPS. Smith entered the suite with two Wells Fargo cashier cheques for $500,000 each and another half million in $50 and $100 bills. The meeting was aborted when a snarling Don King arrived and chased Smith out of the suite shouting threats and obscenities.

In September 1979, Hearns and Steward boarded a Los Angeles-bound aircraft for a meeting with Smith. MAPS had widened its scope from amateur boxing into professional boxing and was keen to meet with the potential superstar and his trainer. When the two Detroiters entered the offices, Smith was seated behind his expensive desk whilst his executive secretary, Teri Key, busied herself making drinks for the guests. The MAPS office was in keeping with Smith's sense of style, with lush wall-to-wall carpeting and potted plants.

One long hallway had huge portraits of Muhammad Ali and other boxers whom Smith had signed to box under the umbrella of MAPS. The views along Ocean Park Boulevard into Santa Monica were also spectacular. It all looked impressive to Hearns and Steward.

Smith immediately got down to business and stunned Hearns when he started discussing purse money. He offered $500,000 for Hearns to challenge World Boxing Association welterweight champion Jose Cuevas and offered a cash incentive of $100,000 if they signed a contract with immediate effect. They signed straight away. In their book *Empire of Deceit*, former United States attorney's special prosecutor Dean Allison and reporter Bruce B. Henderson recount how Smith sent someone over to Wells Fargo to get a cashier's cheque. At this point in his career, Hearns's biggest payday had been $85,000. The stunned boxer walked out of Smith's office that same morning with more than that in his pockets and another $400,000 to come, with an additional $25,000 for training expenses.

The three men left in a limo and headed for the airport. They boarded Smith's private jet and headed straight to Mexico City, where Smith had arranged a meeting with Cuevas and his manager. After some brief discussions, in which Cuevas was offered a purse of over $1 million, he too signed the contract to fight Hearns in Detroit.

The deal struck in Santa Monica had included an agreement that Hearns would box on a MAPS tournament at the Los Angeles Sports Arena, against Mexico's Jose Figueroa. The tournament was also a benefit night for the legendary Joe Louis, who was confined to a wheelchair after a stroke. Figueroa had a respectable record of thirty-one wins with only four losses. On a previous MAPS promotion, he had fought against the highly regarded Andy "The Hawk" Price, who was managed by the soul singer Marvin Gaye. Although Price was awarded the decision, it was unpopular and the crowd booed and threw chairs. Figueroa was seen as an opponent who would offer a stern test for any up-and-coming young fighter. Most significantly, however, he had been stopped by Pipino Cuevas in a recent fight and Hearns and Steward saw it as an opportunity to benchmark themselves against the champion, his imminent foe. Hearns knocked out the Mexican inside three rounds.

What no one knew was the source of Smith's seeming endless supply of cash: embezzlement. Smith had charmed, bribed and cajoled two accomplices, Ben Lewis and Sammie Marshall, to help steal money from their employer, Wells Fargo, the nation's eleventh largest bank. They did it by exploiting a flaw within the bank's computerised systems. "Every bank that has branches in different places has to have some kind of system for allowing customers to walk into a branch that's not theirs and draw money on the account," explained Dean Allison, who prosecuted Smith for embezzlement. "Obviously, the bank has to have a way to keep track of the money that a customer takes out of Branch B, when the customers account is in Branch A. At Wells Fargo, that system was called the branch settlement system." Each transaction would generate two halves of a ticket, one for the branch where the money was withdrawn, the other for the branch where the customer's account was held. These two halves had to be entered into a computer and matched up within ten days, to balance the debit and credit on the same account. The flaw was that, if a corrupt employee charged both parts of the ticket at the *same* branch, money could flow out of the system without being flagged up.

In 1979, the first year of the fraud, Smith stole about $200,000. A year later, it was up to a staggering $15 million, the biggest fraud of its kind in US history up to that point. It was this stolen money that allowed MAPS to break into big-time boxing promotion.

THOMAS HEARNS'S NEXT next fight was held back home in Detroit, where Steward had picked a particularly tough opponent. Saensak Muangsurin, from Thailand, was a former two-time WBC light-welterweight champion. After an early and successful career in

Muay Thai, he converted to boxing and won the world championship in only his third professional fight, a record. He made a number of successful defences but had lost his last two bouts and appeared to be on the slide. Nevertheless, he was still a difficult proposition, a rugged southpaw with an awkward style. Six thousand fans came along to watch Hearns celebrate his coming-of-age twenty-first birthday. Muangsurin's tactics seemed to be to retreat to the ropes and lure Hearns onto counters, but the Detroit sensation simply hit too fast and too hard for him and he took a sustained beating. Referee Bobby Watson stopped the massacre in the third round as the game but dazed Thai, having already been dropped by a straight right, took a vicious pounding in his own corner.

In November, Hearns ventured to New Orleans, where he was matched against Mike Colbert, a fully-fledged middleweight. It was a genuine risk. Colbert, whose real name was Adolfo Akil, once had visions of becoming the middleweight champion, but fell to Marvin Hagler in a bout that was actually recognised in Massachusetts – though only Massachusetts – as for the world title. Losing to Hagler was no disgrace and Colbert had beaten a number of middles on the fringes of title contention. He would also be, physically, the biggest opponent Hearns had fought to date.

In an absorbing ten-rounder, Hearns was declared a clear winner on points. While he was not able to get Colbert out of there, he broke the heavier man's jaw and proved that he could go in the trenches with a big, strong, experienced middleweight. It was a smart piece of matchmaking, and now everyone was sitting up and taking notice of the young Detroit wonder.

NINETEEN EIGHTY WAS intended to be Hearns's coronation year. His ascension began in February, when he boxed "Fighting" Jim Richards, from Curacao. Details of Richards' fight record were sketchy. He was reported as having only eight professional fights before taking on Hearns at Caesars Palace, Las Vegas, and was expected to provide little threat, but there was no point in the Detroit camp taking chances with a title bout looming. Richards tried his best to stay away from Hearns but in the third he was forced to the ropes and was floored by a left hook. He got up only to be dropped again by two rights to the head, and the referee stopped it as he rose again and sagged into the ropes.

In his next bout, for the vacant United States Boxing Association welterweight title, Hearns faced a much sterner test. His opponent, Angel Espada, was the former WBA welterweight champion. The Puerto Rican's record was formidable. He had won the vacant WBA crown in a fifteen-round battle against Clyde Gray, a former Hearns victim, and had defended it against Johnny Gant before beating another mutual foe, Alfonso Hayman, despatching him more quickly than Hearns had managed by an eight-round knockout. When then pitted against the dynamic left-hooker Pipino Cuevas, he finally met his match and had to be pulled out of the fight in the twelfth round with a broken jaw. He had a swiftly arranged rematch against Cuevas to regain his title but was stopped again, this time inside ten rounds.

It was just four months after this latest loss that he agreed to box Hearns in the Joe Louis Arena, Detroit. Despite his defeats at the hands of Cuevas, the media acknowledged that Espada was still a force to be reckoned with. When he faced the Hit Man, however, he was made to look a shadow of a once-great fighter. Hearns gave a consummate display of controlled aggression in a bout which lasted for just four rounds before the referee was obliged to step in and halt the one-way traffic.

Hearns remained active by taking on Santiago Valdez in the Caesars Palace Sports Pavilion twenty-nine days later. Valdez, from Phoenix, had a decent pedigree of fourteen victories in nineteen contests, including a knockout over Hearns's stablemate, Danny "Mad Dog" Paul. There was a hint of vengeance in the air as Hearns flew out of his corner at the opening bell and hammered Valdez unmercifully until the referee Joey Curtis stopped the slaughter. In a ringside interview, Hearns fired a salvo to any watching belt holders. "I don't think there's anybody who can stay with me because of my punching power," he said. "And that includes Sugar Ray Leonard, Pipino Cuevas, Roberto Duran or Wilfred Benitez."

In a final warm-up bout before meeting Cuevas, Steward was eager to ensure that his charge should meet a wily foe and decided to pitch him in against the experienced Nicaraguan Eddie Gazo, a former WBA light-middleweight champion. Gazo had won forty-two of his forty-nine fights and had fought in Japan and South Korea, where he had successfully defended his crown three times before losing it on a disputed points decision to Masashi Kudo. He had since enjoyed a five-fight unbeaten run. He never came close to making it six as Hearns demolished him with a thunderous first round knockout. Steward declared that it was now all systems go for the much awaited world welterweight championship clash between Hearns and Cuevas. Hearns trained at the Kronk before moving out a month before the fight to the isolation of a rural camp in Berrien Springs, a hundred miles from Detroit. After putting in his work, there was horse riding and fishing, minibiking and card games to help him relax and take his mind off the daily grind. By the time he weighed in, at 10st 6½ lbs, the rake-thin challenger was in the best condition he could be.

A thunderstorm followed by a heavy downpour cleared the muggy air on the morning of the fight but the electricity in the city remained. Hearns's fight plan was to back up Cuevas, something few opponents had ever been able to do, and to land his punches first. Cuevas, however, was confident: "No-one can ever knock me out," he bragged. But his Mexican handlers feared that his hotheadedness would lead him into a punching war with Hearns, and that could leave him open to shots from his longer-limbed opponent. Defence was not Pipino's strong suit.

So it proved. And after just five minutes and thirty-nine seconds of concentrated violence, Hearns was crowned king of the world. The lede of *Boxing News* reporter Graham Houston said it all:

> Turning in a awesome display of two-handed punching, Thomas Hearns blasted his way to the WBA welterweight title by overwhelming Mexican Pipino Cuevas in two totally one-sided rounds before a wildly-excited home crowd of around 14,000 at the Riverside Joe Louis Arena.
>
> The scenes of enthusiasm that greeted Hearns' victory were the most frenzied I have seen anywhere. Spectators were standing on chairs all around the ringside section, shouting, jumping up and down and thrusting clenched fists in the air while an exulted Hearns grabbed the ring mike and yelled, "I'm the champion – you'd better believe it."

Observers compared his dismantling of Cuevas to Joe Louis's famous destruction of the German Max Schmeling back in 1936. "Hearns," admitted a chastened Cuevas afterwards, "is too tall and too long to be a welter."

THANKS PARTLY TO Harold Smith, boxing had made Hearns wealthy, and the first people he looked after were his family. He bought and furnished a ranch home in a fashionable northwest Detroit neighbourhood for his mother and siblings, showered Lois with jewellery and bought her a Cadillac, complete with driver as she didn't drive. For himself there was a string of luxury cars – a Rolls Royce, a black Corvette – and a palatial home with a grand piano. He always dressed sharp.

Still, leaving Helen Street provoked a burst of nostalgia. Hearns told one interviewer how he drove around his old neighbourhood and caught up with some old friends. "I still think back to the old days, when I was living on the east side. When I was not in training, I would often play basketball and the fruit machines with my friends. I know that when I was with them, I can relax and speak my mind." When reporters told Emanuel Steward about Tommy's recollections, he smiled and said this was important for his progression as a fighter. "His training camp entourage is large but that is because of the number of Kronk fighters and trainers. But the glitterati that surrounded other fighters are not present with him. It is a working camp, not an ego trip. Thomas still surrounds himself with the same people, the same old buddies. He knows that it's very important to stay close to reality."

Hearns still struggled in public; he was shy and gauche yet fighting to overcome it. He attempted to explain his personal philosophy in an interview with *Sports Illustrated*'s Bob Ottum: "You know what it is? Man, it's like life is one big chance. Look. You could get mugged, you could get cut or robbed today. So if you're going to do anything in life, you got to take the chance, man. You got to take it, and if you're fighting, you got to put some *hurl* on him. I look forward to the, you know, the *com*bat. It's the chance." It was a view conditioned both by his ghetto upbringing and by his strong sense of ambition. When Tommy saw "the chance," he was going to hold nothing back.

# 6 CHAMPION

ON SATURDAY, 6 December, Thomas Hearns maintained the furious pace which characterised his career and stepped back into the ring to defend his crown against Luis Primera, a thirty-year-old Venezuelan, in the Joe Louis Arena. Primera was on an unbeaten roll of fifteen fights. He looked suitably mean and tough and gave the impression that he had lived a colourful life. Although he spoke no English, his interpreter, Pedro Aponte, was happy to paint a picture which supported the powerful impression he created.

After boxing as an amateur, Primera had quit the sport for seven years. During this exile from the ring, he had opened an automobile paint shop in Caracas, which he operated with two of his eight brothers. He also played baseball and sang in a Latin jazz group. His interest in boxing was reignited when he visited a gym to watch a friend spar and he turned professional in 1976. All his fifteen fights had taken place in the Venezuelan capital, Caracas, and twelve of them were won by knockout, a run that had earned him the world number five ranking. When he arrived in Detroit, his first time on American soil, he was shocked to see snow and suffered with the bitter cold, as he had brought only light summer suits with him. Once he had acclimatised, however, his workouts impressed Detroit's worldly onlookers. Primera looked a natural athlete, with good footwork and quick hands.

He attributed this to his amateur baseball days as a shortstop and pitcher.

Hearns was determined to make his first defence a successful one and he set a fast pace from the first round. Primera was undeterred and met the champion with his own attack, forcing him to use his left jab to ward him away. The Detroit fans were thrilled at the fast-paced contest and sportingly applauded both fighters as the bell to end the first round sounded. In the second, Hearns seemed to find his range and began to find Primera's jaw. Two violent right hands saw him drop to the canvas. Primera had recovered by the count of nine and displayed huge reserves of courage by responding with a stunning right cross which cautioned the Detroit assassin from making any reckless attacks.

The fight ebbed and flowed through the next three rounds, with Hearns giving a passable impersonation of Muhammad Ali in his prime, dancing on his toes and holding his left hand low to try to tempt Primera into leading, before unleashing his own blur-fast ripostes. But Primera keep his guard high and tight and his chin down, plodding forward and winging back with hooks. In round five, Hearns got down to business. He stopped bouncing around, held the centre of the ring and closed the distance, looking to pick his spots and throwing punches with what Mike Tyson would call "bad intentions." His left hook, in particular, lashed again and again into the body of the Venezuelan. Primera refused to buckle and continued to hit back, but just before the bell a particularly violent series of blows, concluded with a right cross, sent him to the canvas, gasping for air. Once again, his fighting instinct brought him back to his feet and he finished the round.

The end was imminent though, and it came amid some confusion in the next round. Primera missed with a couple of huge left swings while Hearns continued to enjoy success with his own sickle-like left. He finally cut it deep into Primera's ribcage, causing him to pitch forward to the floor, howling in agony. While he attempted to find his feet, his own corner waved frantically to alert referee Ismelia Fernandez that they wanted to stop the fight. Fernandez ignored their request and instead counted out the brave Venezuelan. This was the Hit Man's thirtieth win and twenty-eighth stoppage victory.

IN APRIL 1981, Randy Shields, a blond-haired, blue-eyed fighter from Hollywood, California, was sanctioned as the opponent for Hearns's second world title defence. Shields, the world number four, was perceived as a legitimate opponent who had consistently mixed in good company throughout his forty-four professional fights, and was expected to present a decent test, although Hearns was the overwhelming favourite. As an amateur he had been a Golden Gloves champion and had achieved the rare distinction of winning a decision over Ray Leonard, though Leonard avenged this over ten rounds in the pro ranks. He had also fought WBC champion Wilfred Benitez, losing on cuts in six rounds. In January 1979, he had taken Jose Cuevas the full fifteen rounds before losing the decision. He had recovered to win a further five consecutive fights. Shields was both managed and trained by his father, Sonny, a former fighter and a stuntman in Hollywood.

Shields was experienced enough to know what he had to do, and honest enough to admit what he was up against. "I'm going to go through all the styles I know," he said. "If one style doesn't work, I'll try another. If that doesn't work, I'll try something else. If that doesn't work, something else. If that doesn't work, then I'm in trouble." In the Hearns camp, Emanuel Steward promised there would be none of the showboating apparent in the Primera fight. "From now on," he said ominously, "it's gong to be all business."

The fight was staged in Phoenix's Memorial Coliseum, in front of a live crowd of six and a half thousand as well as an international television audience via ABC's *Wide World of Sports*. Hearns started at his usual brisk pace, employing a fast, stinging left jab mixed with combinations of rapid-fire two-handed punches. A clash of heads caused a slight cut over his right eye, but it was patched up by cutman Don Thibodeaux and didn't bother him. Early in the second round, an ugly welt began to appear below Shields' left eye. Hearns targeted this injury whilst building up a comfortable lead on points. In the fourth, he hammered Shields across the ring but the challenger could take a punch and stayed on his feet, even hitting back with a good left hook. Hearns acknowledged his guts at the end of the round by tapping gloves with Shields.

The champion stumbled over in round five but it was ruled a slip, and he continued to box well within himself while racking up a seemingly insurmountable lead. In the ninth round, a low chant started at the back of the hall and soon hummed throughout the whole Coliseum: "Randy! Randy! Randy!" The crowd seemed to realise that Shields had no chance of beating the champion but they acknowledged his immense courage. He stared at Hearns through bloodied eyes, his back was scorched red from rope burns and he had started to raise his right arm above his head, not as a gesture of superiority but an attempt to alleviate what was later claimed as bursitis of the shoulder. The chanting was taken as an affront by Hearns and he increased the ferocity of his attack, again targeting the damaged eye.

This increase in the tempo of the attacks led Dr. C.D. Lake, the ringside physician, to closely inspect what was now a deep cut over Shields's left eye, but he ruled that the fight could continue. By the end of the twelfth round, however, Shields could no longer see how many fingers the doctor was holding up in front of him. Sonny Shields's paternal compassion finally overtook his boxing concerns and he threw in the towel to end the fight. The three judges showed Hearns in front by a wide margin, with scores of 120-109, 119-111 and 119-110.

Some criticised Hearns for a lacklustre showing. "I tried boxing him, and it worked for a while," said the champion. "Then I tried to muscle him, and that worked for a little while. Finally I tried to go up and down when his eye started to close, to make him look in two directions. Each style I tried worked for a while, and then he was able to adjust. He made it difficult for me to get to him." Sonny Shields suggested that Hearns had been over-confident, and claimed that the day before the fight he had played tennis in the boiling sun and hadn't arrived at the Coliseum until forty-five minutes before the fight was scheduled to start. Other critics expressed their disappointment that the Hit Man hadn't exploded his famed bombs and flattened Shields. Some questioned the legitimacy of his supposed ferocious knockout power and many argued that when he fought Sugar Ray Leonard, he would be exposed. "Before this fight," said promoter Bob Arum, "I thought Hearns certainly would beat Leonard. But now I see a very close fight." Arum's aide, Jerry Kearney, a long-time boxing writer, went further: "I think Leonard's going to beat him."

Emanuel Steward sprang to his charge's defence. He maintained that it was difficult to fight a man whose sole intention was survival. He also pointed out that the twelve rounds were a vital part of Hearns' education as it was the longest he had been in the ring for any fight. He also stated that the four-and-a-half-month hiatus from boxing was the longest lay-off which Hearns had had in his twelve years of fighting and Steward argued that this had a big effect on his sharpness.

IN JULY 1981, Steward flew to Syracuse to watch Ray Leonard box Larry Bonds. The real purpose of his mission was to meet with Leonard's attorney, the astute Mike Trainer. The meeting had been initiated by Trainer, who was keen to iron out a deal for a world welterweight championship unification superfight between Leonard and Hearns. Initial discussions were straightforward. Both men agreed that it would be one of the richest confrontations in the history of boxing, topping over $30 million in revenue – a figure which was eventually dwarfed. The only sticking point came when Steward demanded parity when it came to dividing the purse money. After hours of haggling, with Trainer arguing that Leonard was the major star, they agreed a compromise. Ten days later, when representatives from both camps met to finalise details, the agreement stood that Hearns would receive $5 million and Leonard $8 million, with each fighter also getting twenty-five percent of any revenue beyond $21 million. Part of the deal was that both Hearns and Leonard would box selected opponents on the same bill at the Astrodome, Houston, in order to build up the publicity for the big fight.

Mexico's Pablo Baez was nominated as Thomas Hearns' third challenger for his WBA welterweight championship. The critics, who had been circling since the underwhelming Shields defence, wondered quite how Baez, who had won only fourteen bouts against eight losses, had qualified to fight Detroit's finest. The twenty-three-year-old Baez offered a spirited defence of his status and pointed to a seventh-round knockout over Zeferino Gonzalez and a second-round knockout of Jose Palacios in February. "I am not worried about Tommy Hearns' punching power," he said. "Nobody knows me but I am just waiting for this moment. I'm just waiting to prove my point at the fight. After that, everything will change." Hearns also built up his opponent in public. He told *The Detroit Free Press* that whilst others might scoff, he had a great deal of respect for Baez. "The Mexican fighter is a thinker," said Hearns. "They're the kind of fighters who are difficult to fight. I expect a difficult fight from him. I watched him work out when we were in California last January and he boxed well against Milton McCrory in a sparring session and other fighters in the gym."

Sugar Ray Leonard's opponent was the much tougher Ayub Kalule, the WBA light-middleweight champion. While Leonard was a clear favourite to take the title, Kalule, a Ugandan who fought out of Denmark, was unbeaten and was highly regarded by more knowledgeable boxing followers. Both Leonard and Hearns, however, seemed to have their minds on their impending clash, and did their best to fan the flames. Fans were invited to watch both men train at separate times at the same gym. The contrast between the two was heightened by these sessions. When Leonard entered the gym, he seemed bored and would go through his training ritual in a quick, quiet fashion, looking precise, polished and professional. He didn't talk and nobody was invited to talk to him. When it was over, he took the microphone and thanked everybody for coming to watch him train. He delivered the well-worn line that he employed in whichever city he was based, that he had been to a lot of cities "but Houston was number one on my list." When he met the press he responded with great confidence.

Two hours later, when it was Hearns's turn to train, he jumped into the ring with Emanuel Steward to do pad-work, firing two-handed punches in rapid combinations, which looked very impressive to the crowd. He then pounded the heavy bag before inviting a number of young onlookers into the ring with him, where he gave a little coaching session. He concluded with callisthenics and appeared to be thoroughly enjoying the hard work. It was only when invited to meet the press that he looked uncomfortable. He was a man whose natural home was inside the ring.

From the opening bell, Hearns used Baez as target practice. The recent criticism of his punching power seemed to inject extra sting into his attacks. He used his long reach to outscore the brave Mexican and let his right hand go like a rocket with increasing frequency. Each time it landed, it shook Baez right down to his toes. Baez was simply unable to get close enough to land a reply.

In the second round, Hearns got up on his toes to dance. After a minute had elapsed, he caught his foe with a swift right cross, followed this with another peach of a right and a left hook for good measure, driving Baez back into the ropes. Surprisingly,

Hearns stood back and didn't follow through this attack. Instead, he retreated and invited Baez to reply. Hearns stayed on the ropes for nearly half a minute and used Baez's flailing punches as an opportunity to practise honing his defence. He drove in an occasional left hook and a right cross whenever he wished to check his game challenger.

When the end came in the fourth round, it was brutal. Hearns came off his stool in earnest and immediately began brandishing his jab. Baez appeared distracted by this unexpected fury and the champion exploited his surprise by catching him with a straight right smash directly onto the unguarded chin. He followed up with a string of punches onto the groggy Baez, who was trapped in the corner. Hearns's attack was relentless and he barely drew breath when continuing to blast away until the Japanese referee, Ken Murito, managed to pull him away. Baez, with a deep gash over his left eye, offered no protest but drunkenly slumped against the ropes, stunned and with legs shaking like jelly.

Leonard fulfilled his part of the bargain, impressively dismantling Kalule in nine rounds. The next morning, the press turned their attention to the now inevitable showdown between the two men. Leonard's charisma put him at an immediate PR advantage. Respected sportswriter Joe Falls – who had memorably summed up Hearns's latest victim with the words, "Pablo Baez, like Joan Baez, is non-violent" – reflected on the difference between the two rivals. "At 8 am, the morning after his fight with Kalule, right on schedule, Sugar Ray walked into the small conference room wearing a sailor's cap and a smile as bright as the Texas morning sun," he wrote. "He was eager to help all the writers conclude their various pieces and assure himself of the maximum publicity. When the reporters asked Steward, who had attended to represent his fighter, where Hearns was, we were informed that he was still asleep. This may seem unimportant but it was a major reason why Leonard could command eight million dollars and three million more than Hearns ... Not only does Sugar Ray's publicity man rush into the coffee shop and pull guys away from their scrambled eggs, he then stands at Leonard's side and repeats all the questions so not a word was missed by anyone."

This episode prompted other journalists to mount the band-wagon and contrast the Hearns camp with Leonard's, who were far better organised. Falls later reflected that Hearns had been badly advised when he had posed for the cover of the December 1980 edition of *Ring Magazine* dressed as a member of Al Capone's Purple Gang. "He was wearing a 1930s trilby, had his coat collar turned up and cradled a machine gun. He looked surly and uncom-municative. This was a stark contrast to the sugar-coated Leonard who jealously guarded his public image." The gun was actually a plastic replica of an M-16 and Hearns did not have his collar up, but it didn't matter: the image, later reproduced in other publica-tions, was so powerful that it endured, along with the "Hit Man" nickname.

BEFORE THE HEARNS–LEONARD showdown could take place, the world of boxing was rocked by its biggest scandal since the Mob hearings of the early 1960s. Harold Smith, the bumptious, money-laden promoter, had been planning his greatest show yet. It promised to be a bonanza of fistic action to be staged in the Mecca of boxing, Madison Square Garden. Larry Holmes against the latest Great White Hope, Gerry Cooney, was the main offering, while Thomas Hearns was contracted to box Wilfredo Benitez as an appetiser. Smith also promised two other world championship fights. Within a month of the announcement, however, the media had the real story. The news finally broke of Smith's breathtaking embezzlement of Wells Fargo Bank, to the tune of $21 million. Early reports referred to a larger-than-life character who the press dubbed "the Black Jesse James." The FBI and the Los Angeles

District Attorney's office confirmed that they wanted to speak to this character, who they revealed was Harold James Smith. Smith, however, had left the country in a hurry. Press reports had him in Puerto Rico, Mexico and Switzerland.

FBI Special Agent Dale Taulbee began to unravel a complex web of lies and deceit, with Smith at the centre. When Taulbee tried to carry out a background check on him, searching all the public and private records, he was troubled when he couldn't find anything earlier than 1974. It was a few days after his name had been made public that a man, who gave his name as Dewey Hughes, contacted the FBI claiming to have valuable information on Smith. Hughes was a Washington-based disc jockey and had known Smith through the city's nightclub scene, where Smith owned the Sammy Davis Jr club. He revealed that Smith's real name was Ross Eugene Fields, a man with a history of fraud.

Smith/Fields was arrested re-entering the country in April. Two days later, he appeared before magistrates charged with offences dating back to 1967. These included six charges of fraud and false pretences. One of these charges alleged that between 1973 and 1974, Smith had cashed over one hundred fraudulent cheques across the country. It was also revealed that his wife, Barbara Lee Smith, was actually Alice Vicki Darrow, wanted in Alabama for interstate transportation of fraudulent securities. When he was asked to respond, Smith, who represented himself, gave an impassioned defence, stating that he had set up a scholarship fund for disadvantaged youths in the name of Sammy Davis Jr. He screamed out, "I am a man of God. I've been to the mountain top!" whilst proclaiming his innocence in the Wells Fargo scandal. His bail was initially set at $200,000, although this was doubled the day after.

After a lengthy trial and eight days of jury deliberations, Smith was found guilty of thirty-one separate charges. The total amount he had stolen from the bank, much of it spent on boxers' purses, was a staggering $21 million. His last bid for leniency was a crude but typical attempt at flattery, as he told the female judge, Consuelo Marshall, that she was "a most beautiful black woman." Judge Marshall was unmoved and sentenced him to ten years in the federal penitentiary. Benjamin Lewis received a five-year sentence and Sammie Marshall got thee years. MAPS was no more.

# 7 SHOWDOWN IN THE DESERT

SUGAR RAY LEONARD was equipped with speed, knockout power, an over-abundance of boxing ability and bags of natural charisma. He had filled the void created by Muhammad Ali's retirement in 1981 to become boxing's superstar and one of the most recognisable sportsmen in America. Like Hearns, his family had moved north from a southern state – in his case, from Wilmington, North Carolina, to Washington, D.C. – in search of opportunity, before eventually settling in Maryland. An uncommonly gifted amateur, he leapt into the wider public consciousness when winning a gold medal at the 1976 Montreal Olympic Games. He turned professional amid reams of publicity, which he justified when winning the world welterweight title in 1979, stopping Wilfred Benitez in the fifteenth round of a classy contest. He entered the 1980s as a world champion and would end it as one. In the decade between, he would win an unprecedented five world championships at five different weight classes and compete in some of the era's most memorable fights.

The promoters for the Hearns–Leonard fight were Main Event Productions, based in New Jersey. Thirty-seven-year-old Shelly Finkel, a bald-headed rock music promoter and boxing manager, was one half of the team. Dan Duva, a twenty-nine-year-old lawyer, was the other. Duva, who took an extended leave-of-absence from his Newark law firm to work on this fight, ensured that the Duva name would be closely associated with it. His wife Kathy dealt with publicity whilst his sisters, Deanne, Donna and Denise, took care of the box office and all travel arrangements. Dino, his kid brother, was an accounting major and worked on the Main Event books. Overseeing the whole operation was the family patriarch, Dan's father, Lou, who had been in boxing as a fighter, trainer, manager and promoter for decades.

That Main Events were working on this superfight was entirely down to Leonard's attorney, Mike Trainer. He liked Finkel and the Duvas and believed they would put on a great show. Moreover, he specifically didn't want to work with Bob Arum or Don King, and as long as he controlled Leonard, the biggest draw in sports, he didn't have to. He simply instructed Finkel and Duva to come up with the guarantee of $8 million for Leonard and to satisfy Hearns, and the fight was theirs to promote. "Bob Arum thinks I took the fight from him," Finkel later said. "The thing was, he never had it in the first place because Mike Trainer would not deal with him and neither would Emanuel Steward." However, Main Events did agree to bring in Arum and use him to deal with foreign rights sales, and his associate Mike Malitz was employed to supervise the technical side.

In July, they staged the official press conference at the Grand Hyatt Hotel, New York, to formally announce the welterweight unification championship bout would take place on 16 September 1981. The two fighters tossed a coin to decide who would speak to the press first. Hearns won and insisted on going first. He appeared nervous before visibly warming to his task. "I've waited over two years for this moment," he said. "I don't think Ray is a pushover. I don't think he's a guy you can walk over. I think he deserves respect. But I do really feel that it's time Ray Leonard got what he's got coming." When he sat down, he received a polite smattering of applause. Leonard ignored him as he bounded up to the podium, smiling broadly and eager to respond.

"I'd like to personally thank Tommy Hearns for those kind words," he beamed. "I consider this will be the greatest boxing match in history. You're in for a boxing lesson, Tommy. I'm going to pop your head. You called me a chicken and it upset me. I'm looking forward to it and, buddy, you had better be ready because I have been waiting for this fight." Leonard then ratcheted up the mind games by claiming that Emanuel Steward had quietly told him that after he knocked out Hearns, he would join his training camp. He then began flicking his left hand near to Hearns's head in an attempt to rile his impassive foe and show how he planned to use his quick jab. Eventually Hearns responded with a chilling warning: "It's only gonna take one shot, Ray. You'll be lying up in the hospital after just one shot. It'll be short."

Dan Duva refused to disclose the size of the purse even though it was now common knowledge that Hearns would get $5 million, ten times more than he had ever been paid before. Duva did confirm that the two champions would earn more from the percentages from the various gate and related receipts, pushing the figures higher than anticipated. He also admitted that Leonard would receive the lion's share of money. Hearns remained unperturbed. "I would have fought him for less than what I'm getting," he told the press, "I just wanted to finally fight him."

The two champions then posed for magazine and fight posters. They had previously always shown respect for each other, but now the gloves were off, so much so that observers recalled the rancorous build-ups to the famous Ali-Frazier fights. "There was no bullshit here," said Lou Duva. "The antipathy was real. What a hatred they've developed for each other." Leonard told Hearns, "I'm going to cut you down to size. I'm gonna do a job on your belly. And when I get you down, you're gonna stay down." When Hearns was posing for solo publicity pictures, Leonard sneaked into another room, grabbed a microphone and began taunting, "Thomas Hearns your time has come." Hearns eventually responded, "Keep you're mouth shut while you can, because I'm gonna break you up in September. All those endorsements and commercial deals are going down the drain."

With the publicity machine working overtime, the fight attracted some powerful interest. Dan Duva phoned Mike Trainer and told him he had received a call from the White House requesting tickets to the fight. Duva, who had never been in this situation before, asked Trainer if he had ever had dealings with the White House and wondered what the protocol was. "Do we just give it to them or charge them or what?" asked Duva. Part of the deal for both fighters was an agreement to tour the major American cities for two weeks in a publicity drive to help promote the fight on closed-circuit television. The barbed insults continued throughout the tour. When Leonard was asked how he intended to handle Hearns, he reasoned that his speed would be a big factor and speculated that Hearns had never been forced to endure the incredible levels of hype and publicity this match-up entailed. "Hearns will become a psychological victim when he sees all those people, hears all that noise and have to go through all the media hype. All of this can get to you and turn most fighters' legs to jelly," he said.

On another occasion, Hearns suggested that people should stop calling Leonard by his nickname "Sugar." He argued that it was just another publicity gimmick to add to his marketability, and was an insult to a legend. "Sugar Ray Robinson was a great champion and a great person and nobody should be using his name like Leonard is doing now. He should use his own name." Without missing a beat, Leonard said, "Thomas Hearns has a very unique nose and I'd like to do an operation on that. As tall as he is, something has to hang loose. That will be my target." Hearns looked riled and retorted, "He also has a big target. A big head."

During the New York leg of the two-week promotional tour, Hearns played in a softball game in Central Park against a team of media people. He appeared relaxed and seemed to enjoy the break from boxing training. Reporters were positive about Hearns and one reporter commented, "Tommy has gotten into the swing of things. In fact, so far he has out-Leonard Leonard, the master showman." Hearns shed his image of the strong, silent type and was offered a guest spot on *Saturday Night Live*. He also went to Harlem, where a crowd of over 4,000 watched him give a boxing clinic for youngsters.

Whilst Hearns was charming New Yorkers, Leonard was touring Detroit. He recognised the need to afford his opponent due respect in his home town but said Hearns was important to him merely from a business aspect. "Now the time is right from the interest I've given Thomas Hearns through TV magazines and talk shows. This fight doesn't need hype, no gimmicks. It's a natural. We have no communication problems. Two American fighters. The public is aware." He beamed his 1,000-watt smile and assured the fans that he had no animosity toward Hearns. "We're not good friends. But there's no hatred. However, there is a distance between us." But he went to great pains to say that he was misquoted in a magazine when it said he would destroy Hearns's family. "What I said was I would destroy Hearns physically, destroy his followers spiritually and his manager financially. I was hurt by the misquote. His mother's a lovely person." He then turned his attentions to Emanuel Steward. Calling him by the nickname "Sonny," which Steward was said to hate, he employed a mischievous divide-and-conquer tactic. "They called him Sonny Steward. They say he's a genius and he is. Do you know he's getting more endorsements than his fighter? Tommy's not seeing what he thinks he's seeing. I hope Thomas Hearns opens his eyes and sees whether or not something funny is going on in his camp."

When the training camp began in earnest, Hearns and a thirty-strong team of Kronk boxers and officials moved to Michigan's spectacular Sugar Loaf ski resort, an area of outstanding natural splendour with picturesque mountains overlooking Lake

Michigan, which shimmered on the horizon. Hearns was relieved to complete the promotional tour and was delighted to hear how it had paid dividends, especially in Philadelphia, which reported that it had sold every one of its closed-circuit television tickets and was planning to open more theatres. The gleeful promoters were now talking of an astounding $52 million gross for the fight.

Hearns now focussed on the fight itself and asked his sparring partners to simulate Leonard's style. One of them, his light-welterweight stablemate Dujuan Johnson, who was known as "Mr Excitement," gave him plenty of problems. They boxed eight three-minute rounds and Johnson soon began to whirl his right arm in the windmill fashion which Leonard had used to dramatic effect on the evening he forced Roberto Duran to quit in New Orleans. The Kronk team encouraged Johnson, much to the chagrin of Hearns, and he repeatedly mimicked Leonard, his wind-milling right hand being followed by a quick, sneaky left jab aimed at Hearns's head. Eventually, Hearns found an antidote, and as the left jab was cocked the Hit Man delivered a fast jab of his own, which hit Johnson smack on his forehead. The power of the punch drove him back into the ropes. The whoops and hollering from his stablemates made Hearns smile.

One of the more fascinating sideshows to the big fight build-up focused on the two men who would be in the corners on the night: Emanuel Steward and Angelo Dundee. Mike O'Hara, the *Detroit News* staff writer, declared, "Emanuel Steward stands at the top of the Kronk Empire as a man who is unshakeable in the belief that he can control the course of his fighters, in a business where loyalty lasts no longer than a three-minute round." He acknowledged that the thirty-seven-year-old Steward's guidance of Hearns towards the showdown with Leonard "was a masterpiece."

Steward was more than happy to take the plaudits, and was not slow to blow his own trumpet either. "I take my hat off to Mike Trainer but it's not a hard job to do when you have a multi-talented gold medal winner like Sugar Ray Leonard," he said. "I was starting out with a kid called Thomas Hearns, who hardly anybody knew. He was regarded as a good dime-a-dozen fighter. I knew that he was a good kid and he became the champion of the world in just thirty-six months, most importantly he did it with no help from the big consortiums." This kind of "help" seemed like a dirty word to Steward. "It means selling a fighter's services to one of the major promoters but Hearns is tied to nobody. If a promoter puts up money, he would want authority and I never want to get into that kind of situation."

Amidst the swell of praise, Joe Falls, a Detroit journalist who had followed Steward's and Hearns's careers from the beginning, wrote an article which offered the rapidly emerging trainer some advice. "Emanuel Steward is a good man but I wish he would stop talking about how much money he has made for Thomas Hearns." Steward had reacted badly to some caustic remarks by world heavyweight champion Larry Holmes, to the effect that Steward was cheating his fighter out of money. Leonard had made similar remarks in the build-up. Falls cautioned, "He's got to stop letting people like Holmes get to him with their barbs. Nobody with any real knowledge has ever hinted that Emanuel Steward has been anything but fair with Thomas Hearns or any of his other fighters. He should get himself a publicity man who understands the boxing business and the matter of dealing with the media because this constant responding to financial matters is costing his boxer some money in bad publicity."

Opposing the relatively young Steward was the veteran Angelo Dundee, a man commonly described as the best trainer in the boxing business. While Steward claimed to have been influenced more by coaches outside boxing, men like gridiron legend Vince Lombardi and basketball great Bill Russell, Dundee was steeped in boxing history, having learned his trade at the feet of masters like Charlie Goldman, Ray Arcel and Chick Ferrera at the famous

Stillman's Gym in New York. It was Dundee who had quietly masterminded Muhammad Ali's victory over George Foreman in Zaire and who repeated the feat when Ali won the title for an unprecedented third time by beating Leon Spinks in a rematch. He had also tutored Leonard to win his title back, with a dazzling array of tricks and cunning, when he outsmarted Roberto Duran in their return fight. Mike O'Hara, another Detroit boxing writer, mused, "The corners will be crucial in this fight. The re-supply system in the sixty-second span between rounds is where a fighter receives strategy, psychology, repairs, admonishment, a scouting report and sometimes nothing more scientific than a whiff of ammonia. Angelo Dundee has proven himself to be the best sixty-second man in boxing. His record attests to that, with champions from Luis Rodriquez to Muhammad Ali and Ray Leonard." Dundee, for his part, admitted he was excited but would check his emotions at the ring apron once the combat started. "I'm all juiced up and I'll be juiced up until the bell rings. When you lose your cool, you're no good to the fighter."

The arrangement between Leonard and Dundee was quite different to the relationship between the two men in the opposite corner. Mike Trainer explained that Janks Morton was Leonard's official trainer and Angelo Dundee only arrived two weeks before a major fight to fine-tune his charge. Dave Jacobs had also been with Leonard since he was a junior but he had subsequently left the team after the loss to Roberto Duran (he would heal the breach and return to the team years later). "Angelo Dundee's role is clearly defined," said Trainer. "He is officially listed as Leonard's manager but he isn't involved in any negotiations or the business side of things. Janks Morton trains Leonard and gets him into condition before Angelo comes into camp. He then puts the finishing touches together and works the corner. When the bell sounds, Angelo runs the corner."

Both trainers claimed that their unique approaches would give their charges an edge. Steward believed that his relationship with

Hearns was based on a mutual respect forged through the amateur ranks. "It's not that I might be a better corner man. I think Angelo's effectiveness is diluted because Leonard doesn't listen to him. Tommy has the advantage because he has a corner he respects and he uses his corner. As great as Angelo is, I don't think he has that kind of input." Dundee was non-committal. He laughed, "I respect Emanuel and this kind of comparison just juices things up. If it gets people talking about the fight, that's got to be good."

People were certainly talking about the fight; indeed the boxing world was talking of little else. *Boxing News* called it, with only slight hyperbole, "the most eagerly anticipated fight probably since the 1971 clash between Ali and Frazier." The magazine ran a poll of some of the sport's most prominent writers and practitioners to see who they were tipping for what was dubbed "The Showdown," and found the pundits were split down the middle. Some seemed very confident that Hearns would blow away Leonard, while others believed Sugar Ray was much more seasoned and would be too cool and clever for his younger foe.

"I like Tommy Hearns," said master trainer Eddie Futch. "He's such a good puncher that most people overlook his boxing ability. He's got great use of his left hand, mobility and speed." Former featherweight great Sandy Saddler, himself a rangy bomber like Hearns, went for the Detroit sensation. "Sugar Ray has to come to Hearns to make the fight. That will be his downfall," he said. "Hearns has the punching power, boxing ability and physical advantage to control the bout." Lightweight champion Alexis Arguello, another tall, smooth puncher, also went with the Hit Man. "As the fight goes on, Leonard will lose his power because he'll be frustrated by Hearns's height and reach," he said. "Both will get hurt and the tide will change several times. But Hearns, the natural puncher, will win." And light-welterweight champ Aaron Pryor had no doubts who he was picking: "Thomas will dominate Leonard completely. He will hit too hard and too often. Ray is not used to that kind of punishment. I beat Hearns in the amateurs but he was a different type of fighter then. He'll knock out Leonard in the middle rounds."

Others begged to differ. "Leonard is smarter, faster, very hard to hit," said the former light-heavyweight champion Jose Torres, now a successful writer. "Hearns has to hit his opponent to feel encouraged – and Leonard is not the kind to get hit too hard too often." *New York Post* writer Mike Marley thought Leonard would "baffle Hearns with constant in-and-out movements," while Mickey Duff, the widely travelled British promoter, also favoured the Sugarman. "His hands are much faster," he said. "Leonard's edge is that he has more experience against major opponents. He always handles a super-bout with great coolness."

Sensibly Larry Holmes, the WBC heavyweight king, refused to be drawn on such a close call. "I just don't know," he admitted. "The guy who wants it most will win."

IN THE DAYS preceding the fight, tensions nearly boiled over in both camps. In true Kronk style, no quarter was asked or given in Hearns's sparring sessions. Wearing eighteen-ounce gloves, he broke the jaw of the talented Marlon Starling (a future world welterweight champion) with a terrific arching right. He also hammered and cut the eye of Dujuan Johnson, who was one of the top contenders in the light-welterweight division, while world-ranked middleweight "Caveman" Lee was battered and bruised. Six members of Ray Leonard's team watched the session and were forcibly ejected when they were suspected of filming the events. Emanuel Steward stopped the session until the group were made to leave. Prentiss Byrd, the camp co-ordinator, said, "If this keeps up, we will physically fight them to keep them out. We're sick and tired of it. They're not professional and we're not going to take it anymore." Steward agreed, "They are starting to stoop real low."

There was also controversy over the sanctioning of what would be the richest fight ever, with a projected global audience of 300 million. As it would bring together both the WBA and EWBC welterweight champions, it was logical the outcome would decide the undisputed belt-holder. However, both organizations demanded sanctioning fees to recognise it as a title bout, with the WBC seeking an eye-watering $500,000. Mike Trainer, who was unafraid to play hardball with the best of them, made WBC president Jose Sulaiman a much lower, take-it-or-leave-it offer. Sulaiman swallowed his not inconsiderable pride and caved in, though just to rub it in the promoters made no mention of either the WBA or the WBC in their promotional material.

In the final twenty-four hours before the fight, Hearns sought quietude, relaxing in his room with a few close friends like Prentiss Byrd, watching television and even singing the odd Temptations song, even while his friends and well-wishers partied and danced at a premature "Victory for Detroit" shindig. On the day of the fight, he rose at eight o'clock, and an hour later, when half of Las Vegas was just going to bed, the two welterweight champions stepped on to the scales for the official weigh-in. Hearns was recorded at 145 pounds, a pound lighter than Leonard and two pounds under the welterweight limit. This caused eyebrows to be raised: the tall Hearns had been expected to come in right on the weight. Both combatants barely glanced at each other and left without saying a word. The war of words was over. Back in his hotel, Hearns ate a hearty breakfast of pancakes, steak, five glasses of orange juice and lots of honey before spending the day at rest. He was visited by the Reverend Jesse Jackson, who came to wish him luck. In the final few hours, he watched Bruce Lee's *Enter The Dragon* to keep himself in a combative mood.

Both fighters arrived at the packed Caesars Palace Pavilion an hour before fight time and gave some final media comments. Leonard predicted, "I'll be moving as much as the little white ball on the roulette wheels at the casino. Thomas Hearns is going to fall before the tenth round. He will still be seeing my fists go pop-pop-pop in his dreams for weeks to come." Hearns replied, "Everybody talks about how great a boxer Ray Leonard is, especially Ray Leonard himself. He is going down for the count in the fifth round and when he wakes up on September 17, he will still be wondering what hit him."

BEFORE THE RING entrances began, the 24,083 sell-out crowd in the makeshift arena were introduced to the ringside celebrities, a sporting and Hollywood Who's Who. Bill Cosby, Dean Martin, David Brenner, Jack Nicholson, Muhammad Ali, Cher, Burt Reynolds, Richard Pryor and John McEnroe all received generous applause. Many tens of thousands more were watching live on closed circuit TV in arenas from New York to New Orleans, Seattle to Los Angeles. In all, the fight was aired at 298 locations in the United States and Canada and in more than one million homes on pay TV. The tension was reaching fever-pitch when Hearns, wearing a dressing gown with the words "Winner Take All" plastered across his shoulders, entered the ring. Hearns clapped Leonard's introduction, but then stalked him across the ring and fixed him with a baleful glare. Angelo Dundee responded by moaning to the referee about the amount of grease on Hearns, but was ignored. By the time the American national anthem had been sung by Lou Rawls, the temperature in the ring topped one hundred degrees.

Leonard was first out of his corner to score with a short left to the ribcage. Hearns's response was immediate: he fired back a straight left jab to Leonard's body and then used the momentum to come forward and catch him with another left to the face, followed by a right cross. A left hook then connected on the chin of Leonard and the noise level in the arena escalated. The Detroit man was instigating the action from the centre of the ring with Leonard keeping outside and looking for openings to launch sporadic attacks. He snaked out a left jab which connected with Hearns's temple but received an immediate counter to the kidneys. Hearns's younger brother, Billy, maintained a stream of invective throughout the action. "Stand up and fight, you chicken!" was one of his politer refrains. At the sound of the bell, Leonard feigned injury whilst smiling but Hearns copied his brother and responded with insults and sneers.

During the minute-long respite, Steward reminded his charge to use the advantage of his seventy-eight-inch reach, which was longer than all but four previous heavyweight champions, to the ultimate. The second round assumed much of the same rhythm as the first, with Leonard moving in a circle and trying to stay away from Hearns, who continued to score with left jabs to the nose and body. When another left caught Leonard flush in the face, it seemed to stir him to action and he retaliated with a left cross to the body. Despite this, the Detroit man enjoyed the most notable success when a stinging right cross knocked Leonard's head backwards. This undulating pace was maintained for the following two rounds, with the Hearns jab followed by the straight right cross, honed to perfection in the Kronk gym, having a significant effect. Leonard still managed to look classy without scoring much and slipped most of the bigger punches coming his way. He always looked dangerous on the counter-attack but he sustained a swelling under his left eye in the fifth round.

Perhaps spurred by the threat to his vision, the sixth round heralded a sustained effort from Leonard to exert his will. He opened up and scored with direct shots to Hearns's head and body. One particular short, power-packed left hook sank deep into his slim torso and drove him back into the ropes. Just before the bell sounded, Leonard visibly increased the pace further to cement his impressive superiority in the eyes of the judges and launched a relentless two-handed attack.

The seventh round looked like it would follow the pattern of the preceding one when Leonard opened with a left jab to the jaw of Hearns. However, in an instant, he hit back with a left and right to the head. Leonard then slipped inside Hearns's long jab to score with his own left jab and hook. Hearns caught him with a short right to the jaw but then took a stunning left and right, which jarred him and stood him rigid. Leonard sensed an opening and moved in to deliver a beautiful left-right combination, which required the Hit Man to quickly bring his gloves up to his head for protection. For the first time in the fight, referee Dave Pearl had to step in and break up the two fighters. After he wrestled them apart, Leonard was first to attack and he hit Hearns with three straight lefts to the head. He seemed to understand that he had established superiority and suddenly oozed confidence. With seconds to spare before the bell, Hearns stepped forward, bent to the left and delivered a powerful hook to Leonard's body. Leonard came straight back with two left hands to the face and took his second consecutive round by a clear margin.

In the eighth round, even Hearns appeared to understand the change in the tide as he stayed on the outside as Sugar Ray established the centre of the ring as his base. Both connected with effective body punches. Hearns landed with a short left hook to the chin which saw Leonard back up. Shortly afterwards, he caught Hearns with an overhand right which grazed the jaw and a following left hook that rattled his senses as he was moving away. Leonard pursued him and they moved along the ropes, locked in an absorbing battle of wills. Leonard scored with a right hand in the final few seconds to secure another round.

Neither boxer landed a punch during the first few seconds of the following round, although it was obvious that Leonard, dominating the ring's centre, was the aggressor now. He dug a hurtful left hook into the body, which prompted Hearns to get up on his toes, showcasing his footwork. This time, Hearns landed the final blows, connecting with two left hooks to Leonard's stomach before the bell. When they both retreated to their respective corners, spectators were divided about who was in front and the noise level increased by several decibels, as each fighter's supporters sought to give their backing.

The tenth round was another even session as both fighters appeared to have won the other's respect and seemed content to conserve energy for one final frenzied push for victory. There were protracted periods without either man landing a punch. But the lull was brief. Hearns landed a stiff left jab to the body and then Leonard threw a fast right cross to the side of his face before following through with a hurtful left hook to his unguarded body. Both men allowed the rest of the round to ebb away before they retreated to their respective corners to compose themselves for the imminent conclusion to their brutal ballet.

Leonard instigated the action when he leapt from his corner and charged at Hearns, grazing him with a right cross. He followed with a searing left hook to the body. Hearns matched his increased pace and both men traded jabs to the head before Hearns made his foe wince with a stinging straight right to the jaw. He ruthlessly doubled up on this by throwing an overhand right to the head and then connected with a jab. His best moment of the round came when his right-left combination was followed by a left uppercut directly under the chin. Hearns drove Leonard backwards and targeted his left eye, which was now almost closed. Despite this sustained attack, Leonard's fighting instinct still drove him to offer the round's final word, when he stormed back with a left-right as the bell sounded.

The following round continued in the same vein. Hearns threw the first shot, a heavy left jab flush in the face of Leonard, who was having obvious difficulty seeing out of his left eye. He followed this up with a hard right to the body, which sent Sugar Ray back onto the ropes, and another power-packed right into the ribcage, which landed with a thump. Hearns was in full flow and was only warded off when Leonard threw a looping right to the head. This bought him time and kept him outside the length of the longer arms of Hearns. He managed to avoid being trapped against the ropes again but he was rocked when a hard right hammered into his jaw just as the bell rang.

Leonard squinted through his quickly closing eye as he returned to his stool. Angelo Dundee, the sixty-second master, greeted him with an exhortation that would become famous: "You've got nine minutes. You're blowing it, son. You're blowing it. This is what separates the men from the boys. You're blowing it!" At the same time, he worked feverishly to reduce the swelling over his boxer's eye. His words galvanised Leonard, who opened the round by hitting Hearns with a fast one-two. Hearns retaliated with two jabs but slipped briefly to the canvas. They continued to trade punches but Hearns was first to back away as Leonard pursued him, punching with both hands. His relentless assault drove the Detroit man back into the ropes, where he slipped halfway through between the second and third strands and sat down on the ring apron. Hearns shook his head to signify it was not a knockdown, and again referee Davey Pearl concurred. Leonard, however, sensed blood. He had now become the predator as he hit Hearns with a left hook and right cross to the body and was almost wild, like a shark that has tasted blood. Leonard caught Hearns with another left and right that had Tommy dazed before he increased the pace of his attack again and had him on the ropes, hitting him with unanswered punches. Hearns's legs looked rubbery and Pearl was obliged to intervene and count to the mandatory eight just as the bell rang. It was a clear round for Leonard and the beginning of the end.

Leonard started the round by summoning some hidden energy and unleashing a blur of rights and lefts. He then dug a powerful right into Hearns's tired body and then staggered him with a headshot, which turned his long, slender legs to jelly. Although these seemed to betray him, his courage didn't and he tried to fight back, but the unremitting salvo of punches prompted the referee to move in close and check the damage. Before he could make an assessment, Leonard launched a further unanswered volley and referee Pearl had seen enough, finally waving it over at one minute and forty-five seconds of the fourteenth round.

There seemed to be a brief moment of silence. It was as if the crowd collectively realised that they had just paid witness to a modern-day classic. Then they erupted. Sugar Ray threw his hands skywards in a salute of victory. Hearns looked shell-shocked and sought solace amongst the desolate Kronk entourage.

When he stayed to hear the official announcement, it merely served to rub salt into the open wound of defeat. According to the three judges' scorecards, Hearns was ahead at the conclusion of the fight. Judge Duane Ford scored it 124-122, Judge Charles Minker had it 125-121 and Judge Lou Tabat scored it 125-123. Had he hung on for one more round, he would have won. In the following days, there would be a furore about these scores. The bout was one of those that divided expert opinion. Many good judges felt Hearns's skilful boxing had outscored Leonard's more potent but more erratic flurries, while others felt Leonard's greater aggression and harder blows should have received more credit. The venerable American broadcaster Don Dunphy had Hearns well ahead, as did colour commentator Dr Ferdie Pacheco. *Boxing News* editor Harry Mullan had Leonard three points in front, while his colleague Graham Houston gave Hearns a wide lead. Hugh McIlvaney, the doyen of British sportswriters, called the scorecards "scandalous" and the *Los Angeles Herald Examiner* was so outraged that it commented, "The scoring was an absurdity of near-felonious proportions." It was, of course, academic. Hearns had lost the richest fight in history.

While fireworks illuminated the Las Vegas night sky, the mood was funereal in Detroit. Over 10,000 tickets had been sold at the Cobo Arena and another 18,000 fans had packed the Joe Louis Arena to watch the live broadcast, whilst a staggering 27,000 had filled the Pontiac Silverdome to see the fight on the big screen. The denizens of the Motor City went into mourning. But even in his hour of defeat, Hearns had words for them.

"Detroit," he said, "I shall return."

# 8 COMEBACK

THE MORNING AFTER the night before saw Thomas Hearns, bedecked in a garish yellow tracksuit with the words "World Champion Thomas Hearns" etched across the back, attend the post-fight press conference. Both he and Leonard hid their emotions – and bruises – behind dark glasses. Hearns made a point of stating that the words on his ensemble should not be used to describe him. "Don't call me champion," he said. "When I get it back, then you can call me the champ." Although he confessed that he was feeling terrible about the result, and planned to quit boxing, it was with the caveat that he would not do so until he had reached his goals. When questioned what these were, he answered without hesitation, "Still four more world championships."

Just before he left Caesars Palace, Hearns went to see Jackie Kallen, the stunning blonde-haired PR agent for Kronk, who had held his jewellery for safe-keeping. She slipped a gold chain over his head and then handed him a ring, which had the words "World Champion" inscribed on it. Hearns quietly told Kallen, "I don't need that any more. I'll put it away until I become a world champion again."

Once back in Detroit, Hearns didn't leave his house for weeks. Defeat had hurt his pride deeply, and the inquest was loud and bitter. *Boxing Today* magazine led with a headline, "Leonard–Hearns: What Happened behind the Scenes?" which was heavily critical of the Kronk preparation methods. Ray

Leonard had studied over one hundred hours of footage of Hearns. In contrast, when Detroit NBC journalist Dan Shane had interviewed Hearns prior to the fight, he admitted that he hadn't looked at or studied any film of Leonard's fights because "that would only mess me up." He justified this by suggesting, "He won't be able to fight me like he did those other guys and I will have to adjust my style to him when the time comes." This lack of regard for his opponent was a consistent trait. Two days before Pipino Cuevas had defended his WBA title against South Africa's Harold Volbrecht in early 1980, in his only nationally beamed TV fight before fighting Hearns, Hearns was unaware that the fight was being broadcast. When he was informed, he told Dan Shane, "I probably won't get to watch the fight anyway, since I'm going upstate to watch my brother John box in the AAU championships."

There was also some apparent discontent within the camp. Don Thibodeaux, Steward's assistant trainer, was reported to have said he didn't like the way training was going in Las Vegas. He believed that Hearns was sparring too many hard rounds. This was supported by a Vegas fight fan named Bob Cerbe, who had watched both fighters' preparations and admitted that he was surprised to see Hearns spar for fifteen rounds just five days before the bout, at a time when Leonard was winding down his heavy workload. Others were perplexed by Hearns's tactics in the fight. "It was all kind of silly," said Duke Durden of the Nevada Boxing Commission. "All Hearns had to do was either stay away, or grab and hold Leonard – spit in his eye, or anything – the rest of the way, and the fight was his." Countless others wondered why Hearns didn't stay away from Leonard or clinch. Hearns was also asked why he didn't fire across more right hands: "You go with what works, and the right wasn't landing. I don't feel I hit him square with the right all night."

Rumour-mongers speculated that Hearns had struggled to make the weight. He had certainly spent time in the sauna just two nights before the fight, a move which would have left him drained. Another whisper was that Hearns was required to do roadwork twice a day in order to shed the excess weight. *Sports Illustrated's* boxing correspondent, Pat Putnam, mused, "The boxing grapevine knew that by the morning of the fight, Thomas Hearns had spent much of the previous two days steaming down. At the weigh-in, when Hearns tipped the scales at one hundred and forty-five pounds, a full two pounds lighter than what was required, he shot a glare in Steward's direction. The glare seemed to ask, 'What in hell did you let my weight get so low for?'"

There was strong criticism of the Kronk team, notably Steward, who refused to face the press until six days after he returned to Detroit. He held a press conference in the city's Ponchatrain Hotel and the reporters sneered that it had taken him so long to respond because he was busy rehearsing his excuses. Steward began by saying, "I already know what your questions are so I'll just start by issuing a statement that will answer a lot of your questions." He talked about a rematch after three comeback fights and said he had already discussed this with Mike Trainer. Although he had spent a lot of time telling reporters before the fight that Leonard would get increasingly tense, he conceded that it had been Hearns who had made this mistake and "got so involved, worrying about the people back in Detroit, that he wasn't himself in those last two days." He described Hearns's training programme as "the best I ever saw," but he did admit, "I felt maybe a pound more in weight would have helped." He refused to be drawn on the rumours about steaming down but instead cited a number of other excuses, including the spurious assessment that "Tommy's biorhythms weren't right." He then delivered his final statement and left, saying, "God works in mysterious ways. It just wasn't meant for us to win that night."

Some years later, Steward would offer a series of excuses for the defeat to the *New York Times* sportswriter Dave Anderson, which Anderson published in his book *Ringmasters; Great Boxing*

*Trainers Talk About Their Art* in 1991. He said he had lost control of the training camp, allowing Hearns too much leeway. For example, Hearns had defied a Steward edict not to indulge in friendly softball games in the afternoons at his Sugar Loaf training resort. He also sparred two days before the fight despite having been expressly told not to, and didn't eat properly the day before the fight, according to Steward. Hearns then came in too light at 145 pounds and, as a result, lacked the strength and energy to resist Leonard's punches as the bout wore on. "People said, 'Look what Ray Leonard did – ain't that great?' But we lost that fight in our own damn camp," said Steward. Hearns's views were not recorded.

ON 5 DECEMBER 1981, the *Detroit Free Press* featured an in-depth interview with Kronk stalwart Hilmer Kenty, who had not fought since losing his World Boxing Association lightweight title to Sean O'Grady in April. Since then, Kenty had undergone delicate surgery to repair a torn retina in his left eye and had received the all-clear to resume his boxing career. He was in full training for his comeback, due within the following two months. He also explained that he had severed his connections with long-time trainer Emanuel Steward and the Kronk.

Kenty's departure was the first major break from the tightly knit group of sixty amateur and professional fighters assembled by Steward. In a thinly veiled attack, Kenty said that his departure was due to "financial arrangements and the amount of time which Emanuel could spend with me." He recalled, "In the week of my title fight with O'Grady in Atlantic City, Emanuel had to go back to Detroit for three days in order to look after other Kronk fighters who were also boxing in a tournament." He also offered a glimpse into the tightly guarded world and hinted at unrest between the fighters, who all craved Steward's attention. "There were always three main fighters – Hearns, Mickey Goodwin and me," Kenty told the journalist. "Steward's a busy man. There were too many other fighters for him to devote time to me." This lack of personal attention was exacerbated by financial pressures. It was rumoured that Kenty was dissatisfied that his contract called for a fifty-fifty split of all purses. Kenty finally revealed that he would transfer to a new gym established by Don Thibodeaux, the assistant trainer who had himself split from Steward after the Leonard fight.

Three months after one of the most talked-about boxing matches of all time, Thomas Hearns started to focus on a comeback fight against Ernie "Grog" Singletary, a grizzled bulldog from Philadelphia who had established his record of twenty-four wins and three defeats whilst campaigning at middleweight. The fight was to take place on the undercard of what would be Muhammad Ali's last contest, against Trevor Berbick, at the Queen Elizabeth Sports Center in Nassau, Bahamas. Singletary was a tough campaigner who presented problems for any middleweight he faced. Before his meeting with Hearns, he had traded bombs in a war against Frank Fletcher for the United States Boxing Association title, which he had lost in eight fearsome rounds. He had also been to London to take on former middleweight champ Alan Minter in another bitter dispute, which he lost on a decision. Furthering his reputation as a fighter prepared to travel, he had fought in Cape Town against South African prospect Cameron Adams and won on points.

There was some concern in the camp about whether Hearns would be strong enough to campaign as a middleweight. He had been put on a diet requiring him to eat up to four substantial meals a day, including consuming steaks and protein milk shakes in order to help build him up to the middleweight poundage. Singletary had the opposite problem. He was a late substitute for the Mexican Marcos Geraldo, who initially had been deemed the ideal opponent for Hearns on his comeback trail, and the Philadelphian fighter reputedly had to shed nineteen pounds in eleven days to make the weight. "I had to starve myself for the last four days before I fought Hearns," he later recalled. "I didn't really have time to feel prepared for the actual fight, and during the fight, I tried to pace myself and take a shot when I had one."

In truth, he had very few opportunities to take a shot. Hearns, eager to impress, kept him away with a lightning-fast left jab, especially after his eye was cut open from a stray head butt in the opening round. Although the blood flowed down his face like an open tap at times, it was never a significant factor in the bout and his superior technique was enough to establish a wide lead. The robust Singletary occasionally looked dangerous with his wild swings but had to wade in close in order to land a punch on the fleet-footed Hit Man, and usually came second best in the exchanges. In the ninth round, Hearns opened a cut over Singletary's left eye and later said, "I thought the fight should have been stopped." He said, "The man couldn't see and I'm not the type of fighter who will hit a man when he's helpless." Hearns won a unanimous decision.

Despite the comfortable win and the boost to his confidence, the fight did create some doubt in Hearns' sense of his own destiny. He also had to have a large number of stitches inserted in the cut on his head. Before his next assignment, against Marcos Geraldo, another middleweight, he addressed the difficulty of moving up through the weight divisions. Before the Leonard fight he had spoken openly of winning an unprecedented set of titles at welterweight, middleweight and light-heavyweight; now he began to revise these targets. "Weight makes a great difference," Hearns told reporters, "I finally realized it when I fought Ernie Singletary in the Bahamas. I must have hit him a hundred times with everything I had and I still couldn't put him down. I was giving away ten pounds and I realised that bigger guys might carry more punching power but the big thing is they can absorb heavier punches. Roberto Duran learned that lesson the hard way. He knocked out

A smiling Thomas Hearns at the Kronk Gym early in his career, before the development of his more intimidating "Hit Man" image. *Photo by Chris Cuellar*

Members of the team that put Kronk on the map: (from left) Don Thibodeaux, Hearns, Emanuel Steward and Walter Smith.

TOP: Master trainer Emanuel Steward with Jackie Kallen, the publicist who coached a reticent Hearns in how to handle the media.

BOTTOM: Former world champion Angel Espada felt the power of the rising Detroit sensation in 1980 and slumped to defeat in four rounds. *Bob Ryder Collection*

TOP: Square-jawed welterweight champion Pipino Cuevas was a notoriously hard puncher and presented the sternest of tests. *Chris Cuellar*

BOTTOM: Cuevas reels from Hearns's deadly assault. The Mexican was dethroned in two explosive rounds. *Chris Cuellar*

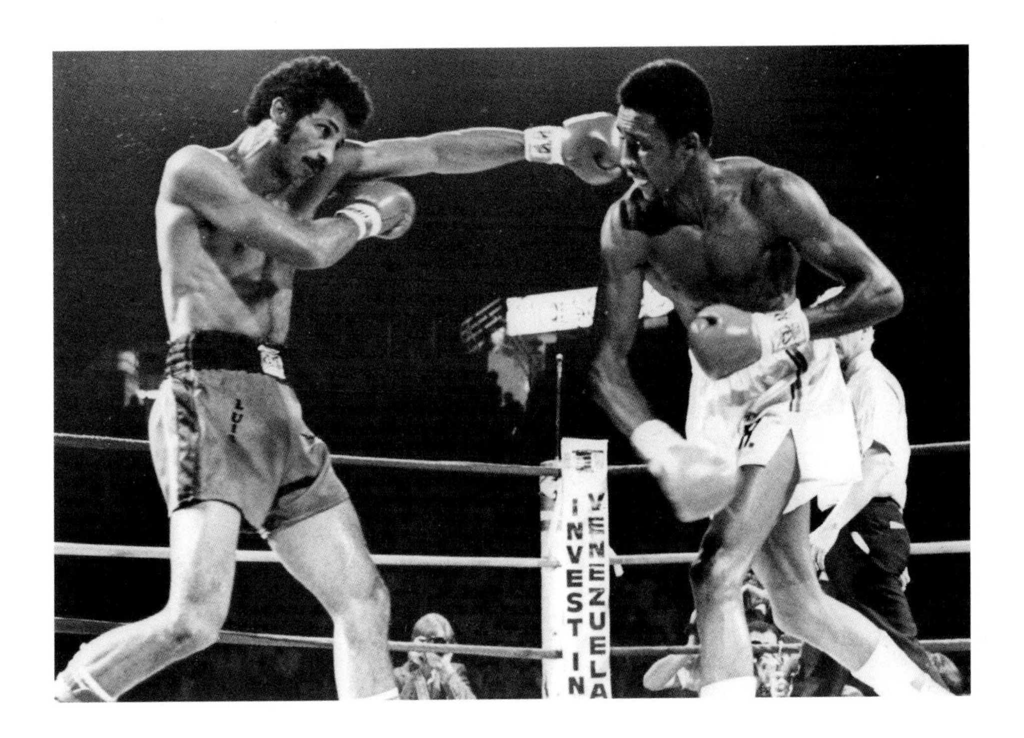

MUHAMMAD ALI PROFESSIONAL SPORTS

PRESENTS

THOMAS HEARNS
vs.
LUIS PRIMERA

WBA WELTERWEIGHT CHAMPIONSHIP OF THE WORLD

plus...
•Benny Ray Trusel
•Danny Paul
•Forest Winchester

MIDDLEWEIGHT
Caveman Lee

JR. WELTERWEIGHT
DuJuan Johnson

SATURDAY, DECEMBER 6, 1980
8 P.M. – JOE LOUIS ARENA

TOP: Challenger Luis Primera feels the force of Hearns's booming right hand. *Bob Ryder Collection*

LEFT: The Primera bout was promoted by MAPS, run by fraudster Harold Smith with money stolen from Wells Fargo in the biggest bank fraud in US history.

ABOVE: Ray Leonard catches Hearns flush with a fast left hook in their classic contest at Caesars Palace.

RIGHT: The end is near against Leonard as Hearns slumps through the ropes.

A relaxed Thomas Hearns faces the press. At his peak, in the mid-1980s, he was one of the most recognisable sports stars in the world. *Bob Ryder Collection*

everybody when he was a lightweight but when he moved up to welterweight and light-middle, he was seen as just another fighter."

The next fight took place at the Aladdin Casino's Theatre for Performing Arts in Las Vegas. Geraldo, whose birth name was Marcus Lopez, had been around the boxing scene for years and had fought a litany of famous names. The fact that he had gone the distance with both Marvin Hagler and Sugar Ray Leonard was testament to his toughness. He stood five feet and eleven inches tall and, significantly, his reach, at seventy-six inches, was only two inches shorter than Hearns's famous span. This was a useful addition to the armoury which had stopped thirty of his forty-nine opponents.

At the opening bell, Hearns strode purposefully from his corner and began stalking the Mexican. His jab was thrown briskly and he caught Geraldo's head and body with ease. It was also evident that his jabs contained plenty of power, as they pushed Geraldo backwards. However, it was not all one-way traffic as the orthodox Geraldo delivered some snappy lefts of his own, and midway through the round he issued a reminder of his own power when he sent over a powerful right cross that narrowly sailed past Hearns's head.

Within a split second, Hearns threw a terrific right lead that landed flush on Geraldo's mouth. The power of the punch drove him backwards into the ropes, his senses reeling. Hearns struck like the cobra of his nickname, sliding closer and finishing his prey with another short right followed by two devastating left hooks to the jaw. They sent Geraldo to the canvas and fight referee Joey Curtis waved Hearns away so he could begin his count. The Mexican groped towards the ropes and attempted to pull himself upright but fell backwards as the referee waved his hands to signal that the fight was over.

Hearns punched the air in delight – then quickly walked straight into another confrontation. Sugar Ray Leonard was analysing the action for CBS television and his questions were designed to rile his old foe.

"Why don't you admit you lost to me?" Leonard asked, with a big grin on his face.

Hearns was visibly annoyed and replied, "I'll never admit that I wasn't able to continue. You may have thought that I was out but I wasn't."

The two fighters continued to bicker when Leonard asked why Emanuel Steward had admitted that the fight should have been stopped. Hearns, enraged that Leonard was choosing not to dwell upon his impressive single round victory over Geraldo, quickly snapped, "I will speak for myself." Instead, he challenged Leonard: "Tell the world that you'll give me a rematch."

Leonard, not to be outdone, replied, "I'll give you a second fight if I hear you admit that the fight should have been stopped and that if the public demand that I give you a rematch."

It was typical Leonard. He loved to be in control, and his popularity with the huge US TV audience gave him the financial clout to call the shots. If Leonard wanted a fight, he got it, and if he didn't, no amount of baiting could draw him into one. Hearns would have to wait. For how long, nobody knew.

THE OFFICIAL ANNOUNCEMENT was made at a New York press conference on Monday, 22 March 1982. Thomas "Hit Man" Hearns would challenge "Marvelous" Marvin Hagler on 24 May in Las Vegas for the world middleweight championship. The figures that each fighter was due to receive were not as high as either could have earned against Ray Leonard, but they were enough to satisfy both. Hagler, as the reigning champion, would make $5 million. Hearns would take home more than $3 million.

Despite the vast sum on offer, there were those who believed Hearns was rushing needlessly to disaster. At twenty-three, he had time on his side. Hagler was six years older, heavier, stronger, more experienced and a formidable prospect. Why rush? "He is a child in a toy store," said *World Boxing* magazine of Hearns. "He knows what toy he wants, but he is not willing to wait until he is ready to play with it." Hearns wouldn't have any of it. "Benitez won't fight me," he said. "Leonard won't fight me. Marvin's the only one giving me a chance to fight. I know what I'm capable of doing. My strategy is to go in there and box." Emanuel Steward chipped in that Hagler was actually a small middleweight and Hearns had the physical advantages. But Hagler had a nasty habit of rendering such arguments obsolete. "All you got to do," growled the intimidating champion, "is bring the tall man down to your size and put his lights out."

Hanging like a spectre over the fight announcement was the figure of Ray Leonard. He was on holiday in Mexico City when he was asked for his reaction. He admitted that before he had announced his latest retirement, he had wanted to fight Hagler and suggested that he would have received $20 million as his purse. The only stipulation he demanded was that Hagler would weigh less than 155 pounds, despite the middleweight limit being 160 pounds. When Hearns was informed of this, he was scornful: "Marvin Hagler is the world middleweight champion. Why should he have to come to the scales at one hundred and fifty-five pounds?" Emanuel Steward sensed an opportunity to win PR points and agreed that Hearns would be happy to accommodate Leonard's demands and come in at any weight he wanted. In fact, Steward clarified that Hearns saw the Hagler match as a stepping stone towards eventually getting back in the ring with Leonard. Hagler refused to be drawn into the discussion and offered, "I'm just happy to see the fight materialize. It shapes up as by far the biggest payday of my career."

It was soon after this announcement that plans for the promotion started to go awry. Whilst doing his roadwork, Hearns tripped, and he sprained a finger in trying to break his fall. He later reported that he "felt like needles were shooting through my arm" when he landed a right hand during sparring. Doctors instructed him to desist from sparring for at least thirty days. When the news came out, Hagler was scathing. "Thomas Hearns is a sissy," he spat. "Boxers are used to fighting with pain. I suffer with sore hands all the time. In fact, all great fighters have sore hands. For a million dollars they could cut my finger off." This reaction caused an outrage amongst the Kronk fraternity. Emanuel Steward reassured them that Hearns was in great shape and wanted the fight to go on. He also denied claims that they were delaying the fight to allow Hearns to put on more weight and improve his condition. Steward pointed out that Hearns had fully participated in all the public appearances during the nine-day, eleven-city promotional tour to hype the fight, in contrast to Hagler, who cited flu as the reason for his non-attendance, even in Boston, just twenty-three miles from his hometown of Brockton.

Yet despite the positive news from Hearns and his team, fight promoter Bob Arum announced that the fight would be postponed. This was a contradictory message completely at odds with the fighter's own statements. Hearns conducted a Detroit press conference to announce that the May bout was still on. Within hours, Arum issued a statement from New York declaring, "The fight was postponed indefinitely." Arum claimed that the injury to the little finger on Hearns's right hand was the sole cause for the postponement. To support his actions he claimed he had consulted the three doctors who had examined Hearns and all three had attested that he should rest the hand for at least thirty days. This was in direct contrast to remarks made by two doctors who had appeared at Hearns's press conference.

It appeared that the real reason for the delay was more complex. In a Los Angeles federal courtroom, Judge Laughlin Waters had issued a temporary injunction on the bout, ruling against SelecTV and a pay television company which had the rights for a home telecast of the bout. Home Box Office, another pay television company, had filed suit claiming that Arum had granted it the rights for the Hagler versus Hearns bout. The judge's injunction effectively precluded the fight from going forward. Court insiders told press reporters that Arum's contract for the fight expired on 31 May, after which the promoter had no rights to the bout, and more importantly, no financial liability. For Bob Arum, the postponement of the fight beyond the contract expiration date allowed him to absolve himself of any financial liability which may have resulted in case of a judgement against him.

Hearns put the Hagler postponement behind him and agreed to box a ten-round contest at the Cobo Arena on Sunday, 25 July. The fight was scheduled to be televised by CBS for a national audience, although it was not broadcast within a one-hundred mile radius of Detroit in order to entice fans to attend. There was a palpable sense of relief by all parties about this return to action. Apart from Hearns, who was simply relieved to be back in the ring again, it was especially welcomed by Steward, who was reeling from the loss of two world championships (lightweight Hilmer Kenty had also lost his title) as well as the embarrassing first-round destruction of his middleweight prospect William "Caveman" Lee by Marvin Hagler.

The Cobo Arena bill was promoted by John Yopp, who had put on several Kronk-dominated tournaments and was a big fan of Hearns. Yopp was thrilled by the prospect of the prodigal son returning to his hometown. His opponent, twenty-four-year-old Jeff McCracken, was based in Los Angeles and was a highly regarded former amateur champion with an undefeated professional record of nineteen fights. Despite this unblemished record, McCracken was something of an enigma. He wasn't ranked amongst the top middleweights and he refused to attend the press conference called to announce the fight, further heightening the sense of mystery surrounding him. It was revealed that he had once been a sparring partner for Hearns, who confessed that he couldn't recall sparring with him. Hearns admitted that he had not viewed any recent films of his opponent as he had been preparing to fight for the past three months. Several opponents had been cited and a number of dates had been changed.

Hearns used the press conference to touch on a number of issues surrounding his future. He admitted that he was still annoyed about the circumstances that caused the Hagler fight to fall through and the subsequent failure of the camps to agree on venues and purses for a rescheduled contest. He also declared that he would not box as a welterweight again but would surrender the division to his friend and stablemate Milton McCrory, who was anointed by Hearns as the next champion. Finally, he expressed regret that a future return bout against Leonard looked to have been jeopardised. Leonard had been diagnosed with a detached retina and, despite surgery to repair the damage, it was looking increasingly likely that he would retire.

Observers could have been forgiven for thinking that Hearns's mind was not on the job at hand and that he might be dangerously underestimating his opponent, an impression reinforced when McCracken entered the ring. He looked in fine physical condition. He had picked up vital experience as a Marine Corps fighter and was a reputed body-puncher who had won all but two of his professional bouts by knockout, often in the early rounds. Reports suggested that he had a potent right hook and fought out of an exaggerated crouch, with his gloves held at chest height.

However, when the bell rang it was soon evident that he was not in the same class as Hearns and the Cobo Arena crowd was treated to a lesson in accurate, hurtful punching. Hearns dropped McCracken in the second, rocked him in the sixth, bruised and cut his face and eventually forced a technical knockout after one and a half minutes of the eighth round. The referee, Harry Papacharalamabous, was obliged to step in and stop the Hit Man from hammering McCracken, who had staggered, defenceless, onto the ropes. McCracken looked bewildered as he was led away to hospital with a broken nose.

Afterwards, Hearns sat in his dressing-room, wearing a crisp white tracksuit and a sailor's cap, and casted an uncritical eye over his own performance. He had wanted the fight to go a few rounds so the fans and critics could witness his range of skills and punching power. He expressed satisfaction at his patience in getting McCracken into a position where he could unload his big punches, although he was concerned that his hands had started to hurt after he had his opponent down twice in the second round. "My hands were starting to become very painful and there comes a time when you have to tell yourself 'forget it,' some guys just don't go down," he said. He reminded reporters that McCracken had only once before been on the canvas as a pro.

Again at ringside, microphone in his hand, was Sugar Ray Leonard, working as an analyst for CBS. He confessed that he had been mightily impressed by the calculating manner in which Hearns had gone about his business. He refused to take the bait from his hosts and make jokes about Hearns, as he had so frequently done since their celebrated showdown. Instead, he showed Hearns the respect he felt was merited, saying, "He is a legitimate middleweight now. No question about it."

Leonard would officially retire from boxing that November, ruling out the bout that Hearns most wanted. Instead his next title challenge would come against another of the sport's great stars, an equally brilliant talent who, like the Hit Man, was trying to rebuild his reputation after defeat to Leonard.

# 9 THE BOY WONDER

SIGNING THOMAS HEARNS to fight Wilfred Benitez was the easy part. Finding a promoter was more difficult. The arrest of Harold Smith had taken out one reckless spender, and a worldwide economic recession meant everyone was tightening their belts. Emanuel Steward tried various promotional organisations, to no avail. Hearns and Benitez were even required to participate in a bizarre promotional tour on which they couldn't confirm where the fight would be held. This was a soul-sapping chore for all concerned. Steward reflected, "It's strange but nobody is really pushing the question, 'Does anyone care about this fight?'" Steward ruminated that this signalled an end to the big money fights in boxing and that Hearns's match with Leonard represented a zenith for the sport.

Eventually Don King stepped in with a $6 million package, and advanced the two fighters nearly $1 million each. He prided himself on being an international boxing promoter and embraced the only option which appeared to be open to them, which was to stage the fight in Caracas, Venezuela, as most of the major boxing venues in North America had been approached but politely declined the offer, citing lack of money as the main reason. The driving force behind the Caracas deal was Graphite Cedeno, a local tycoon, who vowed to put up $1 million to stage the contest and also provided fifty round-trip tickets for each party. King was eager to clinch the deal and shamelessly invoked a bogus racial solidarity between promoter and boxer, as he so often had in the past. "I assured Steward they would get a fair shake in Caracas. After all, I'm black and Tommy Hearns is black, and I wouldn't let anything happen to him," he said. "They have no reason not to fight there. They already know that Hearns is the most popular fighter in the world with South Americans."

In truth, Emanuel Steward had few reasons not to accept it. The real stumbling block was Hearns, who was reluctant to fight outside the United States. Steward argued that while they could call off the fight, it would seriously damage his credibility, given the similar farrago with middleweight champion Marvin Hagler just a few months earlier. "I can't say Caracas is out but it's not in yet, either," he told the press. Steward tried to get Hearns to see the bigger picture, that economic woes were likely to reduce his earning options in America.

This final point was captured by Detroit sportswriter, George Puscas, who wrote a Don King-influenced article headlined "Boxing's Gold Mine Runs Dry." Puscas mused that King had asked the fighters to reduce their purses by $250,000 each to reflect the sad state of his business. King was of the opinion that most fighters had a wildly exaggerated view of their worth and a wake-up call was awaiting them. He blamed the economic slowdown and bemoaned the lack of genuine superstars, excepting the retired Ray Leonard, who had followed Muhammad Ali as boxing's number one money-maker. King believed that "Hearns has possibilities to develop like them. He has a different kind of charisma, if only he would develop a smile."

Hearns was still reluctant to fight outside America, which forced the increasingly desperate King to persuade bosses in New Orleans to host the fight. He assured them that "under normal circumstances, we'd expect to have fifty thousand people in the Superdome to see this fight" and said he would guarantee at least half that number, which would still allow them to make money. He took a hit, however, on ticket sales for closed-circuit television, a market that seemed to have collapsed. Even in Hearns's traditional stronghold of Detroit, the Windsor and Allen Park theatres cancelled showings of the fight, leaving the Joe Louis Arena, the Pontiac Silverdome, and the Royal Oak, Americana and Mai-Kai theatres as the only venues to show the fight. They would eventually draw only 10,000 fans each. King used this as a bargaining chip to persuade both Hearns and Benitez to take the $250,000 reduction in their $1.5 million purses. Finally the date was set for 3 December 1982, on a bill dubbed as "The Battle of Champions." Sharing top billing with Hearns and Benitez was a great fight between the fabulous Wilfred Gomez and the all-action Mexican Lupe Pintor for the super-bantamweight crown.

FOR ALL THAT it had been such a hard fight to sell, Hearns-Benitez was an intriguing contest, matching one of the most explosive punchers in memory against the most gifted defensive boxer of his generation. Wilfred Benitez was born in the Bronx, New York, on 12 September 1958, the youngest of eight children to Puerto Rican immigrants Gregorio and Clara Benitez. Life in the Bronx required the Benitez children to grow up quickly, and at just four years old Wilfred's father introduced him to boxing. By the age of seven, when Gregorio decided to move his young family back to Puerto Rico, young Wilfred was showing a natural aptitude and was perceived as exceptional by his junior coaches. At fourteen, he was selected to represent Puerto Rico in the 1973 Central American and Caribbean Games, in Costa Rica. He was drawn against the Olympic champion, an experienced Cuban, and although he lost it was only by a split decision. A short while later, with a record of just six losses in over 100 amateur bouts, he applied for a professional licence. Because he was under the required age of consent, his father, who also acted as his manager, lied about his age and entered his son's date of birth as 12 September 1956.

In November 1973, aged seventeen according to his licence but fifteen in reality, Benitez took his first steps in the professional ranks and knocked out Hiram Santiago in one round. His ascent thereafter was rapid. Benitez stood at five feet ten inches tall and possessed a reach of seventy inches (compared to Hearns's seventy-eight inches). His array of boxing skills, allied with his devastatingly accurate counterpunching ability, earned him the nickname "El Radar" in Puerto Rico. He became the youngest-ever world champion when he defeated light-welterweight king Antonio Cervantes at the age of seventeen, and went on to beat Carlos Palomino for the welterweight title. His seemingly inexorable rise was halted when he met Ray Leonard in November 1979, in a battle of the prodigies. He took Leonard to the limits of his abilities before losing near the end of the fifteenth round of his welterweight title defence. "It was like fighting the image of myself in a mirror," Leonard later commented. "He was just as quick as I was." Benitez quickly bounced back to win the WBC light-middleweight title in emphatic style from Britain's Maurice Hope and had defended it twice, including a surprisingly straightforward points win over Roberto Duran. He had lost only to Leonard in forty-six fights.

His rapid rise at such a young age seemed to curtail Benitez's maturity. Gregorio was the dominant force in his life and would whack his son hard across the face during a training session or fight if he thought he was not performing to his high expectations. This led to impulsive and erratic behaviour from Benitez, who would threaten to retire from boxing altogether after unsatisfactory displays, such as his draw with Harold Weston. It was this part of his nature that seemed to stop him being embraced in popularity by boxing fans. He was acknowledged as technically perhaps the finest boxer in recent years – including Ray Leonard and

Muhammad Ali – and was admired for winning his third world championship before the age of twenty-four. But Benitez wanted the respect he felt he had earned. He was now managed by Jim Jacobs, who had helped negotiate the million-dollar purses for the fights against Leonard and Duran, and Benitez had outlined his new ambition was to win four world titles. He viewed his match against Hearns as the most direct route to Marvin Hagler, the undisputed middleweight champion.

Benitez was a notorious trash-talker, and during one of the pre-fight press conferences he sneered, "I want to beat Hearns really badly. In fact, I hope he dies out there. That will be better for him." Apart from the inflammatory nature of his comments, it was an especially insensitive remark, as it came just two weeks after Korean lightweight Duk Koo Kim had died following his bout with American Ray Mancini. The public furore was predictably intense but at his next meeting with the press, ten days later, Benitez chose to repeat his crass statement rather than apologise for it. Sitting in the bowels of the Superdome with a towel covering his dyed red hair, he dismissed Hearns, claiming that he had only seen one round of him on film, and assured the outraged reporters that he meant to carry out his threat.

"Wilfred, are you sorry you said that you hoped that Hearns died in the ring?" asked one.

"No," he said. "That's boxing."

Hearns declared that beating Wilfred Benitez was more important than beating Ray Leonard because he didn't want to taste the bitter pill of defeat again. He admitted that he had seriously considered quitting boxing several times, although it wasn't the loss to Leonard that had caused these doubts but the increasing frustration in trying to resume his career. He said, "Every time a fight has been arranged and then cancelled it has brought back the same reaction, which is to think, 'To hell with it!'" He was eager to clarify the situation surrounding the collapse of the fight with

Hagler as well: "I know a lot of people blame me for that fight never coming off. The thing is, I waited all day in a New York office for Hagler to come and sign the contracts. We were both going to make less money than was initially promised but I was there to sign. He never showed up." He reasoned that if he could defeat Benitez, his status within the boxing world would be restored and he wouldn't experience the frustration of not getting regular fights. "Rated fighters will always fight a champion. They believe that they might get lucky. If you haven't got a title, they haven't got a reason to fight you."

He turned his attention to Benitez and expressed his bemusement at the violent threats that the Puerto Rican had made. "It is only when I'm not there that he says these things," Hearns said. "He claims to be a friend of mine but he's afraid to speak his real feelings when I'm around." He repeated his earlier claims that he rarely watched fights on television but argued that the help he offered when training his Kronk teammates had given him a keen insight into the strengths of other fighters. "Benitez is much classier than Leonard," he said. "In lots of ways, he can be more difficult than Leonard because he's smarter. Leonard repeats his punches a lot even when they don't work but Benitez never shows you the same thing twice." To counter this approach, Hearns claimed that he had adapted his own style. "I won't be in Benitez's face to get hit by him. I won't be running but I'll attack him from different angles."

Hearns settled into the luxurious Sheraton Hotel two weeks before the fight and his training routine intensified. He was a stickler for punctuality and decided that at precisely 5:42 a.m. he should meet nine of his Kronk teammates and head to the City Park for a daily dawn run of four miles, which he completed in twenty-one minutes. Back at the hotel, he would return to his bed for an hour of sleep before rising again at eight o'clock to order room service. His breakfast was also precise and consisted of two eggs, hash browns, muesli with strawberries and a large glass of milk. Except for two oranges and an occasional treat of his favourite Chinese food at dinner, this was all he would consume for the day. He would then spend the whole afternoon in the gym but he also resolved to take heed of Don King's warnings and vowed to be more co-operative with the media for the Benitez fight, agreeing to conduct four interviews a day.

Throughout the build-up, Hearns had shown his rival the respect he felt was deserved. This approach changed when he felt that it was not being reciprocated. Both fighters had agreed to ride on a float through downtown New Orleans during one of the city's celebrations in order to drum up more ticket sales for the fight, which were not going well at the box office. Hearns arrived on time and was infuriated that Benitez did not appear at all. When they next met at the pre-fight weigh-in, Benitez tried to stare down Hearns. Rather than indulge him, Hearns studiously ignored Benitez. Emanuel Steward told Walter Smith, the veteran cornerman, that he had never seen Hearns look so serious.

When the Detroit Hit Man and The Radar finally stepped through the New Orleans Superdome ropes, Benitez repeated his tactics, marching across the ring to confront Hearns. The two stood chest-to-chest in a prolonged stare-out as their respective camps watched and hurled insults. But once the bout began, Hearns set the early pace with fast footwork, snappy jabbing and a willingness to use the whole ring. By the end of round two, a red mark had appeared under Benitez's left eye. Hearns was in the ascendant, and in the third, Benitez noticeably showed respect for his pulverising right, ducking out of range whenever it looked as though the challenger was about to pull the trigger. Benitez finally came to life late in the round when he scored with a solid left hook, but Hearns again won the points. Hearns squandered a point in the fourth round when, despite continued warnings from Mexican referee Octavio Meyran, he held the champion's head down. This seemed to spur on Hearns, and in the following round he felled

Benitez with a thundering right cross which landed directly on the jaw. The champion dropped down on his gloves but immediately jumped up to take a standing eight count.

This notable success had a strange effect on Hearns. His tactics, which had been proving highly effective, changed and he seemed gripped by caution, electing to win the fight on points rather than force the advantage he had so obviously seized. Benitez sought to lure him to the ropes, where he intended to drag him into a brawl – the Puerto Rican was exceptional at infighting with his back against the hemp. Hearns declined to follow and stayed in the centre of the ring. There was a stand-off, which Hearns tried to break by drawing out Benitez. Benitez stuck to his guns and refused to be suckered, making for a dull strategic fight rather than the classic it had promised to be.

Hearns did enjoy some success. He nearly finished Benitez with a sizzling right hand with just ten seconds left in the sixth round. The champion sagged into the ropes but was rescued by the bell. In the eighth round, Hearns threw another solid right that connected on Benitez's head, but then winced in pain. It was obvious that he had damaged his fist. This punch was to have prolonged repercussions over the coming years, as it shattered several small bones in his wrist, which popped through the linear muscles at the back of his hand. The injury spurred Benitez on to become the aggressor and he was rewarded at the end of the ninth when he caught Hearns with a short left hook which put him on the seat of his pants. Hearns protested that it was more of a slip than a punch and he jumped back to his feet immediately to prove it.

The tenth round was the best of the fight as both fighters elected to throw off their caution and went at it in a series of toe-to-toe exchanges in the centre of the ring. Benitez caught Hearns with a stinging right cross and was greeted with a left hook in return. Benitez had won the last two rounds in some style and during the minute-long break, Emanuel Steward reminded Hearns to get back to the basics and employ his left jab to re-establish his lead. Whenever Benitez threw his own jab, Hearns was quick to counter with a left and then a right hook, causing Benitez's nose to bleed continuously.

The champion's frustration showed and Hearns felt obliged to twice implore the referee to stop Benitez butting him. Although both men attempted to outjab each other, it was mainly the searing left of Hearns which dominated. In the final round, Benitez made a final effort to retain his title and hit Hearns with a right lead which shook him down to his toes. The exchange embodied the pattern of the whole fight as Hearns responded by snapping Benitez's head backwards with a stinging left hook before landing the two last punches of the contest, a left and right to the head, just before the bell sounded.

It went to the judges' scorecards. Dick Young favoured Hearns by the wide margin of 146-136 whilst Tony Castalano gave it to Hearns by 144-139. Yet Lou Fillipo called it a draw at 142-142, a score which baffled the vast majority of onlookers. Emanuel Steward explained their conservative ring strategy, using the "we" beloved of boxing managers. "We wanted to outbox him and so we made the fight a footwork contest," he said. "We countered his counters." Hearns accepted the congratulations and pronounced himself "very happy to have accomplished another one of my goals – to become a world champion again."

At the post-fight press conference, Hearns continued to be magnanimous in victory and he brought his mother Lois along to hear him agree to a rematch. "I'm not the type of person who forgets a favour," he said. "He gave me a chance, so I'll be glad to give him one." Benitez, however, could not resist continuing his boorish behaviour, shouting, "I won the fight. I knocked Hearns down and he knocked me down. I am the true champion. It was only the judges who beat me." Gregorio Benitez was even less sanguine. As the chief cornerman, he was asked why he had instructed his son, before the fifteenth and final round, to take it easy because he had won the fight. He screamed, "How could you *not* think that? What fight were you watching?" Few agreed with him.

Once back in Detroit, the new WBC light-middleweight champion went to hospital for an examination of the collateral damage he had received in winning the fight. His right hand was more seriously damaged than initially thought; he had suffered a dislocation of two bones in his forehand. Dr Frederick Lewerenz, the Kronk team physician, told the media that Hearns "had suffered a separation of the carpal and metacarpal bones in his hand and wrist, which had lifted whenever he threw a punch." Hearns predicted that it would keep him away from the gym for only six weeks. In fact it would keep him out of competition for seven months.

Wilfred Benitez would never again reach the lofty heights of greatness. He fought on for another eight years – and was even handled by Emanuel Steward at one point – but his magic deserted him and he lost almost as many as he won. In 1996, at the annual induction ceremony at the Boxing Hall Of Fame, in Canastota, New York, came an unforgettably sad spectacle when Benitez was called forward to be honoured. The shambling gait and laboured speech of boxing's youngest-ever world champion was a salutary reminder that not all sporting heroes live happily ever after. Benitez ended up not only penniless, with all his money gone, but suffering from an incurable degenerative brain condition, post-traumatic encephalopathy, caused by the punches he took in the ring.

# 10 THE HIT MAN UNLEASHED

WHILE THE NEW champion's broken hand was taking longer to heal than expected, Emanuel Steward was delving deeper into the internecine world of high-level boxing politics. Steward entered initial negotiations for future fights with Don King, someone he had previously vowed he would never do business with again; Steward had worked with King when promoting his boxer Milton McCrory's fight against the Welshman Colin Jones for the world welterweight title and found the experience deeply unpleasant. At the same time, he met with Bob Arum, King's nemesis. Steward and Arum had previously tried to put on the match between Hagler and Hearns. What did surprise most fight observers, however, was the unlikely alliance between Steward and Mike Trainer, who joined forces with him to enhance the career of Tommy Hearns.

Trainer was the Maryland lawyer who had orchestrated the career of Ray Leonard and helped make him a multi-millionaire, an American idol and the most popular sports figure in the country. Steward had been impressed that Trainer had been behind the two extremely lucrative Leonard–Duran fights and was equally impressed with his ability to cut through bureaucracy to arrange the Leonard and Hearns fight, which was then the richest fight in history. Steward was most impressed, however, by Trainer's ability to turn the tables on the powerful promoters. Rather than allow them to select the fighters and make the matches, he chose the promoters he wanted and made them bid against each other to elicit the best deal for his fighter. It seemed obvious for Trainer and Steward to enter an alliance. Trainer explained that his role was to go to the networks and secure a regular schedule of fights for Hearns, which would allow the Kronk team to be more independent. "When Tommy got his purse cut by King before the Benitez fight, he didn't like it," he said. "Hearns is one of the brightest fighters out there and the networks are out there looking for fights. It makes sense to facilitate the two parties."

The superfight of 1983 was to be Marvin Hagler versus Roberto Duran, but even before it went ahead there was more speculation about a Hagler–Hearns bonanza in 1984. Hearns needed to keep winning, but his only bout in 1983 was a disappointing ten-round points victory over the light-hitting Murray Sutherland in July. Sutherland, who had twice fought for the light-heavyweight title, was a late, over-the-weight substitute for James Green, who was to have challenged Hearns for his light-middleweight title. Some ring rust was inevitable after Hearns's lengthy layoff through injury and he received criticism for not blasting out the Michigan Scot, even though he landed some heavy shots and was in control throughout. "Many in the crowd booed the verdict but this seemed more a matter of sympathy for the underdog than anything," reported *Boxing News*.

Hearns knew that after being out of the public eye for so long, he needed to begin 1984 with an impressive performance. Various opponents were suggested and rejected for a variety of reasons until the name of Luigi Minchillo, known as the "Italian Warrior," came up. Minchillo had won the Italian amateur welterweight title and participated in the 1976 Olympic Games. After the Montreal Games, he was offered the opportunity to turn professional in America but he declined because he wished to remain in Pesaro with his wife and two young children. He had joined the police force at the age of eighteen and forged a respectable career within the ranks whilst boxing in his spare time. He had put his police career on temporary hold in order to pursue his career and his aggressive, durable style soon began attracting nationwide attention. He had never been knocked down in his forty-four professional fights and his only two defeats were to Roberto Duran on a points decision and Alvaro Scarpelli early in his career.

Three months before losing to Duran, Minchillo had won the European light-middleweight championship with a close decision over Louis Acaries. In March 1982, he defended this crown by dominating the former world light-middleweight champion Maurice Hope. He then announced his retirement and declared his intention to return to the police. Only the offer to face Hearns enticed him to return to boxing. "I have the greatest possible respect for Hearns," Minchillo said through his manager and interpreter, Giovanni Branchini. "He is a great, great champion." Minchillo was several inches shorter than Hearns and gave away a lot of reach advantage. He argued that this would allow him to get inside his long reach and use his aggression to stay on top of Hearns for twelve fast rounds. The Italian had won forty-two of his forty-six professional fights.

The bout was originally scheduled to take place in Las Vegas but the Katz Sports Syndicate, which was going to televise the fight from Caesars Palace, pulled out of negotiations at a late stage. The fight was switched to Detroit's Joe Louis Arena instead and the date was changed from 27 January to 11 February. This switch meant that there would be no telecast of the fight in the local area but this mattered little to the champion, who was thrilled to return to his hometown for the third time in over three-and-a-half years since winning the welterweight title from Cuevas. Emanuel Steward, who was also preparing Milton McCrory for a title defence against Milton Guest, suggested that the Hearns fight would be a forerunner for regular monthly tournaments to be held at the Joe Louis and Cobo arenas. He had been working with Detroit Mayor, Coleman S. Young and the arena-owner Mike Ilitich to create a long-term boxing programme. The shows would be promoted by Gold Circle Productions, a new company fronted by Bill Kozerski, a Polish-American ally of Steward's.

The plan, however, provoked an outcry when Detroit City Council voted, by a close 5-4 majority, to spend $100,000 to become the official sponsor of the Hearns–Minchillo fight. Mayor Young supported the plan as part of his "Do It in Detroit" campaign to boost the city's bleak image, but dissenting councilmen said the money would be better spent upgrading services in a city with appalling social problems. Howard Cosell, the nation's most recognisable television sports announcer, got in on the act by suggesting that Detroit would be the "laughing stock of the nation" if it spent taxpayers' dollars promoting boxing matches. Mayor Young argued that the funding was an important part in advertising the city to attract extra tourist and convention dollars.

A crowd of 18,500 fans turned up at the Joe Louis Arena to demonstrate that the drawing power of Hearns in his hometown was still as strong as ever. They watched him take a lot longer than anticipated to win by a unanimous decision over twelve rounds against the brave Italian champion. Despite his pre-fight boasts, Minchillo didn't seem to have any answers to Hearns's long, probing jabs and hooks, his right hand leads and sustained sharp body-punching.

Hearns opened with a combination of class and power but early in the second round, he sustained a cut across his right eyelid, which bled profusely until his corner could stem the flow. This was a spur to change up his gears and begin to dictate the tempo of the bout. In the eighth round he connected with a dizzying combination of lefts and rights to Minchillo's kidneys, forcing him backwards, his face contorted in pain. Minchillo did respond with some solid right hands in close but he failed to deal with Hearns's longer reach. The tenth round ended in confusion as Hearns thought he had heard the bell and began walking back to his corner. His Italian foe thought that Hearns had quit and began celebrating. His victory dance lasted three seconds before Hearns realised his error and resumed the fight. In the twelfth round, Hearns opened up and came close to knocking out the robust Italian with a straight right, providing further evidence that his damaged right hand was once again fine.

Although it was a commanding display, Hearns – who would later say it had been his toughest fight, tougher even than Leonard – did show some flaws. Occasionally, Minchillo was able to easily trap him on the ropes, where he was able to nullify the long reach and get close to causing damage. Hearns was almost too eager in his desire to throw right leads off his front foot, instead of positioning his weight behind them. Still, he emerged as a big winner on all three judges' scorecards: Mexico's Abraham Chavarra scored it 120-110, Guy Jutras of Sweden had it 118-109 and Puerto Rico's Cesar Ramos scored it as 120-109. Hearns declared himself satisfied. "I am pleased with my performance and the fact that my right hand held up all the way. Minchillo is a person who is able to take a lot of punches," he said. "I landed lots of shots and he just kept taking them all." Emanuel Steward, however, was not so easily pleased. He told aides that Hearns had lacked stamina and his legs were gone in the last five rounds. And he told Hearns that he would need to improve before he faced Roberto Duran in the summer months, a fight for which negotiations were already well advanced.

Before he could face Duran, Hearns had to deal with a more complex and ultimately more damaging battle which would rumble on for many years. In May, the *Detroit News* headlined, "Michigan Claims Hearns' Unpaid Taxes Are A Knockout." Pete Waldmeir, an investigative journalist, had been digging around in the fighter's finances and claimed that he owed $103,000 in unpaid taxes. His piece said that that Hearns's handlers insisted it must be some sort of a "mix-up," but records on file in Wayne County show that a personal corporation, Thomas Hearns Enterprises INC., that the boxer headed and controlled owed the state of Michigan the money in unpaid withholding taxes. Emanuel Steward declared the allegations to be "news to me." He also said, "Thomas doesn't know anything about it, either. He pays a ton of money in taxes. In fact, every time we turn around, it seems, he's giving the Government taxes." Soon afterwards, another article by Waldmeir alleged that Hearns owed the Friends of the Detroit Library $36,000 after he had pledged $2 from every ticket sold for his fight against Minchillo to the fund, which was intended to keep the Detroit Public Library open. This time Waldmeir went for the jugular, under the headline "Hit Man Hearns is far from a hit as a human being." He called Hearns "a deadbeat" and drew unflattering parallels between the fighter's millionaire lifestyle and the poverty of much of Detroit, asking why the fighter couldn't "come up with a few bucks to keep a promise to a bunch of needy kids." Hearns blamed the fight promoters and claimed, "They told me to stand up and make that promise but I never intended to give [the money] for every ticket sold."

Partly in response to the bad publicity, Thomas Hearns granted Tommy George, a journalist from the *Free Press Sports*, exclusive access to his world during the build-up to his fight with Roberto Duran. Hearns was generous in his hospitality and open with his views on boxing and beyond. He opened the doors to his extravagant Southfield home, a secluded oasis hidden by towering trees and a six-foot-high fence, where he proudly parked his gold Mercedes alongside his silver Rolls Royce. Inside, standing next to a golden suit of armour, were several tributes to Elvis Presley, including a huge photograph of the "King" and an ornate, black baby-grand piano. There were few reminders, however, of the sport which had afforded him such luxury. Hearns casually explained that he had grown tired of seeing his boxing belts, trophies and other items of memorabilia, so either gave them to friends or to his mother.

Hearns viewed life with an endearing simplicity. He enjoyed nothing better than spending time with his friends from his younger days. They would play for hours on the various computer and arcade games which Hearns had acquired over the years and he admitted that his warrior's instinct was sometimes evident during these competitions, because he "absolutely hated to lose at anything." He also spoke about his ambitions outside the ring. As a teenager he had wanted to become a policeman. He had enlisted for fifteen weeks' training at the Detroit Metro Police Academy and became one of the city's fifteen hundred police reserves. He eagerly volunteered his time at least three times a week, which involved riding in a scout car, carrying a gun and making arrests along with his regular partner, Terry Hodge, who had been a Detroit policeman for over eleven years. Hearns explained that he did it simply because "it was something I like doing. I couldn't just sit around and box all the time. I'd get bored."

His police partner, Hodge, said, "He's not at all fearful. In fact, he has a great deal of common sense. When we encounter a situation, he's very quick to perceive what is happening and to act. When we hear about a fight on the radio, he wants to be first on the scene. His influence shows, especially with kids, because when Tommy shows up in uniform, the fight is over. They're more interested in knowing about him and playfully sparring with him." He recounted, "I've seen the guy get up from a meal and go out and stop a couple of kids scuffling on the streets. The kids' eyes magnify ten times their size. A lot of regular police officers wouldn't get up from a meal and go and do that. He's not like a world champion on the job. He's a partner."

Hearns was especially candid about his relationship with his family. His blood father, Thomas Jackson, had died a few months before in Jackson, Tennessee. Hearns had attended the funeral and expressed regret at never having had a relationship with him. "It was sad that I never met him but I actually felt more sadness for my half-brothers and sisters who were there." He was effusive in his praise for his mother and all she went through with her nine children. "I've tried to show her that I care for her, but you can only do so much with money. I've stopped trying to buy her things and just show her with my heart. That means a lot more than trying to go out and buy her the world."

He also used the interview to address rumours about alleged cocaine abuse and his supposed involvement in a fight at Southfield's Blend Disco, where a man was fatally shot. Hearns had been at the disco during the killing and the rumour mill had gone into overdrive. Tommy George put the allegations to him, including one that he had found the gun in a trash bin and another that he had chased the gunman and held him until police arrived. Hearns denied all these rumours. "I've always considered my health and I don't drink or even like to be around people that smoke. There was never any interest in that or cocaine or any other substance for me. People always try and say bad things about me. I have lots of friends from childhood who were involved in lots of things, but that doesn't make me guilty by association. I don't judge what anybody does. The other stuff about the gun is all untrue. I've heard it all and I have learned to take no notice. People will talk no matter what I do."

When he discussed his relationships with the Kronk gym, Hearns was effusive in his praise for two particular individuals. He thanked Prentiss Byrd and Emanuel Steward for helping him cope with the status his boxing success had bestowed on him. Byrd was an adviser, a public relations man and a big brother. "He's more than a PR man to me," said Hearns, "he's more like my buddy. I depend on him." When he spoke about his relationship with Steward, his voice dropped to a soft whisper, "He's like a daddy. I have a great deal of love for Emanuel. He was there for me when no one else was. Emanuel is the one who made my career happen. Without him, I would not be the fighter I am today even with all the determination I have." However, when asked about reports that he had earned $12-14 million through boxing, or about the management deal he enjoyed with Steward, Hearns refused to comment. He regarded their financial relationship as confidential. He did concede that he had carefully invested his earnings through a business called Thomas Hearns Enterprises Inc. Finally, he spoke about his career vision. "I want to show every man on earth that I can win four world titles in four different weight divisions. No other man or woman, no human being has ever done that."

Writer Ralph Wiley also visited Hearns before the Duran fight. He found a complex, sometimes contradictory character, restless to prove himself. "Fighting was Hearns's single abiding interest," wrote Wiley, in his boxing memoir *Serenity*. "He bought a Young Chang grand piano and didn't learn to play a note. He ordered the construction of an ornate bar in his home, but didn't drink. He built a glove-shaped pool, but didn't swim. He talked of becoming a businessman, while talk of business easily bored him. He said he wanted to be an actor, yet his expression never changed. A confirmed bachelor, he drove a gold 500 series Mercedes Benz. But he was not a carouser. He'd rather spar with you than speak to you."

ROBERTO DURAN WAS a genuine living legend. So when the Detroit Hit Man signed to box "Hands of Stone" for the World Boxing Council light-middleweight championship, boxing fans smiled in anticipation of a classic encounter. It was a fight everyone wanted to see.

Bizarrely, it was initially destined for the unusual location of a beach in the Bahamas, but was relocated to Nevada because of logistical problems and lack of support for such an inaccessible venue. The event was promoted by a consortium of three men with little experience at the highest level of boxing promotion, though one of them, Sheldon Saltman, had been involved with the Ali-

Frazier fights of the 1970s. The other two were Bill Kozerski, a close ally of Emanuel Steward, at Gold Circle Productions and Walter Alvarez, who was based in Miami. The promotional establishment of Bob Arum and Don King were quick to scorn their efforts and the bout was dogged by fears over money. Steward later claimed that he was only persuaded not to pack their bags and take Hearns home by a personal guarantee from the president of Caesars Palace.

Hearns stayed in training after the Minchillo fight. He was excited to be facing Duran, who was a figure he had admired from afar for a number of years. The thirty-three-year-old Panamanian legend had a well-earned reputation as a teak-tough warrior with a solid punch and vastly underrated defensive skills. In his eighty-one-fight career he had beaten the very best, including Leonard. He boasted a record of seventy-six wins, fifty-seven by the short route, with only five defeats.

In the months leading up to June, the Kronk was a hive of activity. The 1984 Olympic Games were to be held in Los Angeles, and Steward had been asked to help coach the boxing team. Many of the Olympians trained there for several months, including Frank Tate and Steve McCrory, who were both already Kronk members, while team star Mark Breland was earmarked to join Kronk. They were pitched in alongside top professionals such as Mike McCallum, Milton McCrory and Hilmer Kenty, and all sparred with Hearns, helping to sharpen him up. Hearns boasted that it was the best preparation for a fight he had ever enjoyed and predicted that he would finish Duran within the first two rounds.

Arriving in Las Vegas to conclude his preparations, Hearns had to contend with an unexpected volley of taunts and insults from fight followers. Initially, he couldn't understand the hostility, as he had always been popular with the Vegas crowd. He had not accounted for Duran's massive appeal, nor for a horde of Duran supporters from Panama who had pitched up in Nevada to support their idol. Part of his popularity lay in his devil-may-care approach. For instance, he invited Hearns and his Kronk teammates to watch him training. His reasoning was that Hearns could see everything he did because he intended to beat him regardless of anything Hearns had to offer.

Roberto Duran was born in utter poverty in a Panama slum, the product of a liaison between a US serviceman and a local girl. He fought for pennies on street corners and trailed his brother down to the nearest boxing gym when he was only eight years old. He was a natural fighter, with boundless energy, aggression and power. His big break came when he was spotted by Carlos Eleta, a millionaire businessman with an interest in sports. Eleta took over the young urchin's management and soon he was cutting a swathe though the lightweight division. He captured the world title in 1972 and defended it a dozen times before moving up in weight to challenge the unbeaten welterweight champion, Ray Leonard. In one of the great fights of the era, Duran sensationally outpointed Leonard over fifteen bruising rounds. He was generally acknowledged as the best pound-for-pound boxer in the world.

Yet glory was followed by disgrace. In a rematch five months later, Duran stalked while Leonard danced. Neither fighter inflicted significant damage on the other, but Duran grew increasingly frustrated at his inability to catch his elusive foe. In round eight, out of the blue, Duran turned away and shook his glove to signify that he was quitting. He later claimed stomach cramps, but it was an unconvincing explanation, and the "no mas" fight secured him a place in ring infamy.

Duran's weight ballooned between fights, and in 1982, he suffered further losses, to Wilfred Benitez and England's Kirkland Laing in Detroit. Carlos Eleta was so disgusted with him that he vowed to annul their contract and regular promoter Don King also washed his hands of the fighter, while the boxing world speculated that he was finished and even his fanatically loyal Panamanian following began to turn against him. It was the spur for one of the most remarkable comebacks in ring history. Duran punched out former welterweight king Pipino Cuevas, butchered light-middleweight champion Davey Moore, and then gave the mighty Marvin Hagler all he could handle in losing a close decision for the middleweight title in November 1983.

Even as he turned thirty-three years old, Duran was still a daunting prospect, but to take on an opponent of the Hit Man's stature after seven months out of the ring and without a tune-up fight was rash. And for his part, Hearns felt he had Duran's number. Even years earlier he had referred to him as "little Duran." It was not that he did not respect the Panamanian, simply that he felt his style was made for him. During one meeting he had playfully pulled Duran's hat down over his eyes. This normally would have provoked a mini-explosion, but Duran did nothing. "Tommy always intimidated Roberto," Emanuel Steward told Duran's biographer, Christian Giudice. "Even when Tommy was like twenty years old and he was at a fight with Roberto in Las Vegas. I'll never forget because Roberto was talking to someone and Tommy went up and tapped him on the shoulder. Roberto quickly backed away when he saw Tommy. It was like he saw a ghost or an evil spirit."

In the build-up to the fight, Steward was distracted by dissent within his usually stable set-up. The source was his number one rated light-middleweight, Mike "The Body Snatcher" McCallum, who announced that he would be parting company from his mentor. McCallum should in fact have been fighting Duran, but Stone Hands had chosen to fight Hearns for a reported $3 million instead rather than make a mandatory defence against McCallum. Instead McCallum was offered $250,000 to fight Sean Mannion for the vacant WBA light-middleweight title forfeited by Duran. McCallum turned it down, feeling cheated out of a big payday and resentful that his stablemate's interests seemed to have been put before his. Steward told his colleagues that McCallum wouldn't accept that Duran's reluctance to fight him was because it wasn't as lucrative as a meeting with Hearns. In the event, McCallum turned Mannion down and lost out on the national exposure he needed.

Hearns hated waiting around on the day of a fight. Time seemed to drag interminably. He couldn't wait for the hours to pass so he could strip into his fighting garb and get on with the business he understood best. The waiting time on Friday, 15 June 1984, was increased by the need to wake early to make the eight o'clock weigh-in. Hearns left his fourteenth floor Caesars Palace suite and descended to the hotel's pavilion, which had also doubled as his training venue. Hearns had divided his time between the hotel's suite and a private room at the Imperial Palace Hotel, where Steward had secreted him away in the days before the fight to avoid the endless distraction of well-wishers dropping in. When he arrived inside Caesars, he had to fight his way through hundreds of fans who had converged around the cordoned-off set of scales before being met by a sneering Duran, who began his standard routine of attempting to intimidate his opponent. Hearns refused to rise to the bait and told the eager press corps, "I don't hate Duran. I have nothing at all against him. In fact, I think that he's a great man. Tonight, I have a job to do and it has got to be done." Duran was summoned first to the scales and he slipped off his tracksuit and weighed in at 154 pounds, hitting the light-middleweight limit. Before he stepped away, he looked over at the Kronk team and made an obscene gesture to Hearns, who appeared nonplussed as he quickly stripped and stepped on to the scales to show he was half a pound under the limit. Rather than imitate Duran, who buzzed around the podium, he raised both his hands skywards to indicate that he was the champion. "I will knock Duran out in the second round tonight," he told the television reporters. "I'm going to be the Hit Man once again."

It was still daylight when he returned to Caesars, the same

venue where he had faced Leonard, for the fight. The temperature in the ring was recorded at ninety-five degrees when Hearns made his walk to the ring. "Twisting his arms and then shaking them out to the ends of his fists, he breathed intensity," wrote Christian Giudice in *Hands of Stone*. "Reaching the ring, he disrobed to show a wiry but sculpted body. Hearns had been sparring in the Kronk Gym with some of the quickest and most talented boxers in the world. He bounced around the ring and shot blur-fast jabs. The Hit Man had never looked in better shape." In the opposite corner, the dark, brooding Duran looked flabby and unusually pensive by comparison.

After the usual introductions and instructions were issued by Manila's Carlos Padilla, both fighters retreated to their corners to wait for the bell. Hearns was first out of the blocks and immediately landed his left jab. The opening seconds followed his fight blueprint as he employed a range of head and shoulder feints amidst a blur of jabs and right crosses which negated the bullish force of Duran and pushed him backwards. Despite this, the man they called "El Cholo" grinned at Hearns before beckoning him to fight toe-to-toe.

In contrast to his performance against Wilfred Benitez, Hearns obliged and sent in a devastating right cross which left his shoulder like a rocket and put Duran to his knees for only the second time in his career. An earlier jab had opened a cut above Duran's left eye and the blood trickled down his face as he took a count of nine. When referee Padilla signalled the fight's resumption, Hearns sprung from his corner and drove Duran back into the ropes where he unleashed a left hook which sent Duran back to his knees again. Duran's Latin pride forced him back to his feet at the count of two, but Padilla insisted on issuing a standing eight whilst Duran looked over his shoulder, smirking defiantly and waving at Hearns to continue his blazing attack. Before the Detroit fighter could accommodate this request, the bell sounded to conclude the hostilities and Duran's true condition was betrayed when he walked to the wrong corner and had to be led by a cornerman to his own stool.

It took just sixty-seven seconds of the second round for the annihilation to come to an abrupt end. Hearns sensed that he had to press home his advantage, reinforced by Emanuel Steward's instructions to terminate the challenge of the Panamanian firebrand. After some preliminary fencing, he unleashed a thundering right cross directly on to Duran's bearded jaw that spun his head sideways. Duran's knees buckled and he pitched face down, out before he hit the canvas. Carlos Padilla didn't bother to count but waved the fight over as Duran's anxious seconds rushed into the ring.

NO ONE HAD EVER done that to Roberto Duran. Thomas Hearns was now in demand. The inactivity that drove him to distraction after his loss to Leonard would be a thing of the past. Just three months after his sensational victory, he was back between the ropes to fight twenty-five-year old Californian Fred Hutchings, at the Civic Centre in Saginaw, Michigan. The rangy Hutchings had an impressive record of twenty-seven victories, seventeen inside the distance, against just one loss and had been elevated to third in the light-middleweight ratings. Despite this pedigree, he gave the impression of a callow novice meeting an experienced master. At the press conference called to announce the fight, Hutchings constantly referred to his opponent as "Mr Hearns" and described him in awed tones as "class." He spoke with wide-eyed wonder about Hearns's earning power and said he still worked in a gas station, pumping gas six days a week in order to support his wife and infant son, which explained his rather odd ring nickname, "The Pumper." The job did not pay too well. "Right now, I'm broke," he confessed. He expressed his frustration that when he had initially signed to fight the champion in January, he was offered $275,000, yet was now expected to accept half that amount. However, he assured the reporters, "Once I get into the ring, I won't be afraid about doing my own thing and proving my real class."

Despite this bold statement, Hutchings was not given a hope by the sporting press. Their only question was how long Hutchings would last. Emanuel Steward refused to rise to the bait and paid tribute to Hutchings' reputation as a clever and elusive boxer. Hearns followed suit and refused to make a prediction about the length of the fight. Instead, he vowed to maintain his career-long strategy of seeking a quick end by applying non-stop pressure in the opening two rounds and then seeing what was required. He claimed his respect for Hutchings was evidenced by the fact that he had broken with his own longstanding tradition and had actually watched recordings of several fights involving his foe.

Hearns stepped into the ring bang on the division limit of 154 pounds, a quarter-pound heavier than Hutchings. The more significant tale-of-the-tape statistic was that Hearns's seventy-eight-inch reach was six inches longer than the Californian's, and this advantage was leveraged from the opening bell as he stalked his opponent and flashed his left jab like a cobra's forked tongue. Just about everything he threw connected as Hutchings looked like a rabbit trapped in headlights. A straightforward right cross toppled Hutchings to the floor for the first knockdown and a left-right combination dropped him again just before the bell to end the first session. "After the first round, I knew that he would not go the full distance," Hearns later said. "I could feel that my punches were hurting him and so it was only a matter of time and patience before the end came."

During the second round, Hearns stayed relaxed. His rapid-fire jab was working to perfection and he set up The Pumper to receive his fearsome right cross with punishing frequency. The sparse crowd of around 2,500 scattered around the 7,000-capacity centre saw Hearns look imploringly at the referee, Arthur Mercante, to step in and stop the bout, but to no avail. So Steward urged Hearns to resolve the matter himself. At the start of the third, he looked like he meant business and battered his challenger with a fusillade of two-handed combinations to both the head and body. Still Mercante watched the slaughter. After a final flurry of left jab, left hook, right cross, Benny Casing, Hutchings' cut man, jumped into the ring to wave the towel of surrender and stop the bout four seconds before the end of the round.

After the carnage, Hutchings was swift to pay tribute to *Mr* Hearns and confessed, "I've never been hurt like that before." He proved a better post-fight analyst than a competitor, admitting "My performance was terrible," before thanking referee Mercante for allowing the fight to be stopped. Hearns merely noted that his punches were not as powerful as the ones he threw to flatten Duran. "My whole body was into those punches," he said. He used the platform to demand the opportunity to take on Marvin Hagler but requested the chance to defend his title again in November before tackling the Brockton fighter.

Hearns was now at his peak. Having been through the fire of some torrid contests, his early brilliance had been reinforced by experience. He was stronger at the heavier weight, tactically wiser and punched harder than ever. Not even his tangled personal life – he had a one-year-old daughter by one woman and faced a "palimony" suit over the upkeep of a five-year-old son, Ronald, born to a former high school friend, Felicia Dodson – could change the fact that the world lay at his feet.

# 11 WAR

BACK IN THE early months of 1982, promoter Bob Arum had convened a meeting at which Steve Wainwright, Marvin Hagler's lawyer, and Emanuel Steward were present. The purpose was to agree a unique three-fight contract which would see Hagler fight three middleweights from Steward's Kronk gymnasium. First of all, the undisputed world middleweight champion would face the all-action Mickey Goodwin. Next he would take on William "Caveman" Lee. Finally he would pitch himself against Thomas Hearns in the main fight of the trilogy.

The Goodwin fight was to take place in Italy in March 1982, with Arum agreeing that his friend Rodolfo Sabbatini would act as co-promoter. However, a month before the fight, Goodwin suffered a broken hand and Caveman Lee, his tough, hard-punching but less-regarded stablemate, had to step up to take his place. This change of opponent also saw the fight moved from San Remo to Atlantic City, as it was felt the Italian public would not have the appetite for this match after a damning article appeared in the *New York Post* claiming that Lee had been knocked out by Hearns in a sparring session, a claim disputed by Emanuel Steward. They were astute judges, as Hagler clobbered the Caveman in less than a round.

The rescheduled fight against Goodwin was complicated by the fact that the Kronk fighter struggled to recover from his injured hand, so Steward, Arum and Wainwright elected to go straight to the eagerly anticipated match-up with Hearns on 24 May in Windsor, Ontario. Despite the hype, the fight did not take place, to the frustration of both combatants, who spent the next three years facing a variety of opponents yet still demanding it. Hagler travelled to Italy to dispose of both Bob Arum's obligation to his co-promoter Sabbatini, and his erstwhile foe, the unfortunate Fulgencio Obelmejias, within five rounds. He then spent the following three years successfully defending his championship against Tony Sibson, Wilford Scypion, Roberto Duran, Juan Domingo Roldan and Mustafa Hamsho. He also made no secret of the fact that Hearns occupied second place on his personal hit list behind Ray Leonard, who had teased the brooding champion before announcing his retirement in 1982, then re-emerging in 1984 to fight the limited journeyman Kevin Howard, who succeeded in knocking the showman down before he was halted in the ninth round. This lacklustre showing immediately prompted a return to retirement and caused Hagler to revise his sights and elevate Thomas Hearns to the top of his list of targets.

The official announcement that Marvin Hagler and Thomas Hearns would finally meet was made in December 1984 at the same Waldorf-Astoria Hotel in New York which had been used two years previously to promote the same fight. As the sole promoter, Bob Arum oversaw the event and watched both fighters guardedly greet each other. Arum announced that both men would earn in excess of $5 million. In the New Year, the three central figures embarked on what Hagler dubbed the "magical mystery tour" as they visited twenty-two cities in just two weeks to promote their clash. The fighters insisted on travelling in separate corporate jets and would only meet at the press conferences. Caesars Palace provided a state-of-the-art Gulfstream G-11 and Arum leased the second jet, a Falcon, which was slightly less luxurious. In order to satisfy the demands of the two egocentric warriors, it was agreed that Hagler would use the Gulfstream whenever the parties were flying west but they would switch planes when flying back. However, when they reached Las Vegas, Hagler's co-managers, the brothers Pat and Goody Petronelli, told Arum that their man was threatening to return home if he couldn't remain in the splendour of the Gulfstream-11. When Arum explained the situation to Emanuel Steward, he told Arum that Hearns would follow suit if he wasn't granted access to the same jet that Hagler had used. This impasse required Arum to lease an identical plane, so that both boxers could have identical modes of transport for the remainder of the tour.

Although neither fighter claimed to be a polished public speaker, Hearns, along with the rest of the Kronk boxing team, had received some tuition in speaking and elocution from Steward's resident PR adviser Jackie Kallen. A former entertainment journalist, Kallen had Hearns tutored to maintain eye contact with interviewers, to smile a lot and to avoid saying *man* all the time. She also taught Hearns to pause and digest questions fired at him before answering. This was evident in press conferences, where Hearns would now begin every response with the words, 'Well, basically...' in order to buy himself some extra thinking time. Hearns still succeeded in angering Hagler every time he opened his mouth, with what Hagler claimed were blatant statements of disrespect towards him.

This was a tactic that Hagler employed before all of his fights. He would convince himself that he hated his opponent and would look for any perceived slight to support his jaundiced view. Hearns was the latest to feel the force of Hagler's antipathy as every word he uttered about the fight built up a well of animosity between them. Steward tried to take the sting out of the simmering enmity by claiming, "Tommy's trash-talking is strictly business to increase the pay-per-view figures. People must understand just how out of character it is for Tommy to do that." This cut little ice with his shaven-headed rival, who sneered, "This tour has done me good. I may have had a little respect for Tommy Hearns before I spent time with him but now I only hate his ass." He promised to exact his retribution in the ring. "I'm going to do to him what I did to Alan Minter. He had that same kind of attitude."

Hagler planned to stick to the training regime he had employed for his previous twenty-five fights, which included a period of isolation in Provincetown, Cape Cod, before moving to Palm Springs a month before the fight. Goody Petronelli managed to convince him to alter this plan and head straight to the Californian desert, where the Americana Hotel offered him the run of their premises and would allow him to adapt to the searing heat. Although he agreed to a change of location, he maintained the same iron will and steely determination that had kept him at the top of his division. He sparred with Bobby "Boogaloo" Watts (one of only two men who had beaten Hagler, although this loss was later brutally avenged in a second round knockout) and Jerry Holly, both tall, rangy fighters like Hearns, and also with Larry Davis, who had to leave the camp after the first day of sparring when Hagler burst his eardrum with a left hook.

Hagler also based himself at Johnny Tocco's Ringside gym, a shabby, downbeat location which he claimed suited his philosophy. "This kind of place is where my roots are. It is the kind of gym where I started and where I belong. I don't believe in all that Rocky Balboa, rags-to-riches crap. My life doesn't change just because I am successful. You will never see me out there showboating, putting on a show for everyone, acting real cute and saying what you want to hear." He outlined his plans to cope with Hearns, a man whose lifestyle was in contrast to his own, and insisted that there would be no need to rely on any judges' scorecards. "I've brought my own judges," he said and held up both his fists.

Hearns chose to base his camp in Florida before moving to Las Vegas in the final few weeks. Most of his sparring was with a young middleweight named Vinnie Mayes, who supplemented his own boxing earnings with the daily fee of $100 and brought his rugged style to bear. Emanuel Steward instructed Mayes to "let the tiger out of the cage" and he laced Hearns with power-packed body punches for round after round. Apart from avoiding Mayes's swings, Steward claimed that one of their biggest challenges was avoiding the number of people who tried to offer help and advice. "You wouldn't believe the kind of people who are calling," he said. "They include voodoo doctors, an old man who wants to teach Thomas a special punch he claims to have patented in the 1920s, another who has offered a special mixture to soak his hands in, masseurs who believe they hold the key to unleashing his power, hypnotists and nutrition experts."

On relocating to Vegas, Hearns trained in Ballroom Four of Caesars Palace, a setting that was in stark contrast to the sparse surroundings of Hagler's chosen base camp. His routine also offered a contrast with his menacing foe. After starting with some light punching on the speedball, he engaged in sparring with Steward, who boxed in a southpaw style to imitate Hagler and allowed Hearns to aim punches at his open palms. Occasionally, Steward would lunge at Hearns and then sprawl forward to leave the impression that he had just attempted a wild swing and nailed nothing but air. Occasionally, he sparred with southpaw middleweights Cecil Pettigrew and Brian Muller and a Kansas City-based light-heavyweight named Charles "Hollywood" Henderson, while Gino Linder, a support member of the team, helped out with a drill designed to strengthen his midsection that involved Linder hitting Hearns repeatedly in the stomach with a medicine ball.

ON THE EVENING of 15 April 1985, a strong wind blew through the tennis courts of Caesars Palace, where the ring had been assembled for the big fight. There were concerns that a storm was brewing and the fifteen thousand fans inside the arena hoped that the gathering cloud didn't indicate rain; they hoped instead for clouds of war. Bob Arum's promotional team had dubbed this meeting simply as "The War" and the atmosphere was charged by the time that Hearns, wearing a red robe with yellow trim over his customary gold trunks with his name etched along his waistband in red and the Kronk name along the bottom, had marched into the arena with the strains of "Hail To The Victor," the Michigan University fight song announcing his arrival. As the challenger, he was obliged to enter the ring first and, as he dispensed with his robe, he looked in splendid physical condition and primed for action.

Customarily, the champion often uses his status as a final psychological ploy and keeps his opponent waiting for as long as possible before deciding to arrive in the ring. Hagler was too eager to taste conflict to engage in this kind of point scoring and as soon as Hearns had entered, John Philip Sousa's patriotic anthem, "Stars And Stripes Forever" preceded his march into battle. When he stripped from his royal blue robe, his whole body and head gleamed with sweat under the ring's arc lights. He had thoroughly warmed up in the dressing-room and was ready for a quick start. Hagler did not avert his gaze from Hearns throughout the preliminaries, including Doc Severinsen's trumpeted version of "The Star Spangled Banner" and referee Richard Steele's final instructions. As the two physically splendid fighters faced each other in mid-ring, Hagler snarled, "You better hope I don't bleed. It only makes me meaner."

When the bell signalled an opening to the hostilities, both men flew from their corners like dogs let loose from a leash. They eschewed any "feeling out" period and instead unloaded on each other with a wild abandon rarely seen in a boxing ring before. Hagler, usually the more cautious starter, opened hostilities with a looping southpaw right that Hearns ducked. They threw punches at each other as if they had only been granted a few seconds to do so and the dull thud of leather could be heard as the punches slammed into head and body. The crowd, initially awed into silence by the level of menace and commitment, exploded in a frenzy of undiluted excitement, as each fighter took turns to rock the other.

Emanuel Steward was similarly rocked by the level of intensity. He implored Hearns, "Just box him. Stick and move. Don't fight with him" but his pleas were in vain. Midway through this opening salvo, Hagler sustained a deep cut on his forehead, just above his right eye which caused blood to flow down his face like a running tap. The injury, which eventually required four stitches, was caused when he smashed into Hearns's shoulder in his eagerness to attack Hearns. The crowd's bloodlust was heightened further and their noise made it impossible for both men to hear the bell chiming to signal the end of what *The Ring* later termed "the greatest round in boxing history." HBO commentator Barry Tompkins declared, "This may be the most brutal, even round you've ever seen in boxing."

The fight doctor, Donald Romeo, went straight to Hagler's corner to examine the cut and the bruising which had started to swell beneath his eye. Goody Petronelli assured him that the cut could be dealt with and he returned to his seat. The real drama, however, was taking place opposite him. When Hearns retreated to his stool, he said, "My hand's gone. It's broken." This would not be mentioned by either the fighter or his camp in the aftermath. Instead, Steward attempted to calm him and beseeched him to remember their game plan of frustrating Hagler from long range. Goody Petronelli, meanwhile was imploring his own charge not to change a thing apart from keeping his hands a little higher. "Don't worry about the cut," he assured him. "Just keep the pressure up."

Before the spectators had time to get their breath back, the bell sounded. Hearns was already off his stool and met Hagler two-thirds of the way across the ring. Hagler again threw the first shot, a left cross, before Hearns started moving and spearing his opponent with his long left lead. Rather than quell the level of ferocity, the minute-long break had served to stoke it further and they greeted each other with an immediate exchange of heavy punches. Hagler, bleeding profusely, caught Hearns with a terrific right hand and Hearns replied with an equally venomous left, causing the blood to splash into his own face. Hearns appeared to sense that a stoppage was imminent and upped the tempo further still, catching the champion with a series of vicious punches. One scything left ripped open a second cut under Hagler's right eye and made his face resemble a grotesque mask.

Hagler knew that his hard-earned crown was beginning to slip. He responded with a primal, untamed fury and made no pretence of finesse or trying to set his man up. Instead he threw a tidal wave of punches at Hearns in a bid to overwhelm him. Hearns refused to yield and fired back to Hagler's head and body but Hagler just ploughed through and continued to beat away. The ferocity of the encounter threatened to overshadow the sheer range and quality of punches which were delivered by both men. Richard Steele continued to look closely at the injuries which turned Hagler's face scarlet and ringside commentators began to speculate that they would force him to terminate the contest. A deranged-looking Hagler ended the round by catching Hearns with a series of right hands which caused his knees to buckle, and as the bell sounded he turned to his corner on rubbery legs. Hagler looked back with utter disdain.

When they emerged for the third round, Hearns appeared to have taken heed of his corner's instructions and opened up with his snaking jab. Hagler was relentless and continued to bob and weave, never taking a backward step. Petronelli had been unable to stem the flow of blood and had only cleaned the cuts, which had continued to bleed profusely. Richard Steele halted the fight to call Doctor Romeo into the ring to check whether the cuts were significant enough to stop the contest. He asked Hagler if he could see through the blood coming from his forehead. Hagler answered in the affirmative and would later claim that he sarcastically replied,

"Well, I ain't missing him, am I?" The doctor spoke to Steele and allowed the fight to continue.

Hagler knew that it was now or never. He dashed at Hearns and hit him with a right hook which sent him reeling backwards. Hearns's legs went into spasms and Hagler drilled home even more spiteful punches, eventually toppling his challenger to the canvas. Hearns dug deep into his reservoir of courage and clambered back to his feet before the count ended. When Richard Steele assessed his capacity to defend himself further, he looked into the dead eyes staring back and threw his arms around the beaten warrior to signal the fight's conclusion. The most electrifying eight minutes of mayhem ever seen in a ring were over.

Whilst Hagler, his face drenched in a mask of blood, cavorted wildly to celebrate his eleventh successful championship defence, some ringside observers were upset to witness the brave but beaten challenger being held up by one of his entourage like a baby and carried back to his corner. It was several minutes before he could stand on his own two feet and hear the official announcement of one of the sport's truly epic encounters.

IN THE SANCTUARY of his dressing room, Hearns winced in pain as his right glove was gently removed. Dr Fred Lewerenz, the medical adviser for the Kronk boxing team, suggested that Hearns had fractured his hand. "The injury is to the bone leading from the knuckle of his finger," said Dr Lewerenz, and insisted that he have an immediate x-ray. Despite his agony, Hearns refused to mention his injury, sustained in the first round, during his post-fight interviews. He later said that he did not want to take anything away from Hagler. When the two men met outside the dressing rooms, Hearns congratulated him and Hagler told the press, "He seemed to be a little more sensible and less cocky then. We talked and he told me that he thought we had earned our money."

The inquest into Hearns's second professional defeat started immediately. Veteran Detroit sportswriter George Puscas mused, "Thomas Hearns just doesn't know when to run. Invite him to fight and he will fight. He allowed himself to be lured into a brawl with Marvin Hagler." He levelled criticism at the Kronk team, which had allowed Hearns to swallow his own publicity. "A guy can destroy himself by believing in his own beauty and Hearns is narcissistic about the power in his right hand. If he landed it on the moon, the moon would shatter. He's sure of it. The problem was, Marvin Hagler took all his heaviest shots and didn't crumble." Emanuel Steward blamed the unprecedented intensity of the contest. "It was a more physical fight than we wanted and before the first round had ended, I sensed trouble ahead. They fought a twelve-round fight in eight minutes and it was like starting a marathon with a sprint." He later cited the fact that Hearns had a massage prior to the fight, which weakened his legs and prompted such an aggressive opening salvo.

Other observers suggested that Hearns should retire with a reputation as a great fighter who fell just short of being classed amongst the greatest. Steward vowed to talk to his charge when they returned to Detroit. "I'm proud of him. He fought a great, great fight," he said. Hagler's trainer, Goody Petronelli, treated with disdain talk of the loser retiring; he knew just how much Hearns had to offer the sport. "Hearns still has a beautiful future but maybe not as a fully-fledged middleweight," said Petronelli. "He has been a fabulously destructive welterweight but is not the same puncher at middleweight."

# 12 BACK IN THE MIX

HEARNS TOOK TIME out to recover after his epic contest with Hagler and to allow his broken hand to heal. It was eleven months before he finally felt ready to return to the ring. He was desperate for a return match against his conqueror and his desire was shared by the global audience who longed to see a repeat of their classic pairing. Bob Arum resisted these calls and insisted that there was little merit in rematches. Instead, he suggested Hearns prove that he deserved one. Arum pieced together a show which would whet the public's appetite by featuring both Hearns and Hagler on the same card and allowing them to judge if the Detroit man justified a return. Hagler was matched against the tough, hard-punching Ugandan John "The Beast" Mugabi and Hearns was scheduled to fight the highly respected James "Black Gold" Shuler, the leading contender for Hagler's undisputed middleweight championship. Shuler was unbeaten in his twenty-two contests, stopping sixteen of his opponents. Their twelve-rounder would be both a North American Boxing Federation middleweight title fight and a WBC final eliminator, with the winner becoming the next in line to challenge Hagler. As a further incentive, Arum offered Hearns a $500,000 bonus if he disposed of Shuler within six rounds.

The twenty-six-year-old Shuler hailed from Philadelphia and had been a member of the ill-fated 1980 Olympic boxing team which was prevented from competing in Moscow due to Jimmy Carter's boycott of the games to protest the Soviet invasion of Afghanistan. Many observers suggested that the 1980 US vintage had the potential to be one of the finest ever Olympic teams and Shuler was one of its leading lights. He had almost quit the sport following the tragedy of 14 March 1980, when a flight of the Lot Polish Airline, carrying members and officials of the US boxing team, had crashed, killing sixty-four passengers, including twenty-two members of the team. Shuler had been due to travel with the team to a European competition but had withdrawn because of illness. He was eventually persuaded to turn professional and made his debut in September of the same year, winning in two rounds before ratcheting up an impressive twenty-two career victories and forging a notable reputation as a silky fighter. As number one contender, Shuler could have refused the elimination bout and still been next in line to challenge Hagler, but he was tempted by a career-best purse of $250,000. Humble and good-hearted, he was extremely popular with his stablemates and was widely recognised as one of the sport's "good guys."

The legendary Eddie Futch, who had guided fourteen men to world champion status, was in Shuler's corner for this contest. Futch paid tribute to Hearns as "one of this decade's most menacing figures" but was adamant that his latest protégé would upset the 3-1 odds in favour of Hearns and emerge victorious inside the scheduled twelve rounds. "There are quite a few cracks in his armour which have recently been evident," he said. Futch spent hours coaching Shuler to take away Hearns' punching power by sliding inside his long reach and working at close quarters. "Hearns needs time and room to deliver his punches," he told his man. "We won't give him either."

Futch, who as a young boxer had lived in the Black Bottom section of Detroit and had regularly sparred with Joe Louis, had left in the early 1950s for Los Angeles, but always maintained that his roots were still deeply embedded in the Motor City. He would regularly meet up with old friends like Luther Burgess and Walter Smith, who had learned their skills in the tiny Brewster gym situated on the east side of Detroit and were now part of the Kronk team. Futch had some sharp opinions on why Hearns had lost and, despite his friendships with the team surrounding the fighter, he wasn't afraid to express them. "I attribute his two defeats down to his strategy," Futch said. "Against Hagler, he came out and got embroiled in a war which he wasn't able to get out of. When he opened up and hit Hagler with his best shot and stopped him in his tracks, I would have told Hearns to box him." In a thinly veiled dig at Emanuel Steward, he said, "You have to prepare your fighter to have a number of different strategies. If you go out and take a shot at the guy and don't get him, then get on your bike and move." When he reflected on the loss to Leonard, he said, "I was at the fight but had to leave after the thirteenth round when Hearns was winning the fight. When I heard he'd gotten knocked out, I was shocked. Leonard was able to make adjustments when he found out that he couldn't outbox Hearns from the outside and he started to attack the body."

Mischievous reports suggested that Hearns might be getting bored with boxing. He had recently taken up drag racing, having bought himself a 1974 Nova Super Rod which he blasted up to 135 mph on a quarter-mile track. "I tried to talk him out of it," said Steward. "I get nervous just thinking about it." In the days preceding the Shuler fight, there were also concerns that it could be postponed due to high winds and torrential rain. It was only on the day itself that Bob Arum could officially confirm to the 16,000 spectators and Showtime, who were involved in their first ever production and estimated that around $25 million had been taken via pay-per-view, that the bill would go ahead. He still had to hastily assemble heaters to dry out the ring apron.

Hearns's road to redemption began when he strode to the ring where Shuler awaited him. He looked confident as he faced his challenger, though it was one of the few occasions when he didn't enjoy a height advantage, and the pattern of the bout was set in the first few seconds when he exchanged left jabs from a side-on stance and began to move Shuler steadily backwards towards the ropes. He then delivered a surprisingly swift left hook to the body which caused Shuler to drop his hands. In a flash, Hearns launched a long right hand that had the full force of his weight behind it. It crashed onto Shuler's jaw. Shuler immediately tumbled backwards and landed flat on his back and remained there, oblivious to the referee, Richard Steele, tolling the count of ten over him. He remained unconscious for several more anxious minutes before the ringside doctor was able administer a neck massage to alleviate the pain and discomfort the impact had caused to his vertebra, and allowed him to regain his feet.

A short time afterwards, Hearns was coming down the stairs of the trailer that served as his dressing room. Suddenly James Shuler appeared, walking up the stairs. They came face-to-face again; both smiled and shook hands gingerly. "I guess I'll have to get you on the court," Shuler said with a sheepish smile. "But don't ruin my basketball dreams too." Hearns was in a hurry to get ringside, where he was rooting for Marvin Hagler to do a number on John Mugabi. He wanted the big money that would come if and when he crossed gloves with the Marvelous One again; it takes two to make a great fight, and Bob Arum was already teasingly suggesting this one could take place in Las Vegas on 23 June.

Hagler beat John Mugabi in eleven rounds of mortal combat. Twelve hundred punches were exchanged before the champion ended the destruction in the eleventh round with a power-packed right hand. Arum said that Hearns had faced the easier opponent on the night and went so far as to state, "If Tommy had boxed Mugabi, the African would have won." This was a view that was endorsed by some of the press. Mitch Albon suggested, "Hagler

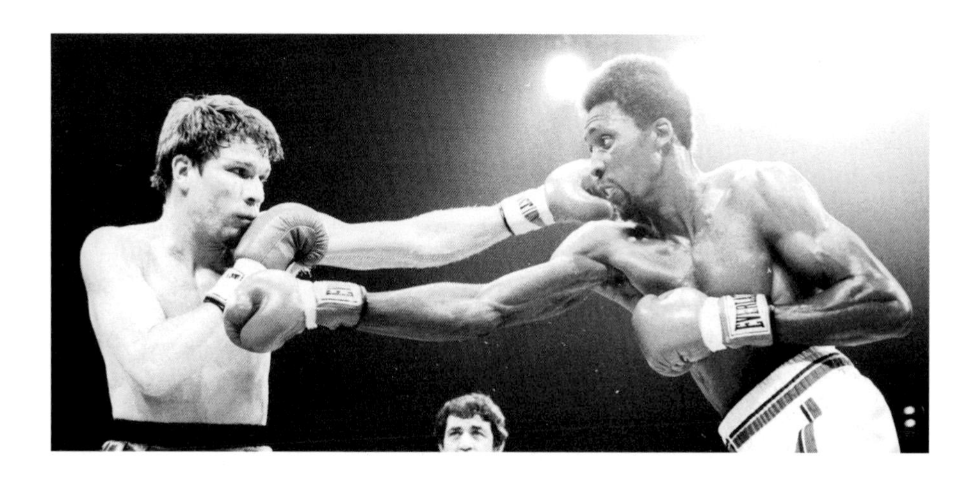

TOP: Hearns slips inside the jab of Jeff McCracken to land his patented right cross, at the Cobo Hall in Detroit. *Chris Cuellar*

BOTTOM: All smiles–for now–as Hearns shakes hands with defensive wizard Wilfred Benitez, whose light-middleweight title he took in 1982. *Chris Cuellar*

The height advantage Hearns enjoyed over most opponents is starkly illustrated against a crouching Luigi Minchillo from Italy. *Bob Ryder Collection*

TOP: The great Roberto Duran fell to the most emphatic loss of his storied career when Hearns blasted him out in two rounds in their 1984 title fight. *Chris Cuellar*

BOTTOM: The Hit Man meets the Brown Bomber: Thomas Hearns with another Detroit legend, former heavyweight champ Joe Louis.

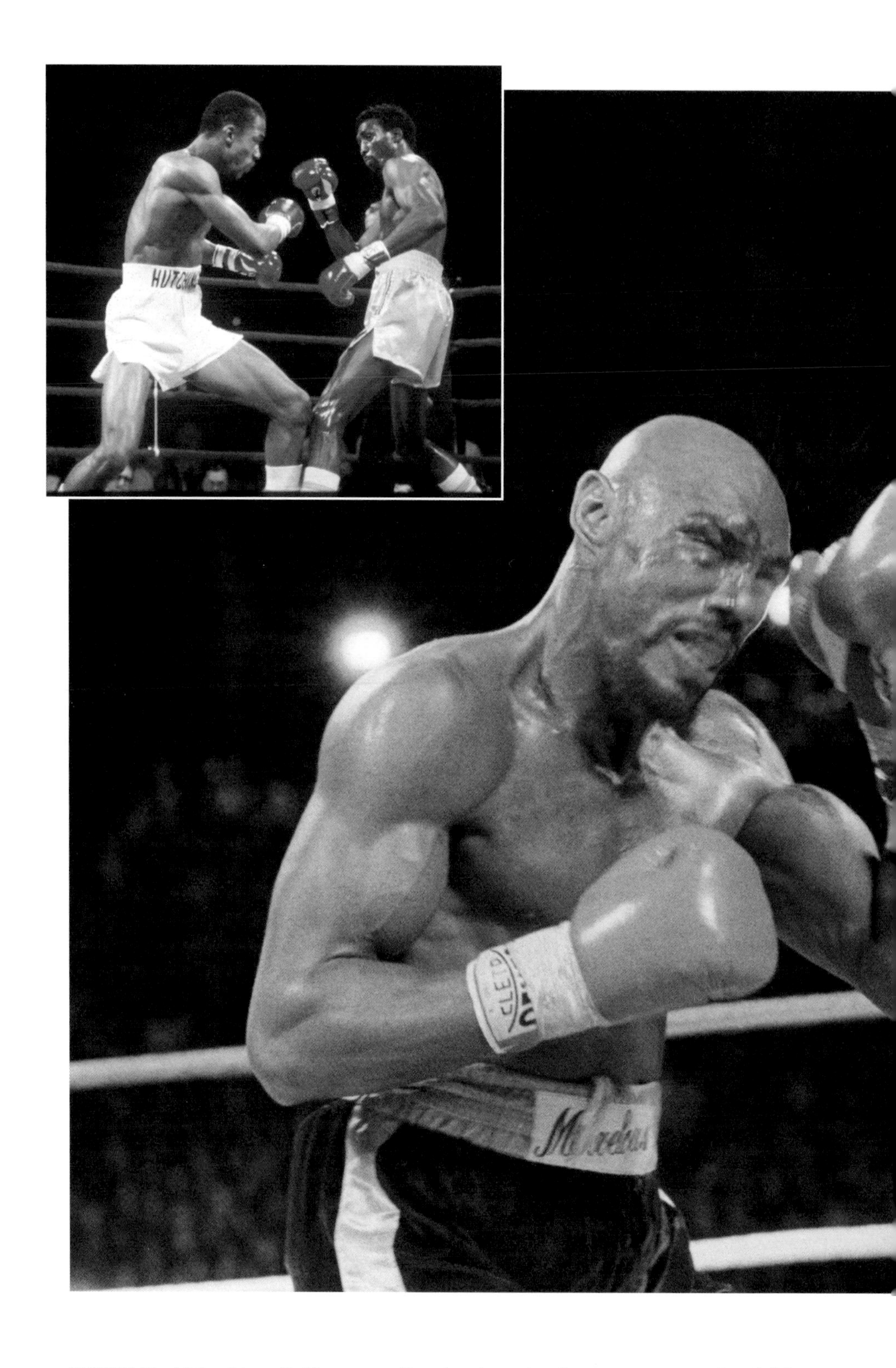

INSET: Fred Hutchings (left) was as tall as the champion but was outgunned and fell in three in a light-middleweight title fight. *Chris Cuellar*

Marvin Hagler and Hearns exchange ferocious blows in their epic middleweight clash in 1985, called the most exciting three rounds of boxing ever. *Bettmann/CORBIS*

TOP: An older, bigger Hit Man with Manny Steward and cutman Ralph Citro. The longstanding Hearns–Steward partnership eventually broke up in acrimony, only to be re-established several years later. *Chris Cuellar*

BOTTOM: Britain's Dennis Andries was incredibly brave but totally outclassed in a bruising encounter for the WBC light-heavyweight title. *Bob Ryder Collection*

TOP: Hearns lines up Ray Leonard for a right hand in their long-awaited return bout. It ended in a draw that many felt Hearns won.

BOTTOM: An almost identical pose as Hearns tees of on flabby cruiserweight John Long in the twilight of his career. *Dan Graschuck*

TOP: The forty-seven-year-old Hearns looks exhausted as he slumps on his stool in his final bout, against Shannon Landberg, in 2006. *Bob Ryder*

BOTTOM: Thomas, now a fight promoter, with his son Ronald, a successful light-middleweight boxer in his own right. *Bob Ryder*

and Hearns fought the wrong opponents. It should have been Hearns against John Mugabi and Hagler fighting James Schuler. If Hearns wants a rematch with Hagler, he should prove he is worthy of it. That was the way boxing once operated. It should have been Hearns taking punishment from a relentless beast like Mugabi so he could put Mugabi down then say, 'Okay Marvin. I have licked this guy. Let's mix it up.'"

Yet the gunshot right hand that had laid out Shuler remained a dominant image of that evening; as hard a punch as any Hearns had thrown before. It would be repeated on television numerous times for several days. Among the cognoscenti, his body punches drew even more praise. "It was as workmanlike a job as he's ever given," said co-trainer Walter Smith. Smith explained that Hearns had watched films of Shuler's fights, and they had decided body shots would bring Shuler's hands down and then Hearns would switch his attack to the head. "It was a knockout of classic stock," wrote Shelby Strother in the *Detroit News*. "But it was boxing smart, on-balance, calculated ring work that put it on the silver platter."

The likeable Shuler approached Bob Arum after the fight to thank him for the dubious opportunity of facing a legend like Hearns. "What can I say? He's a great champion – he's in Marvin Hagler's class," he said. Shuler then retreated home to Philadelphia, where he bought a motorcycle with some of his ring earnings. A week after the bout, Shuler was killed after a crash on his new bike. Both Hearns and Emanuel Steward flew to his funeral, and when he quietly paid his respects at the open coffin, Hearns put his newly acquired NABF championship belt inside.

HEARNS NOW WANTED to remain active and stay ring-sharp to be ready for Hagler when the opportunity should arise. Bob Arum was only too eager to oblige and he shepherded over 13,000 spectators into the Caesars Palace Arena to watch Hearns face Mark

Medal, a New York Puerto Rican who fought out of Jersey City and boasted a record of twenty-four wins. He had also held the IBF light-middleweight crown for six months in 1984. Despite this impressive pedigree, Hearns appeared to be treating Medal's challenge in a cavalier manner. When he made his entrance, bedecked in a shimmering gold and red robe, he adopted a casual air, chewing bubble gum as he lazily strolled towards the ring. When he stepped through the ropes, he spurned the chance to throw any warm-up punches but instead glanced at Medal and blew a huge bubble, like a balloon. Some at ringside speculated that it was a new and unusual way of gaining a psychological advantage by looking utterly unperturbed. Others felt that it reeked of complacency and disrespect.

The first round suggested the former. Hearns threw an immediate one-two combination of right hand and a left hook that forced Medal to drop to his knee, but, despite his best efforts, he was unable to finish him off. Before the end of the second round, the crowd appeared to feel cheated by the fact that they had not been treated to a spectacular ending and began to boo. It appeared that Hearns was coping with the 109-degree heat by coasting, though in truth he had once again damaged his right hand (his camp would later deny rumours that it was broken). In the sixth, Medal shrugged off the handicap of having his left eye closed by Hearns' snaking jab and made him cover up to the head and body. Hearns re-established his almost casual dominance after this and eventually forced the referee, Davey Pearl to stop the fight in the eighth round and award him a technical knockout victory. Some fans cheered sarcastically amid lusty jeers when the Hit Man had his hand raised in victory.

At the ring apron, Emanuel Steward didn't argue when it was suggested that Hearns's performance was the worst since he had won the welterweight championship in 1980. "I didn't like it one bit," he said, though he did try to offer some mitigation, "The bookies' twelve-to-one odds on him winning didn't help his concentration. Medal was not much of an opponent and when Thomas came back to the corner at the end of the first round, he told me that he felt sorry for Medal and suggested that the referee should have stopped the fight right after he had put him down." Hearns himself confessed that he had been mentally distracted – he had started looking forward to a projected rematch with Marvin Hagler that November. "I have to admit that my mind was on Hagler during the fight," he said. "This taught me never to look beyond the fight that you're in." Bob Arum, however, refused to be drawn on whether the fans' reaction had put paid to the Hagler rematch. "Babe Ruth didn't hit a home run every time he batted," was his reply.

Reaction from the press benches was less charitable. "This was one of those days that Hearns should have weighed in, gone to his hotel room in Caesars, laid down, and never bothered to get up and head outside for the fight later that day," said *KO* magazine, referring to Hearns as "the Detroit pussycat."

Hearns was now tentatively scheduled to challenge Marvin Hagler in November, but Ray Leonard spoiled the party by declaring that he wanted to fight Hagler and was not prepared to wait, even though he had been inactive for more than two years. Leonard had retired from the sport due to an eye injury in 1982. He returned for a single, unimpressive fight in 1984, then promptly retired again. But now he said he wanted one more big fight, against Hagler. Hagler and his trainers, Pat and Goody Petronelli, played it coy, keeping both Leonard and Hearns in suspense. Hagler even hinted strongly at retirement himself. But in boxing, money shouts, and Leonard was the money tree. Emanuel Steward could see which way the wind was blowing, and he didn't like it. "If [Hagler] goes ahead and fights Leonard, he's missing a big opportunity," he said, angry and frustrated. His fighter's big rematch was slipping away. "A Hagler–Leonard fight would be a fraud. It would be another Larry Holmes–Muhammad Ali show – a hoax to the public." Hearns also tried to bait both men, suggesting they were afraid of him and bitterly joking that he would like to send them to the Wizard of Oz for some new hearts. But there was nothing he could do.

HEARNS WANTED A quick return to the ring and on 17 October, the day before his twenty-eighth birthday, he was scheduled to end a two-and-a-half-year absence from his hometown to meet a twenty-five-year-old Doug DeWitt in the Cobo Arena. The press were united in their conviction that Hearns needed to deliver an impressive performance and make up for the lacklustre showing four months earlier when he strolled through a victory over Mark Medal.

Doug DeWitt was born in Youngstown, Ohio, but had located to Yonkers, New York, to begin his professional career at the age of eighteen. He had fought thirty-three times, with twenty-seven victories and three draws, and was third in the world rankings. Just three months earlier, he had lost a points decision to Hearns's stablemate Milton McCrory. Noted for his iron jaw, he vowed that he would frustrate Hearns by adopting a dangerous fight strategy. "If I can make him throw his big punches in the first three rounds and avoid them," he said, "I will come back in the fourth and fifth rounds and make a war of it. That is my shot." He questioned Hearns's lack of stamina and believed that his superior conditioning and durability would allow him to emerge victorious after twelve rounds. "I figure that Tommy's got good ability to take a punch but when some people get hit on the chin, their legs go and then it becomes a matter of stamina. Hearns has been hit plenty but only Hagler knocked him out cold, and even then I think that Tommy gave up."

DeWitt was as good as his word. He took Hearns's best shots without flinching and at times managed to drag him down into an old-fashioned street brawl. The champion's best opportunity to end it came in the third round when he landed a booming right cross and followed it up with a burst of two-handed punching, but the bell and fight referee Tommy Watson intervened to prevent the knockout that the 6,000 spectators had come to see. In round six, Hearns suffered a cut over his eye when DeWitt drove him into a corner and their heads collided in a clinch. Blood began to spill down Hearns's face, onto his chin and even to his long, yellow boxing trunks.

Hearns displayed his resolve by repelling DeWitt's wild follow-up attack. The Yonkers fighter was warned for throwing a low punch in the ninth round but Hearns shook it off and appeared content to stay out of the brawl and notch up a unanimous, twelve-round points victory. He finished nursing a jagged cut over his right eye, while his challenger sported a pair of badly bruised eyes and an argument raged in the background about DeWitt's liberal use of his head and elbows. "I wasn't satisfied about not ending it early but I surprised Doug that I could go beyond the fifth round and my boxing performance was excellent." He praised DeWitt as "a man with a lot of heart and a lot of ability." DeWitt was gracious in defeat and although he claimed, "I thought I hurt him," he also conceded that, "In the third or fourth rounds, he caught me in the eye and I couldn't see very well. I think I gave the fight away."

In the post-fight press conference, Emanuel Steward sprang a surprise by announcing that Hearns would step up to the light-heavyweight division for his next fight, against either WBC champion Dennis Andries or WBA champion, Marvin Johnson. Steward admitted that a primary motivation for this step was their frustration at waiting for Hagler, who had announced that he was close to agreeing on the terms to meet Ray Leonard, then making the latest in his long list of comebacks. Bob Arum was instrumental in putting together this match and told the press that Leonard was a more lucrative proposition for Hagler than Hearns. Arum had attempted to assuage Hearns by dangling the carrot of Dennis Andries and the opportunity to win another world title before Leonard did. He suggested that the fight be delayed to allow Hearns's cuts time to heal. "I can't do anything about Hagler's reluctance to fight me again," said Hearns. "But I feel I have the power to move up to the light-heavyweight division and do some damage." He was keen to remind the press corps that he still hadn't given up on his goal of winning four world championships in different divisions before he retired from boxing.

DENNIS ANDRIES WAS a quiet man but a rough, tough fighter. He was also a man who lived in the shadows. The WBC light-heavyweight championship belt was a mantle he wore lightly, much preferring to blend into the crowd. The day after he had captured the title, from J.B. Williamson in his hometown of London, he travelled to the press conference from his unpretentious house in Hackney to the West End via the London Underground and carried his newly acquired belt in a carrier bag. He was bemused by the interest in his mode of transport and told the press, "The tube was the quickest way to get here. If I'd have taken a taxi, I'd have been an hour late and a few shillings poorer too."

He had arrived in England from Guyana as a callow thirteen-year-old, along with his parents and brother. He did not take up boxing as an amateur until the age of nineteen, after a friend had showed him a trophy he had won in the ring. His fought just sixteen times at amateur level and admitted, "I didn't win them all. I knew that I had to lose some to learn but I loved it." This learning process continued when he turned professional in 1978. He lost six and drew one of his first twenty-one bouts, giving little indication of his future success at world level. Andries suggested that this was due to bad management rather than a lack of talent. "When I first started out, I was used mainly as a substitute fighter and would take fights on a day's notice and many of the losses were arguable." His fortunes began to improve when he captured the British light-heavyweight title from Tom Collins in 1982, which gave him the confidence to extend his unbeaten record to fifteen fights over the next three years. His last fight, six months before meeting Hearns, had caused quite a stir when he stopped the highly regarded Tony Sibson inside eight rounds.

Andries had never fought anyone of the pedigree of Hearns. His purse of $200,000 reflected this and dwarfed his previous best of £75,000 for the Sibson fight. Indeed his manager, Greg Steene, was refreshingly honest in his reasons for accepting the match. "We're here for the money," he said. "Hearns is one of the biggest names in boxing and having his name on Dennis's record will help him tremendously." Andries was typically modest about his own chances. "I don't want to be like the majority of fighters and start bragging," he told the Detroit press pack. "I don't like to get myself hyped up and go crazy. I came here to do a job and I will do my job very well."

Behind the scenes, however, the promotion was riddled with the kind of machinations that typified top-level boxing. Jose Sulaiman, president of the World Boxing Council, was demanding $30,000 from Emanuel Steward as a payoff to Eddie Davis of New York, the number one contender for Andries' title. Andries should have fought Davis, not Hearns, who wasn't even a light-heavyweight, but Davis's management consented to allow the Hearns fight to go ahead in return for a tidy sum, or what was known as step-aside money. Sulaiman should have known better. Because in boxing, the fighters might not be tuned in but the good managers certainly were. It occurred to Steward that he and Hearns had been short-changed themselves – by none other than Marvin Hagler, who was due to fight Leonard instead of Hearns. "If we get paid by Hagler," Steward said, "we'll pay Davis. But we don't expect to get paid by Hagler, so Sulaiman and Davis will have to sort it out themselves."

Hearns in the past had paid large amounts of step-aside money to allow him access to big fights. Steward said John Mugabi had been paid over $300,000 to stand aside as the number one contender for Hearns's light-middleweight title so Hearns could fight Roberto Duran, then Hagler. Mugabi then should have fought Hearns in March 1986 but instead took on Hagler while Hearns knocked out James Shuler. This made Hearns the top middleweight contender, with the promise of a rematch with Hagler. But Hagler chose instead to fight Leonard.

To help Andries prepare to defend his title, New Jersey veteran Ken Bogner was hired as his trainer. Bogner's assessment was that Andries was a fighter rather than a stylist. He traded on his immense strength, endurance and dedication but possessed the subtlety of the Los Angeles Raiders' pass rush. Bogner came into the camp six weeks before the fight and focused on trying to improve Andries' jab. "You can't teach him that much in a month," Bogner said in the days leading up to the event. "I have taught him to bob and weave and move his head a little more frequently and he has started to pick it up a little." Bogner was quick to emphasise his good points and waxed lyrical about his strength. "He is one of the strongest fighters I have ever seen," he said. "I had him work for twelve fast rounds and he wasn't even tired afterwards. He has won a world championship, so whatever he is doing must be working."

Hearns devoted himself to the task at hand with an unusual level of commitment. Five weeks prior to the fight, he moved out of his house and lived in exile on the twenty-third floor of Detriot's Pontchartrain Hotel. He called home only three times and immersed himself in solitude in his hotel suite while mentally preparing to win in an impressive manner. "I sit up in my bed and map the fight out in my mind," he said. "I play it over and over again, picking out the right shots, the right punches that will be crucial to me." He refused to dwell on negative scenarios and explained, "I never contemplate defeat. I just don't allow myself a chance to think about any negative thoughts."

There were plenty of others who did this for him, and the pressure on Hearns to capture his third world title began to increase. Bob Arum told the press that Hearns "was at the crossroads of his illustrious career." He explained that the plan was for Hagler to face Leonard and, if he decided to continue fighting afterwards, to face Hearns again. "Tommy is a major fighter again if he can beat this guy, Andries. If he doesn't beat him, he isn't a major fighter anymore. The loss to Hagler did not hurt Hearns. It was the performances against Medal and DeWitt which did. He looked simply ordinary and the thing which I sell Hearns on is excitement. In short, he has to look exciting." This message permeated into the Kronk camp, prompting Prentiss Byrd, Emanuel Steward's second-in-command, to declare, "If we lose this one, we're out of business." Steward chose to focus on the threat presented by their opponent and told friends, "I'm confident but not supremely confident." He reminded the others, "Tommy has never fought at light-heavyweight before and Andries is fifteen pounds heavier than anybody he has fought before." He did accept Arum's loaded warning and told Hearns, "This fight can open doors but it can close them just as quickly." He added ominously, "When the door slams shut in boxing, the lock can rust and the jambs swell."

The pressure and speculation only added to the anticipation of 11,000 spectators inside the Cobo Arena, most of whom had come to see their local boy attempt to become only the ninth man in history to win three world championships in different weight divisions. They felt a fierce local pride in Hearns, who had been representing their city for ten years of his professional life, and they continued to greet him with acclaim from the moment his name was announced until referee Isaac Herrera had issued his instructions. The contrast between the two fighters was not just one of style and personality: Hearns looked sleek and sinewy; his upper body rippling with definition which was accentuated under the harsh arc lights, whilst Andries, at five feet and ten inches, was a stocky but well proportioned human bulldozer.

It looked one-sided from the beginning. Hearns shot out his long, spiteful jab and found the champion with ease as he relentlessly chugged forward, looking to get within range to throw his wild, flailing punches. Hearns was simply the classier boxer and the speed with which he unloaded his combination punches was dizzying. Andries, metronomic in his approach, absorbed the punches without taking a backward step. The second round, however, brought a reminder of Hearns's fragility as he tasted his own blood, which rolled down his cheek from a deep cut along his right eye, caused by a stray elbow. This prompted Hearns to use his jab with even more frequency as he sought to prevent Andries getting too close to cause further damage. "When I felt the blood from the cut, it made me come alive," Hearns remembered. "I immediately thought, 'Go after this guy.'" He changed his strategy and began to hit Andries coming in with right leads. "The left jab was supposed to be the key," Hearns said, "But his ability to counter made me wary."

"Hearns was able to box at his own pace, to pump out the jab and pick his man off from outside," reported *Boxing News*. "By the third he was so confident he waved his left arm up and down as if trying to mesmerise Andries. And the British fighter just couldn't seem to do anything about it."

Hearns kept proceedings at long range until the sixth round, when he dramatically crashed a right over the top of an Andries jab. The blow was so powerful it sent the British bulldog flying backwards and he landed heavily, hitting his head on the canvas. For a few seconds it looked as though he would not make it back up, and when he did manage to regain his feet, he was sent back down again by a brief series of punches, one of which seemed to land when he was on his knees with his arms clutching at his challenger's legs. Hearns bounced on the balls of his feet, eager to attack again, as referee Herrera completed the mandatory eight count and checked that Andries was ready to continue. Hearns was like a blur as he dashed in and cracked home a sweeping left hook before Andries had time to raise his defences, sending him down for the third time. The Detroit Man raised his arms in triumph, sure now that the referee would stop it, and walked to a neutral corner to take the plaudits, only for Emanuel Steward to tell him to concentrate. Hearns appeared unaware that the traditional three-knockdown rule, which meant fights had to be stopped when a boxer was floored three times in a single round, was not enforced in championship bouts sanctioned by the WBC. He later said, "I thought the fight was over and raised my hand before I realised I had to go and try all over again."

The gutsy Andries clambered back to his feet, only to stagger around the ring as Hearns blazed punches at him. He fell again under an avalanche of blows, but rose once more in an extraordinary display of courage and endurance. He even swung an enormous roundhouse right at Hearns, only to miss by a mile and fall once again to his knees, though this time it was ruled a slip. The bout was descending into farce and many at ringside called for it to be stopped, but Hearns seemed to have temporarily punched himself out and the game champion lasted to the bell.

The Detroit crowd acknowledged the champion's courage and resolution when he returned to his corner and this gave him the impetus to stage a rally in the next round. He even managed to connect with some powerful punches, whilst Hearns looked weary and was breathing heavily after his bombardment of the previous round. After the break, he raised his game, although at one stage he was pulled to the ground and the referee warned Andries about wrestling. As they resumed, Andries launched another of his huge right swings. Hearns easily ducked it and countered with a short right of his own, sending Andries down for what was, officially, the fifth time. This time the champion was all in. He somehow dragged himself to his feet but looked in desperate straits and headed to his own corner instead of towards his opponent. Referee Herrera had little option but to stop the fight and declare Hearns the new world champion.

The Hit Man was full of praise for his game opponent, though he felt the fight should have been stopped in the sixth. He also wasted no time in declaring that his real target was elsewhere: the victor of the upcoming Hagler-Leonard fight. "I really want the winner of that fight – I don't care who wins," he said. "It's not the money, I want to be the only man to win four titles." Licking his lips, Bob Arum felt that such a lucrative bout was now there to be made. "Tommy is now an established superstar again," he said. "There's no doubt he'll get a multi-million dollar fight out of this."

On 6 April 1987, Ray Leonard pulled off the upset of the decade when he returned from retirement to beat Marvin Hagler by a close, controversial decision. Infuriatingly for Hearns, Leonard prevaricated for a while before retiring again, leaving the middleweight title vacant.

# 13 THE HAMMER

BOB ARUM URGED Hearns to remain active and keep his name in the minds of the public. His stock had risen considerably. Although the fight he really wanted, against Ray Leonard, seemed to have slipped tantalisingly away, there were other opportunities. Arum mooted plans for him to drop back down to middleweight and meet Juan Domingo Roldan, a rugged Argentinian, for the vacant WBC crown. Hearns and Steward looked into the possibilities, not least because victory would make Hearns the first man to officially win world titles in four different weight categories: welterweight, light-middleweight, middleweight and light-heavyweight. Greats like Henry Armstrong, Roberto Duran and Alexis Arguello had tried and failed to win four titles, and Hearns's place in the history books would be assured. After Leonard's retirement had left the middleweight throne empty, Frank Tate won the International Boxing Federation title, while Sumbu Kalambay beat Iran Barkley for the WBA crown. The WBC belt remained unclaimed, and it was for that that Hearns now signed to fight.

The muscular, broad-chested Roldan, who came from a village in the province of Cordoba in Argentina, was eager to meet him, as beating such a big name was the best way to gain the recognition he felt he deserved. He traded on his nickname, "The Hammer," an apt description of his obdurate, hard-punching nature. One magazine accurately described him as "probably the strongest middleweight in the world." At seventeen, before becoming a boxer, he had proved his inordinate strength in a highly unusual contest. "A circus arrived in my town and they had a bear," he said. "It was a fighting bear, undefeated because nobody could fight him for three minutes without a visit to the floor. The owner of the circus offered a hundred pesos. 'For that money, I will fight the entire circus,' I said. It was a tremendous brawl but the bear could not floor me within the three minutes and I won the money."

Crude but very powerful, he was eventually spotted by Argentina's leading manager, Amilcar Brusa, and was recruited as a sparring partner for Brusa's star, the great middleweight champion Carlos Monzon. "He was as strong as a beast," said Monzon, "but he was very young, not experienced." Roldan toiled away, learning his trade, until he sprang to international recognition with a kayo of Frank "The Animal" Fletcher, a win that earned him a number one contender spot. His first crack at the middleweight throne failed before the cruel fists of Marvin Hagler, but not before he became the first man to knock the fearsome Hagler to the canvas, with a left hook – Hagler claimed it was a slip. He had since won twelve fights on the trot, and had rejected the possibility of meeting Iran Barkley, as he felt Barkley's name did not carry enough kudos. Instead, he had begged his manager to line up the scalp of Hearns for the vacant title.

Emanuel Steward was reluctant to accept the fight. "Roldan is one mean motherfucker," he told Hearns, recounting a well-worn story about Roldan once fighting a wrestling bear in a carnival for $100. He felt that dropping back down the weight divisions to meet such a durable opponent would be an unnecessary risk, but Hearns was unmoved by this reasoning and dismissed fears about losing weight. "Although I felt really strong as a light-heavyweight, I feel just as strong as a middleweight," he later said. He argued that his fight with Andries had been more of a risk. "It is true that fighters grow into heavier weight divisions and don't always carry that vital increase in power," he said, giving the examples of Roberto Duran and Alexis Arguello, who had no longer hit with effect once they took on bigger men. However, he was dropping down to a lighter division and would bring his potency with him. Finally, he was dismissive of the threat the Argentine posed and reminded his mentor that he possessed advantages in height, reach, power and boxing ability. Roldan's most effective weapon was a vicious, chopping right which he liked to throw frequently but which was telegraphed. Hearns believed that this would make it an exciting contest with relatively low risk, as long as he avoided the eagerness to brawl which had cost him so dearly against Hagler.

Bob Arum's well-oiled publicity machine swung into action. The major theme was Hearns's attempt to make history and become the first fighter to win four world championships. The veteran promoter pointed to his victories over Cuevas, Benitez and Duran, saying, "He has enough Latino scalps hanging in his tent to cure baldness." To mobilise the South American community, he reminded them that Argentine great Carlos Monzon had owned the middleweight title for so long that Roldan had a duty to win it back. He said that it was a clash between "the pride of Argentina and the gringo who knocks out all their heroes." The fight was scheduled to take place at the Las Vegas Hilton and half of the 11,000 tickets sold were snapped up by Argentinians.

Apart from the difference in their purses – Hearns was receiving $1 million and Roldan $250,000 – Hearns also possessed a significant height advantage over the five feet seven inches Roldan. He also had a huge reach advantage of seventy-eight inches against Roldan's sixty-nine inch span. This prompted bookmakers to establish him as a 4-1 favourite. Yet Roldan's confidence was contagious. He reportedly placed a $45,000 wager on himself, and his fellow countrymen followed suit to such an extent that, by fight night, Hearns was a mere 17-10 shot.

One day after training, Steward sprung a surprise on his charge when he interrupted a video session to study Roldan's style with some old, black-and-white films of Hearns fighting as an amateur. They laughed at the skinny kid from the east side with arms as long as poles and cringed when he threw a punch and lost his balance. After a short while, Hearns, never one to dwell too long on the past, stopped the show and said, "It is no good spending too much time looking back at yesterday because today will hit you with a punch in the mouth."

Soon afterwards, Hearns was walking through the lobby of the Las Vegas Hilton when he noticed Elvis Presley's famous white sequined jumpsuit displayed in a glass case. Hearns had occasionally cited the Memphis singer and Muhammad Ali as his two heroes and the suit caused him to reflect on his two idols' legacies. He said, "People only remember Elvis Presley for two things: being a great music maker and then looking like a fat junkie." He then drew parallels with his fighting idol: "It is similar to when people see Muhammad Ali. They remember him in two ways. Some look at the soul of boxing, still the most recognizable athlete on the planet. Others only see a helpless invalid." This prompted him to tell members of his entourage that he wanted to stay in boxing as long as he could, and wanted to secure his own place in the sport's history by winning four separate world championships, although he knew it was a race against the clock. "I understand the dangers of hanging around boxing for too long," he said.

Hearns chose to follow Marvin Hagler's example and based his training camp at the Johnny Tocco's spartan gym, situated just off the Las Vegas strip. Emanuel Steward focused on correcting errors he had observed in the previous fight against Dennis Andries. He hadn't failed to notice that Hearns would stagger slightly after taking certain punches, especially right hooks. Steward maintained that Roldan possessed an unrefined style of fighting which could upset their plans, and so he drilled Hearns in defensive techniques for hours at a time. In the last press conference before the fight, he declared himself pleased with the smooth running of his camp and dismissed concerns that weight loss might drain him. "I bulked up to one hundred and seventy-three pounds to box Dennis Andries but I feel even stronger now," he said. "Believe it or not, it wasn't very hard to lose the weight. I did it by just training and working out every day."

Meanwhile, Roldan's camp was rocked by the news that one of his training team had been arrested and charged with shoplifting at a local K-Mart department store. Roldan dismissed the importance of the thief and claimed that he was not one of his primary trainers. But the stigma was hard to shake and Roldan expressed his frustration at being forced to defend his camp at every press conference in the build-up to the biggest fight of his life.

By the time of the fight both men had put aside their concerns and distractions and were completely focused on the task ahead. When the opening bell chimed, the bullish Argentinian tore across the apron and took Hearns by surprise. The opening minute saw Hearns forced on to his back foot and he pawed away with his left jab to keep Roldan at bay. Then, against the early flow of the fight, Hearns thwacked a beautifully timed right cross to the side of the temple and Roldan dropped for a count of six. Mills Lane, the famous referee who also served as a Washoe County judge, appeared momentarily surprised that the Argentinian had recovered so quickly from such a hard punch but Roldan plowed forward again, winging punches and forcing Hearns to hold on. But just before the opening three minutes were up, Hearns smashed home three consecutive right hands which dropped him again. He was saved by the bell before a count had to be administered. It had been quite a round.

Roldan's corner worked furiously on their man during the break, and when the second round began he stormed out again, forcing the fight while the Hit Man was obliged to keep him at the end of his whipping left jab. Hearns remained alert to the slightest opening and he soon delivered another right followed by a stunning left hook, sending Roldan to the canvas for the third time. The end looked nigh, but even a third knockdown could not persuade the Argentine bull to change his approach. He clambered back up and continued to pursue the fleet-footed Hearns fearlessly. He made no attempt at subtlety and didn't bother to slip or bob-and-weave away from any of the long-range punches coming his way. "Showing remarkable resilience, Roldan chugged ahead as if the fight was just beginning," reported *The Ring*. Sensationally, he managed to catch Hearns with a clean right hand which shook him to his boots and left him looking bewildered. Roldan slammed another right hand at him, forcing Hearns to grab hold and wait until his head had cleared. He attempted to counter with two right hands but they were ineffective and the crowd responded wildly to this change in momentum. *Boxing News* reporter Graham Houston compared the round to another classic confrontation: "It was in the same league as the Tony Zale and Rocky Graziano wars of the 1940s."

Round four was equally extraordinary. Roldan stepped out of his corner in a buoyant mood. His wild swings drove Hearns into a corner where Roldan suddenly connected with a sizzling left hook. Not for the first time in his career, Hearns's legs turned to jelly, but the Hit Man ducked, swayed and held on until his head was clear. As Roldan went wild, Hearns began to hit back, firing sizzling punches with ferocious intent. He whipped in a right cross that hit Roldan on top of his head and suddenly it was his turn to stagger. Hearns switched his attack to the body, whipping in left hooks to the ribs to further open up Roldan's already porous defence. And when the chance arose, he unleashed another booming right to the side of Roldan's face, causing him to topple forward against Hearns, who stepped back and watched the courageous South American fall to the floor. He lay there on his front, his face buried in the canvas, before flopping over onto his back with his arms splayed as Mills Lane completed the ten count before waving it off after two minutes and one second of the round.

Hearns, who must have been hugely relieved that his opponent had finally stayed down, celebrated wildly, pumping his fist before throwing his arms aloft as his entourage crowded into the ring and lifted him into the air. He had achieved his long-spoken dream of becoming the first world champion at four weights. The statistics recorded that Roldan had thrown two hundred and forty-two punches throughout the four rounds but just twenty-seven percent had connected. In contrast, Hearns was much more sparing with his punches, delivering one hundred and sixty-three yet he was much more accurate and landed with fifty seven per cent. This accuracy was reflected on the judges' scorecards, with all three having Hearns clearly ahead at the finish. But this fight was never going to be about the scorecards. "It was," said *Boxing News*, "the sort of fight where one daren't take one's eye from the ring for fear of missing something sensational." Months later, Hearns would tell an interviewer, "I have never been hit like Roldan hit me. The more I hurt him, the stronger he got. Thought maybe I shouldn't hurt him so much!"

AT THE POST-FIGHT press conference Hearns was still euphoric and keen to emphasise the historical significance of his victory, even hinting that he might now go after a fifth title, at cruiserweight. "Being in a class all by myself is like living in a country where nobody else is there," he mused. In a pointed reference to Hagler and Leonard, whom he was hoping to lure from retirement and who were sitting at ringside, Hearns said, "I am now my own boss. I call the shots." Steward suggested that Leonard and Hagler must pick up the gauntlet which had been thrown, because "They are fighters and now that Tommy has won, they want a bit of the glory again."

(Leonard, insisting he would stay retired, would only say, "I have no interest in Tommy, but I'm happy for him.")

On 4 November 1987, thousands of Detroit residents flocked to the streets connecting the city's Kennedy Square and the Cobo Arena to pay homage to Thomas Hearns, immaculate in a black suit, sat atop a white Mustang convertible which slowly passed along the route, led by the Central High marching band thumping out a rendition of Michael Jackson's "Bad" and flanked by a police motorcade. The only thing missing from this honour, which was usually reserved for returning astronauts and World Series baseball champions, was the ticker tape. The cavalcade snaked its way to the Cobo Hall, the scene of many of Hearns' greatest days, where Mayor Coleman Young waited, ready to proclaim that 4 November was officially "Thomas Hearns Day" and to award the fight legend and his trainer the keys to the city. Standing beside the looming statue of Joe Louis, Mayor Young declared, "Thomas Hearns has made the city of Detroit feel incredibly proud. One week ago, he achieved something that no other boxer has ever done and it is appropriate that this ceremony is taking place in front of the great Brown Bomber because Thomas is in that class along with Sugar Ray Robinson who was also a proud Detroit citizen." An emotional Hearns responded, "This is truly a great moment for me. It is something I will cherish more than anything and that includes the honour of winning the fourth title."

"Go for number five, Tommy!" shouted someone in the crowd.

While *Ring* magazine was cynical about the legitimacy of Hearns's four-weight record, achieved as it was at a time when numerous governing bodies, the so-called Alphabet Boys, had demeaned the notion of world titles, it nevertheless admitted "there can be no denying the 'Hit Man's' stature as one of the 1980s' greatest and most exciting performers." Bob Arum attended the ceremony and wasted little time hyping future challenges for Hearns. "There are a couple of guys out there called Marvin and

Ray who need to respond to our challenge," he told the crowds. Emanuel Steward also tried to increase the public pressure on Hearns's two conquerors, and said, "I am meeting with the representatives of Sugar Ray Leonard and Marvin Hagler in the coming week to negotiate terms for a fight in May 1988." He speculated that such a bout would reap each fighter in excess of $10 million but insisted that Hearns must get the larger share. "Right now, Thomas is the most popular fighter out there. He is more popular that Leonard or Hagler." The cheering hordes of Detroit fans certainly did not disagree.

# 14 THE BLADE AND THE HEAT

IN MAY 1988, Hearns was based in training camp in Phoenix, Arizona, preparing for his imminent fight against Iran Barkley in Las Vegas when he received news that Kimberly Craig, his one-time high school sweetheart, had been shot in the face and was in a critical condition at a Detroit hospital. Craig, aged twenty-eight, was the mother of Hearns's five-year-old daughter Natasha Alana, although they had become estranged after Ms Craig, an estate agent, had felt obliged to sue Hearns two years earlier to get him to pay a weekly allowance of $600 in child support. Reports suggested that she had been shot twice by a male passenger who was in her car and subsequently fled without a trace. Police chiefs contacted Hearns to inform him and to ascertain if he had any information which could help them discover the assailant's identity. Hearns said that he did not know anything that could help but was prevented by Emanuel Steward from returning to Detroit, so instead arranged to have his daughter flown directly to Phoenix. Steward was hugely sympathetic to his boxer's plight but was determined that nothing would interfere with the preparations for the fight against the unpredictable Barkley. Craig would eventually recover from her injuries and be reunited with Hearns.

After dismantling Juan Roldan, Hearns had embarked upon a frustrating six-month game of cat-and-mouse with Hagler and Leonard, the two fighters he most wanted to cross gloves with again. Eventually both decreed that they would not come out of their retirement to fight him, so he was forced to search for a new opponent. The obvious choice was Barkley, whom he agreed to face at the indoor, 9,000-seater Hilton Centre, Las Vegas, on Monday, 6 June 1988, in a Bob Arum-promoted triple-header of world championship fights, which also included the WBA light-heavy-weight contest between Virgil Hill and Ramzi Hassan and Roger Mayweather competing for the WBC light-welterweight crown against Harold Brazier.

The decision to fight Barkley, whose unusual first name was attributed to his stepfather's love of geography, followed a process of elimination. Hearns had revised his targets and intended to unify the middleweight division by beating the two other 160-pound champions, Sumbu Kalambay and Frank Tate, but both proved too difficult to entice. Barkley, a leading challenger, was first mooted as a possibility in April. He was an aggressive slugger who enjoyed a toe-to-toe brawl. Hearns admitted that he did not know a great deal about him except that he possessed a big left hook, which had dropped the number one contender, James Kinchen, eighteen months earlier on the way to a win that projected him into the world's elite middleweights. Hearns recalled watching this fight before meeting Doug DeWitt and was impressed by the speed of Barkley's hands. His record of twenty-four victories against four defeats, with fifteen early endings, along with an unsuccessful tilt at Sambu Kalambay's title made him an obvious candidate.

As the deal for the fight was inked, Barkley recalled that when he boxed as an amateur, he had hung pictures on his bedroom wall of Hearns, Hagler and Leonard because he dreamed about fighting them one day. He was determined not to let his dream fight pass without making the most of it. He told a journalist from the *New York Times*, "Hearns is shop-worn" and offered the evidence that Juan Roldan had repeatedly rocked him. "What the Argentinian started, he couldn't finish, but if I find a sign saying 'hit me' on

Hearns's chin, I will not make the same mistake." He predicted that he was going to win the title by knockout.

Hearns had resumed training at the start of May and based his camp in Phoenix before moving to Las Vegas and Johnny Tocco's gym. He insisted on employing Milton McCrory as one of his sparring partners. The former welterweight champion had recently lost to Lupe Aquino and announced his retirement from the ring. Hearns had been devastated by the loss and believed that by joining his camp, he could build up his friend's confidence and encourage him to continue to fight again. Steward prepared Hearns to deal with the pressure that would be exerted by Barkley and prophesied a second round knockout for Hearns, who he was confident possessed too much strength. Hearns was buoyed by the fact that Barkley had been found wanting whenever he had stepped into the elite level of boxing and remarked, "He hasn't been in there with anyone close to me either."

He was also thrilled with the results of an operation he had undergone in secret. He had been persistently troubled with breathing problems, which were diagnosed as caused by blocked nasal passages. "I have had a swollen nostril that's been troubling me for years," he said. "On one side of my nose, I was breathing at only fifty per cent capacity and just ten per cent on the other side." Following a two-hour operation, and after the victory against Roldan, he boasted, "My endurance has now improved significantly."

IRAN BARKLEY GREW up in the Patterson Projects, a densely populated grid of public housing in the Mott Haven district of the South Bronx, an area notorious for drugs, gangs and mayhem. "It was so tough that he had to fight his way in and out of his apartment building or pay extortion money to bigger, older youths," reported *Boxing News*. "But he took up boxing on the urging of his older sister Yvonne, a former woman boxer, and had no more trouble."

As the fight date drew near, Barkley seemed to grow in confidence. He enjoyed regaling sportswriters with his life story and telling how Yvonne had taught him how to fight to survive in their Bronx neighbourhood. She would take him to a New York gym despite his protestations to stay at home and play on his drum kit. He had eventually turned professional in 1982 and had fought for six years without troubling the radars of the sport's big hitters. When he had lost to the unranked Sanderline Williams, the boxing establishment prepared to write him off. He was brought in to face Michael Olajide to act as a stepping stone for the Canadian's ascent to the super-middleweight division. Against the odds, he knocked out Olajide in five rounds and it was this victory which had earned him his shot at Hearns. Barkley could be hit and he could be floored but, in the words of his manager, Vinnie Ferguson, "He gets up like a wounded gorilla." He acknowledged that he was stepping up in class but was ready for the fray. "I expect Hearns will be dangerous and come to take me out," he said. "That's fine. I will be waiting and I'll hit him with a shot of my own. If his legs go, then it's goodnight Tommy Hearns."

Hearns was the 4-1 favourite. He had won forty-five of his forty-seven bouts and was twenty-nine years old, an age when many champions are reaching their peak. Yet some observers felt he was nearing the end of the road, and that sooner rather than later, someone – though perhaps not the erratic, easy-to-hit Barkley – would end his middleweight reign. Eight and a half thousand spectators thronged to the Hilton Centre to see whether Barkley could make good on his bold talk.

Hearns set the tone. He left his corner in a confident mood, standing tall and using a string of head feints which indicated his respect for the Blade's lunging attacks. When they invariably came, he countered to the body before suddenly switching target and aiming several right hands to his opponent's head. Hearns looked commanding, staying high on his toes and remaining at long range, forcing Barkley to throw huge, signposted haymakers.

The second round quickly fell into the same pattern and Detroit's celebrated son used every inch of his ringcraft to crash home a number of rapier punches, which started to leave their mark in the tiny swellings and red blotches that appeared beneath both of Barkley's eyes. The challenger's mouth started to fill with blood from a torn lip, and his increasing desperation was evident when referee Richard Steele warned him to keep his lunging punches up higher. When the bell tolled to end the second session, Dr Donald Romero from the Nevada State Athletic Commission ventured to Barkley's corner to inspect his injuries and determine whether he could continue. Eddie Aliano, his cornerman, managed to stem the bleeding and reassured Dr Romero that he could come out for the next round.

"You gotta go for it," urged his co-trainer, Al Bolden. "You gotta street fight. You gotta do it South Bronx street style."

Both men left their stools to start the third round with an air of inevitability. Hearns countered Barkley's wild lunge before being charged into the ropes, where he again threw a fluid combination of lefts and rights with a sting enough to repel the New Yorker and throw him off balance. Hearns connected with two more stinging right hands, while Barkley's replies found only fresh air. Hearns sensed the end was near and piled on the pressure. A right-left combination followed by a double left hook to the body obliged Barkley to grab hold of his tormentor to gain some respite.

Hearns was in total control, and with this came complacency. He often carried his left hand low, allowing him to shoot his jab up from the hip, but it made him vulnerable to a fast hook over the top. As he looked to pick his shots in the centre of the ring, Barkley suddenly threw an arcing right which landed square on Hearns' unguarded chin. The impact of the punch seemed to stop time; one sportswriter later equated it to the moment of calm before an atom bottom lands. Hearns stood rigid for an instant before falling to the canvas.

The referee stood over his stricken figure and began to count. Hearns tried to rise but fell back as the seconds ticked by. By a superhuman effort, he tried again and somehow restructured his scrambled senses enough to clamber unsteadily to his feet before the count reached ten. Barkley roared forward and the raw fury of his attack knocked the clearly defenceless champion through the bottom two rungs of the ring ropes, forcing Steele to grab him to stop him falling completely out of the ring, while at the same time declaring the contest over. Barkley was the new champion after two minutes and thirty-nine seconds of a tumultuous, unforgettable third round.

The bout was one of the most exciting of the decade – and was voted *Ring* magazine's Upset of the Year – yet because it was on pay-per-view rather than live on network TV, it never reached the audience it should have. "Such is the nature of today's society," concluded Jeff Ryan in *KO* magazine, "that an event has to play in America's living rooms to have a deep-reaching impact."

After he had received some lengthy treatment, Hearns responded with magnanimity. He admitted, "I didn't see the final punch but thought I had slipped it." He confessed to feeling disappointed but wanted to pay respect to the new champion. He said, "Tonight, Iran Barkley was the better man. I'm surprised he managed to take a helluva shot but he came to fight." The pictures told a different story to the result as Hearns was completely unmarked whilst Barkley had plasters over both eyes to stem the flow of blood that later required sixteen stitches. The Bronx battler came out with a classic quote when asked about his injuries: "I didn't care about the cuts because I didn't have time to bleed." He dedicated the fight to his brother Alfred and his father, who were both gravely ill with cancer. When he was asked if he would grant his vanquished rival the opportunity of a rematch, Barkley graciously promised, "Any time he wants a fight, he's welcome to it."

When Hearns arrived back in Detroit, he was inevitably pressed about his future. He gave an agitated response to Detroit journalist Mike O'Hara, who wrote, "All fighters get creased and old under the searing ring lights that expose every wrinkle in their skills. There is no vanishing cream for a left jab that cannot be released at the right time. No cosmetic surgeon's scalpel can nip away a halt in the step or tuck the sag in the chin's ability to withstand punishment. Age is now chasing Thomas Hearns and he is at the point where the glory and gold of boxing have intersected and he is only as good as his last round." HBO analyst Larry Merchant also weighed in. "I was surprised, though not stunned, by the outcome," he said. "When Hearns gets hit in the jaw by anybody, it's like a jolt of electricity seems to go through his legs." People were writing off the Hit Man.

"Did I ever say I would retire?" responded Hearns. "I have every intention of winning my title back." Emanuel Steward supported him and offered the view that Hearns should continue boxing because he hadn't taken a long, drawn-out pounding. "Looking at it logically, Barkley took more than eight minutes of sustained punishment during which Tommy was in complete control. The fight ended with the first solid punch Barkley landed."

FIVE MONTHS AFTER his shocking third round defeat to Iran Barkley, Hearns set out to claim world title number five. He was scheduled to step back into the ring against San Diego's James "The Heat" Kinchen for the newly created World Boxing Organization super-middleweight championship. The WBO had been set up by a group of Puerto Ricans and Dominicans who split from the long-established World Boxing Association at its convention of 1988, in what has variously been described as a power struggle and a row over the rules and ratings system. Based in San Juan, it claimed to follow the noble principles of "Dignity, Democracy, Honesty." The Hearns–Kinchen fight was to be its first sanctioned world title contest.

The events which had thrown Hearns, Kinchen and the WBO together were typical of the complex, internecine world of boxing. Hearns, eager to get back into the ring to dispel any doubts that his crushing loss to Barkley was anything more than a fluke, was supposed to box the Venezuelan veteran Fulgencio Obelmejias for the WBA version of the super-middleweight crown but Obelmejias was forced to pull out with a rib injury. Intrigued by Ray Leonard's inability to resist the sport's siren call and his latest comeback against Donny Lalonde, Bob Arum, the show's promoter, wanted to give credence to a possible Hearns–Leonard rematch and contacted Kinchen, who had spent his career on the fringes of the world's top ten, to persuade him to accept his tilt at glory by facing Hearns. A Hearns win, Arum reasoned, would get him back on track for a possible money-spinner with Sugar Ray. He then turned his attentions to the WBO. Hearns was now in the unique position of winning his fifth – and the sanctioning body's first – world title.

At the Las Vegas press conference to announce the fight, the questions about his enduring presence in the sport were the main theme. Hearns stood and politely fielded them all. He admitted that he could understand their perspective, as his rivals such as Hagler and Leonard had bowed out from the cruellest sport. "I am a boxing rarity," he said. "I love what I am doing and I am not eager to retire from active fighting. It's exciting and I love the attention. I also like the money too!" He continued, "When I leave boxing, I don't want people to simply call me Thomas Hearns. I want them to call me 'The Champ.'" Hearns promised that when he faced Kinchen, they would see a new style. "From this fight, I will no longer fool about in the ring. From the opening bell, I am going to forsake boxing and fancy footwork and stop the feeling-out process. I'm not going to do any boxing again. I'm going to come out and get the job done."

If that was supposed to send shivers down Kinchen's spine, it failed. The thirty-one-year-old North American Boxing Federation's super-middleweight champion had come into this encounter as a late replacement. He had returned from a twelve-round victory over Marvin Mack at Lake Tahoe and been home barely a week when he accepted the fight. He was nonplussed by Hearns's attitude and asked, "Has Hearns had his morning coffee yet? He seems grouchy."

Hearns was in a tetchy mood, but James Kinchen was not the source of his ire. His twenty-two-year-old brother Jessie, and his sister Sarah, had been charged with a felony assault resulting from a neighbourhood fracas. The police had alleged that Sarah Hearns had hit a neighbour during a dispute. When the situation threatened to flare up, Jessie Hearns had fired five shots into the air. Although no one was injured, the resulting court case, which saw his siblings cleared, had weighed heavily on Hearns. It was an unnecessary distraction and detracted from the positive image that he had been striving to present. This charm offensive had included a recent visit to a retirement home, where Hearns had asked an eighty-five-year-old widow to dance with him. He also broke camp to host the Boys and Girls Club of America, where he had initiated a day of spirited games. Finally, he completed his annual Hallowe'en visit to the Detroit Beaumont Hospital, where he spent an afternoon charming bedridden children.

Despite the distractions, Hearns was focused on returning to action and beating Kinchen in a convincing manner. He admitted that the Barkley defeat had made him aware of his vulnerability. "I know that the clock is ticking on my career," he said, "and it's not the greatest feeling in the world, knowing what might happen in there." He dismissed any discussion about meeting Leonard in a return encounter after eight years and insisted that he wasn't thinking beyond Kinchen. "Sugar Ray Leonard is fighting Donny Lalonde three days after me. It stands to reason that if I lose to Kinchen or if he loses, there will be no rematch."

Eight thousand fans ventured to the Las Vegas Hilton to see if Hearns could win his fifth world championship in style. Instead they watched an underwhelming display in which he seemed to visibly age in the ring. He looked closer to sixty when Kinchen almost finished him off at the end of the fourth round. He was cruising and in control of the fight when the Californian suddenly sprang from his inactivity and landed a right hand. Without any warning, Hearns' legs seemed to betray him and turned to jelly, causing him to drunkenly stagger to his right, directly into line with Kinchen's barrage of punches which propelled him against the ropes and then onto the canvas apron. Tommy clutched the ropes. He barely beat Mills Lane's count, just managing to rise unsteadily at nine as he grabbed the referee in order to steady himself. "I thought his career was over," revealed Prentiss Byrd, Emanuel Steward's chief assistant. "His whole career went through my mind." Steward violated boxing rules by leaping onto the ring apron to implore his protégé to hold onto Kinchen and allow himself time to recover. He later said, "I thought that it was a repeat of the Iran Barkley fight."

Mills Lane was on the verge of stopping the fight as Hearns struggled to keep upright in the face of Kinchen's ferocious attack. When Kinchen rushed in to finish him, Hearns grabbed his rampaging foe around the shoulders and held on for dear life. When referee Lane tried to separate them, Hearns groped at him and used him to steady himself again. This stopped Kinchen from landing the finishing blows when the Detroiter appeared all but out. "I held onto him like he was my woman," said Hearns. "I had to survive that round. Mills Lane would have had to be Hercules to break us sooner." Amazingly, he used every ounce of his determination, energy and will-power to carry him through the final eight rounds against a renewed and reinvigorated fighter who fought ferociously every step of the way. "I was not going to let this slip away. I had come too far to let it slip away. Whatever it took to win this fight, I was going to give it my all," said Hearns afterwards.

Hearns won the decision by the narrowest of margins, with judge Larry Rozadilla awarding the nod to Kinchen whilst Bill Graham and Cindy Barton both voted in favour of Hearns. Observers were quick to bury Hearns's reputation as a fighter. The popular ringside consensus was that the Iran Barkley knockout had signposted that Hearns's best days were behind him and the listless display against Kinchen had confirmed that they were out of sight. As he walked away from the ring, Hearns's right eye was swollen shut, his right hand was swathed in ice bandages and his joints throbbed from the punishment he had absorbed. He turned to Emanuel Steward and said, "I never, ever want to feel like this again."

Yet when Ray Leonard beat Donny Lalonde to join Hearns as a five-time world champion, it was clear that the path to their rematch was now open.

# 15 LEONARD, PART TWO

IN THE WEEKS following the disappointing James Kinchen encounter, the sports pages were full of reports suggesting a historic second meeting between Hearns and Ray Leonard. Emanuel Steward did nothing to dampen the speculation. He claimed that both fighters had reached a verbal agreement for the rematch even before the Barkley fight. "There are no other major fights on the horizon and we figure that Tommy and Ray will make almost triple the money they made for their first fight in 1981," he said, citing the influence of pay-per-view as a major factor.

The showdown was set for Caesars Palace, Las Vegas, on 12 June 1989. Yet Hearns had a hard time believing that it was finally reality. "Tommy never believed it would happen," Steward later told *Boxing Illustrated*. "It was a funny type of psychological thing. The fight was finally here, the one he had waited eight years for, but he still wasn't sure."

Hearns also harboured hidden but deep doubts about his own durability. He had heard and read so many stories about his chin and legs being suspect that he had begun to believe them. Steward knew he had to build up his fighter's confidence in those areas, so once the negotiations were complete, Hearns began his preparations in the steaming hot Kronk gym. He used an exercise bike to build up his legs, and sparred and punched the pads. He left nothing to chance and spent time at Highland Park's Powerhouse

Gym to strengthen not his punching but his leg muscles, telling the weightlifters who watched his efforts, "I've waited eight long years for this return fight."

Steward also took Hearns to see a medical specialist to test his legs to see if they were weak and if they could be strengthened. They found that Hearns's legs did not have strong muscles in the right places for the movements of boxing, so the doctor developed a special exercise bike to correct these faults. On the days when Hearns didn't run, he rode the bike at the gym after training.

At the same time, Prentiss Byrd took Hearns to a dentist in Philadelphia to examine his jaw in order to design the optimal mouthpiece. "Like most fighters who have been boxing for a long time, Tommy's jaw had actually shifted on the left side and there was a gap which made it very vulnerable when he was hit with right hands," said Steward. "And so Dr Williams devised a particular mouthpiece, designed to push up on the jaw and balance out the pressure so that it could be absorbed throughout his entire jaw and never again be localised in any one spot. If he were to get hit there, it would balance out and he could come back." One further panacea that Hearns refused, however, was some potentially contentious medicine for his longstanding sinus problem, which restricted his breathing. Not wanting to fall foul of a postfight dope test, he refused the medication his management offered and instead drank a herbal tea called Breathe Easy four times a day.

Whether the benefits of the bike, the mouthpiece and the tea were real or psychological, they seemed to work. On the morning of Tuesday, 13 June 1989, Hearns gave his final press conference two days before he was scheduled to fulfil a dream that he had pursued for eight years to meet Leonard, the thirty-three-year-old nemesis who had haunted his thoughts ever since his fourteenth-round loss in 1981. Hearns declared that he was happier, more content and confident than he had been about any of his fights in the past three years. He assured the throng of journalists that his training sessions had gone "exceptionally well," and claimed that he felt physically, mentally and emotionally ready to slay his demons. "I couldn't be better," he said.

Two hours after returning to his hotel, his idyll was cruelly shattered when Hearns received a phone call from his mother, Lois, to tell him that his younger brother, Henry, had been charged with first-degree murder (according to Emanuel Steward in *Ringmasters*, he was told the news by a friend of the family and then broke the news to Hearns and his mother Lois in their hotel room). Henry had shot his girlfriend in the head at Thomas's Southfield mansion. A man of less mental strength might have, but Hearns had learned to compartmentalise his feelings before a fight, to block out distractions and focus on the ring. "It was something I had to put aside," he later said. "My family means a great deal to me. But that day, it meant more to me to get in there and defeat Ray Leonard because I know for a fact that my family and my little brother wanted me to stay there and take care of business."

Emanuel Steward faced the multitudes of press that suddenly descended back on the doorstep and refused to make any comment about the charges. He admitted that the events had not helped his charge but revealed, "Thomas took the news pretty well, everything considered. He's a strong-minded individual, he's very controlled and he has got tunnel vision about this fight with Leonard." He suggested that caution would be the best option until further details emerged. "We don't know much more about what happened than we knew a couple of days ago," Steward said. "We're trying to find out the details."

The details of the second shooting incident involving his family slowly began to emerge. Henry Hearns, aged twenty-two, was being held in the Southfield City jail, accused of killing his fiancée, nineteen-year-old Nancy Ann Barile. The couple had been in a turbulent relationship and had apparently argued in a bedroom at Thomas Hearns's home. A witness reported hearing Henry say, "I'm going to blow your brains out." Then he shot Barile once in the head with a .44 Magnum pistol. Henry, who had been pursuing a career as a musician and who was described by his lawyer as "a very gentle kid," was eventually tried and found guilty of second degree murder and was sentenced to twenty-five years imprisonment.

If extra spice was needed, it was added just a couple of days before the fight when Hearns accused Leonard of bulking up by illegal means. Leonard was furious. "For some crazy reasons, Tommy has got it into his head I have used steroids," said Leonard. "And it's just not true. I take the charges very, very personally. But what annoys me even more is what these allegations have done to boxing. We have enough criticism as it is. For someone like Hearns, who makes a good living out of the sport, to taint it in that way makes him a fool." Hearns, however, refused to back down. "Everyone is suspicious about what it took to get Leonard in the shape he's in today," said Hearns. "It seems like he got pumped up overnight."

The weigh-in took place at noon on the day of the fight. In their final public encounter, Hearns refused to answer questions about his domestic turmoil but admitted, "A fight of this magnitude is never going to be easy." He promised the watching public that they would see the war that they expected. "Somewhere inside the twelve rounds, I will catch up with Leonard and take him out," he predicted. Leonard was less circumspect and suggested that a long tactical contest would ensue. "Hearns usually follows whatever I do," he claimed, and so he planned "to dance around the ring for a few rounds before I pick up the pace in the later rounds." He dismissed speculation linking him with a fight against the middleweight champion, Michael Nunn. "Everyone seems to have it in their heads that this is an easy fight," Leonard raged. "This is Tommy Hearns. I don't care if his legs are weak, if his chin is weak. I'm going into this fight with just one thing on my mind, which is to get him out of there as quickly as I can."

The weight limit for the super-middleweight division was 12

stone. It was something of a surprise then, when Hearns weighed in light at 11st 8½lbs, adding fuel to the speculation that a secret deal had been insisted on by Leonard's camp. Leonard, who came in at only 11st 6lbs, clearly did not want to be heavily outweighed by the bigger Hearns, and for weeks before the fight, stories had circulated that he had insisted his opponent weigh no more than 11st 10lbs. These rumours were denied by Mike Trainer, Emanuel Steward and Bob Arum, yet were subsequently revealed to have been true: Hearns would have suffered a $2 million deduction from his purse had he weighed in over 11st 10lbs. It was the kind of deal at which Leonard and Trainer were adept.

Steward told reporters that the loser of this encounter should retire immediately. He reasoned that both men had been through enough difficult fights and should not risk their health. Leonard had also been showing signs of vulnerability, having been dropped in his previous fight by Donny Lalonde. Steward pointed out that both men could boast vast wealth and should enjoy it. The $11 million he had secured for this bout ensured that Hearns' career earnings were around $30 million. Leonard's attorney, Mike Trainer, mused that his fighter's $13 million payment pushed his fortune to $83 million, the highest amount ever earned by an individual sportsman. Hearns, ranked as a 3-1 outsider, dismissed his manager's concerns and argued, "It is up to each individual when he should retire." He refused to discuss it further because, "I never think about losing and I won't start now."

When Sugar Ray Leonard made his ring entrance, he had the Zulu word for power, AMANDLA, emblazoned across the back of his robe and the top of his waist band in capital letters. The word held dual symbolism: to signify his own intentions and to offer solidarity to South Africans, where the word was often a rallying cry at anti-apartheid demonstrations. Hearns was less profound and had his own name embossed across his own gold robe and shorts but the steely look in his eye signalled his intent.

The contest opened with unexpected caution. Both fighters tentatively left their corners and began feeling each other out. They moved around the ring, waiting for the other to launch the first attack, like fencers looking for the right opening before committing themselves. This absorbing game of brinkmanship lasted for three rounds before both fighters appeared to reach their conclusions and begin to reveal and implement their strategy. Hearns pumped out his long left jab with metronomic regularity, throwing it fractionally short in order to prevent leaving his chin exposed to Leonard's rapier-like counter punches. The Maryland fight prodigy's plan involved throwing a rich variety of right hands to the slim body of Hearns to weaken him for the later stages.

Leonard's body shots consistently fell short of their intended target and he attempted to recalibrate his sights. He dropped his head low and moved closer inside Hearns' long spearing reach to fire a two-handed combination of punches. Hearns immediately countered with a downward chopping right to the side of Leonard's unguarded head and then followed it up with a right hook to deposit Leonard on the apron. He looked stunned at the indignity and scrambled back to his feet to receive the mandatory eight count from Richard Steele. When the action resumed, more than half the round remained but Hearns, wild with bloodlust and revenge, stormed forward and pinned Leonard against the ropes, vainly trying to finish him off and exorcise his demons, but he lacked his customary composure and failed to land a telling punch.

In the next round, it was Leonard who recovered his poise first and he looked increasingly relaxed and comfortable with his antidote to the menace he faced. When the bell signalled the end of the round, he grinned broadly and winked at the retreating Hearns. When they emerged for the fifth session, the reversal in fortune appeared complete as Hearns took a hammering. One quick-fire right hand to his unprotected chin buckled his knees. Before he could quell the rising storm, Leonard unleashed a power-packed left hook flush to the side of his head and caused his legs to wobble again. When he was pinned against the ropes, he was forced to tuck up and defend a ferocious onslaught, which lasted for more than a minute. When he returned to his corner, Emanuel Steward wrapped his arms around Hearns. "This is what makes a great fighter," urged the master trainer. "This is what'll make you great." Hearns gulped in air, then reassured Steward. "I'm feeling great," he said.

Both fighters were now locked in a struggle to establish supremacy and they began to increase the size of the risks they were taking. They took turns to get on top but on each occasion, before they could pull away, the other would storm back and reel in the lead. The instructions from the camps were also changing. "This is a physical fight, Tommy," Steward told his charge. "Forget the boxing and fight the man." Leonard was instructed to attack both sides of Hearns' body and weaken his resolve. In the tenth, a beautiful arcing right cross opened a cut under Hearns's left eye whilst Hearns dominated the next round and issued a whiplashing volley of right hands to drop Leonard to the canvas again.

The twelfth round offered the final twist in this compelling contest. Leonard dug deeply into his reserves, determined to have the final word and leave a lasting impression with the judging panel. He attacked with one last all-out effort to try and finish Hearns, whose legs seemed determined to betray him. He looked spent and tried to halt the onslaught by merely pawing at his opponent to keep him at bay and to reassure referee Steele, who continued to look closely at the Detroit man until the bell ended the contest. Whilst an avalanche of appreciation tumbled down into the ring, Hearns smiled broadly whilst Leonard simply stared at Hearns in amazement.

The three men sitting in judgement were as divided as the watching millions. Jerry Roth voted in favour of Hearns by 113-112 yet Tommy Kaczmarek rated Leonard as the winner by the same margin. Dalby Shirley could not separate either man and scored it a draw, which determined the final decision. All three officials had given Leonard the final round, Shirley by a 10-8 margin, which clinched the drawn verdict.

Neither fighter responded with indignity when the decision was announced. Sugar Ray Leonard told the press pack that he wanted to watch the film of the fight to assess the accuracy of the scoring but accepted that both he and Hearns had, "showed that we are both champions." Hearns was equally sanguine. "You have to leave these decisions up to the judges and I respect their decision," he declared. "I'm proud that I boxed a draw. The judges could have ruled that I lost and so I leave here, thankful for what I have." His final words offered a glimpse into the real relief that he felt in exorcising an eight-year-old ghost. "You have no idea how often this man has been on my conscious," he said.

The decision, however, was far from popular, with a majority feeling that Hearns had done enough to win, not least because of the two knockdowns he scored. Judge Shirley later said that, on a general impression, he thought Hearns had won the fight, but he submitted his scorecards round by round and was surprised to discover he had the two men even at the end. Certainly Hearns looked and acted more like the winner at the press conference the next day, with Leonard appearing unusually subdued while Hearns seemed happy that, at the very least, he had restored his reputation. To his great credit, he refused to make a big issue out of the scoring, and perhaps for this reason there was not as much furore about it as there might have been. Both men again paid tribute to the other. "Tommy proved he was a real champ," said Leonard, while Hearns joked, "Ray, next time, don't fight me so hard!"

Where next for the Hit Man? Marvin Hagler at ringside said he would consider a Hearns fight for $20 million, a ridiculous figure that was never going to materialise, especially as the closed circuit figures for Hearns-Leonard had been disappointing. The company that organised the closed circuit lost money and its boss, Lou

Falcigno, said, "People didn't seem to care. And I think the same would apply to a rematch, or Duran or Hagler against Leonard. I think we have to wait for new and exciting fighters." The great era of Benitez, Duran, Hagler, Hearns and Leonard, the kings of the middle weight divisions, seemed to be drawing to a close.

# 16 GENERAL HEARNS

IT WOULD BE another eight months before the name Thomas Hearns was once again in the sports headlines, when the flamboyant tycoon Donald Trump announced that he would headline his Atlantic City promotion against Michael Olajide. Hearns's appearance alongside the effervescent Trump prompted the *New York Post*'s Phil Mushnick to deliver a withering assessment of both men in his paper's edition of 19 February 1990, under the headline, "Punch-Drunk Boxers No Match For Trump." Mushnick told his readers, "Although it is conceivable that he can still fight [...] at just thirty-one-years-old, Thomas Hearns is already showing unmistakably clear signs that he is punch drunk. Six years ago, Hearns was bright, alert and all together. Now he slurs his speech, which is spoken in an Ali-like whisper. His eyes roll around in his head and he frequently drifts off into unintelligible tangents." Mushnick continued, "All Donald Trump has to do is stop looking in the mirror and listen to the sound of something other than his own voice. Instead, he should listen to Hearns. What's a couple more shots to the side of Thomas Hearns' head if it means another nickel landing in Trump's pocket? That is surely Mr Hearns' problem but just as HBO underwrites the insidious ways and means of Don King, Showtime Network is underwriting Trump's latest self-absorbed 'sports' venture." He concluded by imploring New Jersey's boxing commissioner Larry Hazzard to intervene. "Match tape of Hearns' speech from six years ago to tape of his speech today or match photos of the look on his face then versus the look on his face now. Hearns doesn't need another hit in the head, Mr. Commissioner. On Hearns' fortieth birthday Donald Trump won't be there and Hearns won't know where *there* actually is."

This article prompted a welter of press calls for Hearns to bow out gracefully from the sport. They grew stronger when Ron Katz, the matchmaker for Top Rank promoter Bob Arum, revealed that Hearns had been having problems making the 168-pound super-middleweight limit and could be seriously weakened before facing Olajide. Hearns dismissed this as matchmaker's froth and hype and maintained that he was never more than just three pounds above the limit. Still, the furore over his physical decline would not abate. At a press conference, he had mistakenly dubbed the Taj Mahal casino, where the fight was scheduled to take place, as the Mirage, the new gambling palace in Las Vegas. It was later suggested that this slip of the tongue was down to Hearns's mischief rather than a sign of his mental fragility. Before he had agreed to fight Olajide, Stephen Gwynn, the owner of the Mirage, had dangled the carrot of a $10 million fight against Michael Nunn before him. This offer was withdrawn after Nunn scraped a tediously dull win over Marlon Starling. Hearns was annoyed that he was now only getting $1.5 million dollars for his efforts.

Liverpool-born and Vancouver-raised, Michael Olajide was five years younger than Hearns and boasted a record of twenty-seven wins in thirty-one outings, including two points victories over Curtis Parker and James "Hard Rock" Green, a pair of respected top ten operators. He had lost a decision to former Kronk fighter Frank Tate in a tilt for the vacant IBF middleweight title and had been knocked out inside five rounds by Iran Barkley. The latter loss sparked a bitter split with his trainer-father and he had come under the wings of veteran trainers Angelo Dundee and Hector Rocca, who revitalised his career and propelled him back to sixth in the world rankings. Olajide, who possessed the good looks of a male model, claimed that the canny Dundee had not only re-taught him rudiments like how to effectively block and slip punches but had also had a significant impact on more cerebral matters. "He's more like a psychiatrist; he has worked on my head," he said.

At the final pre-fight press conference, Dundee predicted that Hearns would get more trouble than he had hoped for and warned the press to accept Olajide's rating as a four-to-one underdog at their peril. The man who had guided the careers of Muhammad Ali, Sugar Ray Leonard and many other champions explained that they had prepared plans to upset and disrupt Hearns from building any kind of rhythm in their twelve-round championship fight. Hearns sat quietly alongside his challenger, smiling at the customary predictions, before reflecting, "Everyone in boxing might be a 'little star' but I am like a five hundred watt light compared to Olajide." Hearns refuted the press speculation about his allegedly deteriorating condition and warned his critics that they needed him more than he needed them. "Boxing needs me more than ever before because it is lacking superstars. There is no Mike Tyson walking around as the undefeated world heavyweight champion [he had been beaten by Buster Douglas in February] and the public are fed up of Ray Leonard coming to fight when he decides he wants to before he performs badly anyway. Besides me, there is no one else in boxing to excite people."

On the beautiful spring evening of 28 April, 1990, the fight referee, Tony Orlando called both combatants to the Taj Mahal's ring centre to issue his final instructions. His parting words, "Let's get this fight on," appeared to go unheeded by the challenger. When the opening bell sounded, both fighters ventured out of their corners cautiously, but Olajide in particular seemed content to circle and cover up whenever Hearns threatened to attack, real or feinted. In round two, Hearns increased the frequency of his attacks but couldn't connect with any telling punches, as his timing appeared to be slightly off. He smiled in wry amusement at the extreme caution of Olajide, who covered up furiously at the merest hint of an attack.

This pattern, of Hearns attacking without throwing any meaningful combinations whilst Olajide retreated at an alarming pace, soon began to frustrate the five and a half thousand spectators, who started to jeer and boo. The criticism spurred Hearns to try and lure the Canadian into a toe-to-toe punch-up but the intimidated challenger point-blank refused to take the bait. It was not until late in the fourth round that Olajide finally came out of his shell and scored with a right hand shot that troubled Hearns. Unfortunately for him, Tony Orlando ruled it a low blow and deducted a point as Hearns staggered to a neutral corner to recuperate.

Hearns was the only one who tried to make a fight of it. He came out and started to throw his heavy artillery to Olajide's slim body along with further right hands to the head. Despite his efforts, the spectators continued to heckle and express their disappointment but Olajide appeared impervious to their complaints. Whenever the challenger did come out of his defensive posture to land a punch, Hearns mockingly pretended to stagger to prick his opponent's pride, but to no avail. He began to hook off his left jab and landed to both the body and head but his punches lacked the sharpness to trouble his reluctant foe.

There was some excitement to lift the torpid fare in the ninth round when the Hit Man connected with a stiff right cross which dumped Olajide onto the canvas. He clambered back up at the count of seven and took the mandatory eight count from referee Orlando, but the shock seemed to galvanise him and for the first time in the contest, Olajide became aggressive and began chasing the champion, with some success. He scored with fast left hooks and then mocked Hearns by beckoning him to come and exchange punches. Despite breathing heavily and visibly tiring from the rigour of making the fight, Hearns responded and the final three rounds were enlivened by both men trading leather. Olajide scored with left hooks whilst Hearns responded with chopping right hands and the fans greeted each attack with acclaim. When the bell signalled the conclusion, Hearns was awarded the fight by the widest of margins. Judge Vincent Rainone gave it to him by 119-107, Samuel Conde-Lopez by 120-107 and Cesar Ramos by 119-110.

"Come on Ray, how about it? One more time ... please," he told the post-fight press conference at the Taj Mahal. "I'm looking to be a star," said Hearns. "I'm already a star, but I'm not that shining star, the one that stands out in front of everybody else. I want to be out there in the light, shining. There is new life for Thomas Hearns, another chance to once more rise above everybody else." It was clear, for all of his success, there was still a monkey on his back. "Hearns has always been considered *one* of the best rather than *the* best," said American boxing writer Nigel Collins. "It's a distinction that bothers him."

THIS DISQUIET IN Hearns soon manifested itself in a most unexpected way. Speculation arose about the breakdown of the long relationship between Hearns and Emanuel Steward. Although Hearns strenuously denied it, the *New York Times* reported that he felt his career was stalling after the Olajide contest. The report claimed that Hearns desperately wanted a third fight against Leonard but was frustrated that negotiations had broken down. It also suggested that a dispute had arisen over the size of purses available and Steward's forty per cent slice of them. The issue had been brought to a head by Steward's reported $4 million fee for the last fight with Leonard. Steward refused to comment on the *Times* report but Hearns merely stated that he expected to start training back at Kronk for his next contest in the near future.

In an interview conducted with respected Detroit boxing journalist, Lindy Lindell, Emanuel Steward was more candid about his feelings and his disillusionment with the state of the sport. He expressed disappointment at boxers he had nurtured from the beginning who had let him down and regretted that these experiences had left him "unable to trust anyone." Reflecting on his early coaching career, he said, "When I started the Kronk Boxing Team, it was a programme where everyone within depended on a kind of family-type of loyalty. It was only after I began to get involved with fighters who were not from the Kronk that I realised that this kind of situation didn't necessarily carry over. With the original guys like Jimmy Paul and Milton McCrory, the Kronk was their life and their families were involved as well, like satellite members of our team. This climate meant that we never looked at contracts very closely." Steward maintained that this relaxed approach to the legalities had been a mistake. "When we got involved with other fighters, we were lax from a business viewpoint. Most of the guys who came in, like [IBF welterweight champion] Tyrone Trice, were susceptible to listening to outsiders who would bend their ears. This is a problem common to the business of boxing. This creates jealousy and a bad atmosphere because fighters are very egotistical." The portents of discontent were evident in Steward's words and manner. He knew that the end of his eighteen-year relationship with Thomas Hearns was nigh.

The split, when it came, was a bitterly fought, protracted affair with both men appearing unwilling to take the final step and terminate their partnership. After the Olajide fight, Hearns was eager to press on and fight again quickly, and negotiations for a possible contest with Roy Jones, the IBF super-middleweight champion, began. Hearns was angered by Steward's confirmation of this to the press and his claims that he was haggling for a $3 million purse for his fighter. Hearns stated that he was personally conducting negotiations with Jones because Steward was otherwise engaged with his other fighters, leaving Hearns to negotiate, train and prepare on his own at the Kronk gym. "Emanuel tries to put himself out there in front and make it seem like he's doing everything and I'm doing nothing," Hearns said. "I want this fight, and, I want to show to him and to everyone else that I can go out and speak on my own behalf and have the ability of organising things for myself." Hearns had met Roy Jones near his Florida home and they had discussed boxing each other in the autumn of 1991, with Las Vegas their preferred venue.

Hearns was particularly aggrieved that Steward had been unavailable due to entering the training camp of heavyweight Lennox Lewis to prepare him for his bout with Ray Mercer. "It feels like Thomas Hearns has been on the back burner for a long period of time," he complained. "I think I am the main breadwinner but Emanuel is too busy training other fighters. He doesn't have time to train his own fighters. Instead, I have to look out for myself because the person I used to depend on doesn't have time for me." Yet he refused to confirm that he had split with his mentor, saying "I still have a lot of belief in Emanuel and I'm not closing the door." Though, ominously, he added, "Yet."

JUST WEEKS AFTER this statement, Hearns announced that he had ended his association with manager and trainer Emanuel Steward for "personal and professional reasons." He then shocked even the hard-bitten boxing hacks by declaring that the notorious Harold Smith, fresh from serving six years in federal prison of a ten-year sentence for embezzlement, and Dennis Rappaport, a boxing manager from New York, would now represent him. Smith, despite his record of having promoted major boxing tournaments with stolen money from one of the largest bank frauds in US history, had quietly obtained a boxing manager's licence in California the previous year. When Steward heard of this new arrangement, he struggled to conceal his bitterness. "How about that? Tommy has got himself a conman and a shyster," he sneered. Rappaport, who had previously managed the heavyweight contender Gerry Cooney among others, uttered one of boxing's immortal quotes when asked about his relationship with Hearns: "I don't want to tell you any half-truths unless they're completely accurate."

Although neither man would publicly confirm the reasons behind their divorce, insiders claimed that money was at the heart of the split, specifically Hearns's increasing resentment at the large amounts which Steward deducted from his purse money. "I get ten per cent as the trainer, which is standard in boxing," Steward would later explain. "And I was entitled to twenty-five per cent as his manager, which is the usual fee." Hearns, however, was quick to point out that these percentages were levied on his earnings of nearly $54 million, putting him among the top five highest paid fighters in the sport's history. Steward reminded observers of his early and unrewarded heavy investment in his fighters and claimed that this was merely his entitlement. His bitterness was palpable. "I can now safely say that Tommy Hearns was never a talented fighter," Steward said. "On four or five occasions, I thought that he was finished but each time I built him back up, got him ready for the next chance. I guess that he doesn't remember any of that. If so, then good riddance."

There was a desolate mood in Steward's Kronk gym as he recounted to friends his efforts to rekindle Hearns's career after each of his three professional defeats. He cited the occasion that he had paid $25,000 to help form the World Boxing Organization after the loss to Iran Barkley, in order to secure Hearns a fight with James Kinchen for the WBO super-middleweight championship. "Hearns had to have that title because we knew Sugar Ray Leonard would try to win a fifth championship," he claimed. "If Tommy didn't have that title, we couldn't have got such a huge purse of eleven million dollars for him." He claimed he had found it increasingly difficult to motivate Hearns for certain fights against weaker opponents, and had grown disenchanted with trying to secure bigger purse money for Hearns against such lightly regarded opposition. Hearns's final words to him, a week or so before, had been, "Nobody has ever managed like you but from now on, I want to manage myself."

The boxing fraternity quickly chose sides, with many of the sport's leading trainers rallying to their colleague's cause. Pat Petronelli, the co-manager of retired former champion Marvin Hagler, told the press, "Tommy Hearns has given up a great manager to go with one of the biggest conmen in the world." Sportswriter Shelby Strother said, "This sucker punch was a low blow from Hearns." And promoter Bob Arum was also quick to side with Steward. "This is monstrous," he blustered. "I love Hearns but he will never fight for me again. Not ever!"

Hearns responded to the public backlash by agreeing to an exclusive interview with Mike O'Hara of the *Detroit News*. It was to cause more recriminations. He started by explaining the reasons for the break-up. "Things have been going on for a few years and been building up to a point where I have now decided that I am tired of it and I don't want to deal with it anymore." He went on, "Emanuel would never be frank with me. He'd tell me things to pamper me, to satisfy me for the moment and I got tired of that. He'd talk about certain fights that were coming through but the truth was, he never even thought about doing it, like the [Roy] Jones fight." He dismissed Steward's claims that he only took his entitled thirty-five per cent cut. "My last fight against Leonard, Emanuel took almost forty-eight per cent. The fight grossed twelve million dollars and I received six and a half million dollars. Emanuel got the rest." He added, "I'm doing the fighting, not Emanuel." He claimed that he had not worked with a contract for the previous seven years. "Emanuel cannot talk about me being unfaithful when we have worked together for so long without a contract." He then stated, "I have always paid the thirty-five per cent to him but he suddenly boosted it up. Is that greed or what?" He then asserted, "Emanuel wants to be as big as I am."

He suggested that this move was a clear riposte to those who suggested he was unable to think for himself. "Emanuel wants to have control over his fighters but I am not one to be controlled." He also issued a strong rebuttal to the criticism of Harold Smith as his adviser. "I have heard that the people handling me are incompetent but this is not true. Harold Smith does not manage Thomas Hearns. Harold Smith is not my promoter. Thomas Hearns is his own manager and Thomas Hearns is going to do his own thing."

Finally, Hearns said that he and Steward had actually agreed that they should split up without any public animosity and without bad-mouthing each other. So he was disillusioned when he heard the criticism levelled at him from Steward and Kronk insiders. "I might have plenty of bad things to say but two wrongs don't make a right. I only hope that he gets satisfaction by doing this."

A MONTH AFTER confirming his decision to leave his spiritual home and mentor, Hearns accepted an invitation from the United Services Organisation to take a group of boxers to visit American troops gathered in Saudi Arabia for Operation Desert Shield, the impending assault to liberate Kuwait from the invading army of Saddam Hussein's Iraq. He solemnly declared the ten-day trip to be "the most important experience of my life." Brushing aside criticism that he was neglecting his preparation for a proposed fight against Virgil Hill, he argued, "American people need to support one another and show they care. These troops represent us, the American people and they are sacrificing their lives for us. This is just my way of saying 'Thank you.'" He joked that he wanted to offer his gratitude because, "They are not using boxing gloves in this battle and so I can't help in that way."

Hearns and his group visited bases and were surrounded by hundreds of troops wherever they went. They kibitzed with the military personnel, shook endless hands, posed for photographs and signed autographs. Hearns even sparred in a makeshift ring with a US Army sergeant. "He made the effort to come out here and see us – I respect him for that, and I'll never forget it," wrote one US airman. "I'm a fan for life – to hell with Sugar Ray Leonard!" On his return, a humbled Hearns said, "This is definitely my first real sign of just what I mean to people. People consider me a fighter. The men and women in that desert are the real fighters. I was able to come home after ten days; they had to stay and face the possibility of war everyday." In December 1990, he was made an honorary four star general by US commander General Norman Schwarzkopf, otherwise known as Stormin' Norman, in recognition of his support for the troops.

Once back in the relatively safe confines of Detroit, he busied himself training for his next assignment, an exhibition fight against James "The Heat" Kinchen at Detroit's Cobo Arena. Kinchen had previously lost a decision to Hearns after some worrying moments for the champion, when Kinchen had wobbled him. This time, Hearns explained that their contest had a dual purpose. He was hoping to show his adoring Detroit public that although he had left the Kronk institution, he would never lose his allegiance to his hometown. Secondly, the proceeds from the exhibition would benefit the city's homeless, specifically the Salvation Army and the Capuchin soup kitchen. "I love Detroit," Hearns told reporters, "There is no other city to live. Whenever I go someplace, after two or three days, I'm always ready to come home." Unfortunately, the exhibition had to be cancelled due to a stomach virus that Hearns had contracted on his tour to the Middle East.

During this period of exile from his Kronk kingdom, he also mused about the possibility of pursuing a future outside the ropes. He said that he would like to try his hand at the unlikely possibility of being a comedian. He also suggested that he would perform and record the rap song his jailed brother Henry had written, titled "DJs Make Me Dance." He said, "As soon as the exhibition fight is over with, I'm going straight to the studio and see how I actually sound on track. All I need is a strong beat behind me. If I get that strong beat, then I think I will be successful." He did not want to limit himself to just one career. "I might get a leading role in a movie someday, and I'll bloom after that. I like entertaining people. I like making people happy."

BUT BOXING REMAINED his priority. And when he decided on the man to assume Emanuel Steward's mantle, he sprang another surprise by selecting Alex Sherer, an unknown thirty-four-year-old former member of Steward's Kronk team, as his trainer. Sherer, a communications graduate from Ohio, had been working for the State of California as a public information officer when he met Steward in 1979. As a self-confessed boxing junkie who had fought as an amateur, Sherer was then coaching a Police Athletic League boxing team in Sacramento. He kept in frequent contact with Steward, and in 1983, the esteemed trainer offered him a job as assistant coach at the Kronk, where he would first encounter Thomas Hearns. Sherer acted as a scout for Steward, looking for talented young boxers around the amateur circuit and checking out prospective opponents for upcoming Kronk tournaments. Although he occasionally coached the Kronk's amateur boxers, he had little experience working in the corner of the professional ranks, and much less working in the rarefied atmosphere of world championship fights.

In 1989, he and Steward parted company in acrimonious circumstances and Sherer moved to Washington where he began researching the history of boxing and more specifically, the life of Ezzard Charles, his boyhood hero. He also applied to return to education and enrolled at law school. When he heard that Hearns had parted company with his long-time mentor, he telephoned the fighter to wish him luck. Ten days later, he professed himself "shocked" when Hearns approached him with the offer to replace Steward.

Hearns was attracted to the bookish Sherer for a number of reasons. Since Sherer was not obligated to any other fighter, Hearns believed that he had the time to devote his full attention to training him alone, a focus he felt had been sorely missing. Sherer did not disappoint and spent hours watching footage of prospective opponents and also watching Hearns's daily workouts, telling the fighter, "I'm always looking for an edge. A professor changes his teaching plans from day to day and I try to do the same thing." He even reviewed sessions when Hearns would only shadow box so he could "check his balance, his movement and rhythm and make sure that his hands come back in the proper position." There was also a financial motive for Hearns's decision. Sherer told reporters, "I don't think fighters need to pay their trainers or managers thirty to fifty per cent to simply pick up a telephone. I am being compensated fairly."

ON 11 FEBRUARY 1991, Hearns stepped into the ring for his first professional bout without Manny Steward in his corner. Alex Sherer had been instrumental in arranging two routine contests, against Ohio's Kemper Morton, a twenty-fight veteran, in Inglewood, California, and against Tennessee's Ken Atkins, in the more exotic location of the Aloha Stadium in Honolulu, Hawaii. Hearns routinely dismantled the hapless Morton with a beautiful left hook in round two, sending him into retirement before a good crowd of 8,134 – including rock stars Eddie Van Halen and Sammy Hagar – at the Great Western Forum. Afterwards, he took the ring microphone to present a generous $50,000 cheque to the USO in the Persian Gulf. "This little money's just a start," he said. "We're going to give a whole lot more." Six weeks later, he summarily despatched Atkins after the referee judged a third-round cut to be too severe to allow the fight to continue. Hearns was happy to be active, whilst Sherer declared himself satisfied that these two fights had sufficiently sharpened up his charge to meet the threat of Virgil Hill, his next opponent and an altogether tougher proposition.

Following his tune-up contests, Hearns exiled himself to Southern California, renting a house in Santa Monica. He used the Quake City gym as a training base for the latest chapter in his colourful career, and invited *Detroit News* boxing correspondent Mike O'Hara to his new home to discuss the changes. "It feels great being my own manager," Hearns told him. "It is a relief to know where everything is coming from and know where it is going." His entourage was remarkably similar to his old Kronk crowd and included the former world welterweight champion Milton McCrory, Hearns's younger brother Billy, and camp aides such as Arthel "Bam Bam" Lawhorne, another former Kronk teammate. Hearns said that their company helped but confessed that he hankered after Detroit. Whilst he accepted that he would never again wear the Kronk colours, he admitted that he missed training there with all of his friends. When he had met Emanuel Steward at the Mike Tyson versus Razor Ruddock bout in Las Vegas, he had approached him and tried to embrace him, but Steward refused to reciprocate his show of friendship. He extended an olive branch by admitting, "I regret the bitterness and the after-effects between me and Emanuel. It was not called for." He reminded him, "Together, we made each other a lot of money but we also had a lot of fun; a lot of cherished moments." But he was already looking to the future, not the past.

# 17 THE LIGHT-HEAVIES

VIRGIL HILL RETURNED home to North Dakota from the 1984 Los Angeles Olympic Games clutching a silver medal. He had narrowly lost to Korean Joon Sup Shin in the middleweight division final and, under normal circumstances, his medal success would have heralded a surge of interest from managers, promoters and the public. But following the welter of gold medals that had been captured by his countrymen at the same Games, Hill's silver failed to impress. As a consequence, he did not receive the bonuses and lucrative sponsorship and promotion of his more decorated teammates when he decided to turn professional.

Immediate evidence of this came on his debut, in November 1984, at the fabled Madison Square Garden, New York. Whilst the gold medal winners, including Mark Breland, Pernell Whittaker and Meldrick Taylor, were earning purses of around $40,000 for their early pro contests, Hill earned just $5,000 for beating Arthur Wright in the second round. He knew that his route to the top would be a long one.

Initially, he was promoted by Dan Duva's Main Events organisation, which had signed several Olympians. This exacerbated Hill's feelings of frustration, as he was not promoted with the level of intensity that he felt he merited compared to his more illustrious stablemates. He soon left and signed with Bob Arum's Top Rank, where he continued to improve and learn his trade. He remained unbeaten until he finally got a tilt at world honours, challenging Leslie Stewart for the WBA light-heavyweight crown in September 1987. Hill delivered the finest performance of his career against the Jamaican, destroying him in four one-sided rounds.

Once considered as one of the dullest divisions in boxing, the light-heavyweight ranks enjoyed a renaissance as Hill, Michael Moorer, Prince Charles Williams and Dennis Andries each held separate versions of the world crown. Hill extended his record to thirty consecutive wins, with eighteen early endings and eleven successful title defences, before he faced Hearns. Hill admitted that Hearns was a fight that interested him more than any other and took precedence over a match with Moorer to establish the division's premier fighter. The Hearns name carried more prestige and would earn him his biggest ever payday of $1.5 million, against Hearns's fee of $4 million.

This discrepancy in pay was one of a number of niggles which upset the champion in the pre-fight build-up. He felt that he was not afforded the respect he had worked so hard to obtain in his four years as champion. When he and Hearns were called together at press conferences, the media treated Hearns as the champion and dismissed Hill as a second-rate challenger. This discontent bubbled away quietly. Hill used it as motivational fuel but was unable to contain his disgust at the final Caesars Palace press conference. The traditional etiquette was for the champion to speak after the challenger had delivered his final words, but on this occasion the roles were reversed. To make matters worse, Kathryn Greene, widow of the legendary boxing agent and writer Ben Greene, interrupted the event to present the Ben Greene Humanitarian of the Year award to Hearns. "This is not the Thomas Hearns show," railed Hill. "Hearns is not the champion. I am and I think that you ought to remember that and treat me accordingly."

This demand for respect was not something which Hearns felt he needed to be reminded of. He appreciated Hill's ability and resolve and knew that it would take a sublime performance to wrestle the title from his grasp. He delivered a masterful performance which stripped away the years and the increasing signs of decay to unanimously outpoint Virgil Hill over the fight's twelve round duration. He battered the defensive specialist repeatedly with crisp, fast left jabs followed through with lightning-fast right hands to the head. The plan, according to *Boxing Monthly*, had been devised by Alex Sherer: Beat the champion at his own game. "So, Hearns concentrated getting off first and sharpest with the left jab, nullifying Hill's best weapon, and beating him to the draw with left hooks," reported the magazine. "When Hill countered, Hearns countered right back so that a puzzled, demoralised Hill was in the unhappy position of a fighter who couldn't get into his rhythm, couldn't make things happen to his advantage."

On three occasions, in the sixth, ninth and eleventh rounds, Hearns had Hill in dire straits, but each time the champion relied on his wiles to survive. The champ did land some good shots, particularly a left hook in round five, but told his trainer between rounds that he "couldn't get going" and Hearns generally dominated. The challenger crowned his performance in the twelfth round when he rolled back the ravages of age to crack Hill with three whiplash right crosses, breaking his nose and causing Hill to grope and claw at him to remain vertical.

Judge Chuck Giampa made Hearns the conclusive winner by 116-112, whilst judges Jerry Roth and Art Lurie agreed that he had won his fiftieth fight by the margin of 115-113. Ringside observers declared that it was his best fight in years. He hadn't been wobbled like his 1989 rematch with Sugar Ray Leonard. He had resisted getting careless and staring up at the overhead arc lights as he had against Iran Barkley and he avoided falling below his level of ability as he tended to against Mark Medal and Doug DeWitt, which turned out to be protracted struggles. Hill's presence had made Hearns totally focused, disciplined and sharp. He outboxed a boxer, outjabbed a jabber, and out-countered a counter-puncher to control the proceedings and dominate a champion who had reigned for four years and entered as a 4-1 favourite.

At the post-fight press conference, Hill's trainer Freddie Roach was an agitated presence, in contrast to his battered and bruised charge, who seemed to have taken his defeat with nonchalance. The respected Roach was visibly fuming because his fighter had not followed their detailed fight strategy. "Virgil Hill didn't show up," Roach told the packed meeting room. "He failed to execute the plan and let things happen that we didn't want to." He accused Hill of paying Hearns too much respect and was circumspect in praising the new champion too much. "I'm not sure whether Tommy was very good or Virgil was very poor," he mused.

The press was in no doubt. "Hearns turned back the clock to his glory days," said *Boxing News*. *Boxing Monthly* called it "a superbly executed win over a younger, previously unbeaten opponent." Phil Berger of the *New York Times* suggested, "Virgil Hill must have thought he was fighting a Thomas Hearns impersonator. Hearns was supposed to be a shot fighter yet he bewitched Hill with a consummate display of ringcraft." Mike O'Hara from the *Detroit News* wrote, "It was not vintage Hearns but his right-hand leads and vicious left hooks were hallmarks of his brilliant career," while Mike Marley of the *New York Post* said, "The youngest old man in the fight game, well-trained and following his new trainer, Alex Sherer's strategy, treated the champ like his name was Virgil Molehill." Hearns described it as "my most satisfying night in the ring." He said that it ranked as his greatest achievement in his long and illustrious career: "I'd have to put this one on top. This one here meant more to me than any other in the world. I opened a lot of people's eyes in the boxing world."

His own eyes were also opened when he sat down and reviewed the business side of his new arrangement. Vartan Kupelian, a *Detroit News* journalist, claimed that Hearns had saved an extra million dollars by terminating his relationship with Emanuel Steward. Paying his staff a salary as opposed to a percentage of his earnings had been a sound financial decision. His Detroit-based attorney, Brian Sullivan, told the press, "He doesn't do the detail work but he's not supposed to. He has attorneys and accountants to do that. What I will confirm is that Thomas Hearns is running a smooth, smart and thrifty operation."

After the fight, Alex Sherer was in demand. "It's like everything has changed," he said. "I'm no longer just an amateur coach anymore. One little fight and everybody recognises me." He was a hot item and other fighters wanted him to work his magic on them. Despite this, he was modestly refusing to accept any praise. "Everybody's looking at me differently and everybody's giving me credit. The truth is, I am working with a great athlete. He deserves all the real credit." Sherer was adamant that he would not tolerate the long periods of inactivity which had punctuated Hearns's final years at the Kronk gym. He expected his fighter to taste action at least twice more before the year was finished and speculation was rife that Bobby Czyz, the cruiserweight champion, and Evander Holyfield, the heavyweight king, were the two potential opponents. A win against either – highly unlikely in the case of Holyfield, dubious but not impossible in the case of Czyz – would have made Hearns a six-weight world champion. But he had other plans. He had unfinished business to attend to.

THOMAS HEARNS IGNORED all other potential options and insisted that he be granted the opportunity to avenge his loss to Iran Barkley. He had a score to settle and he agreed to offer his recently acquired WBA light-heavyweight championship as the bait to entice Barkley back into the ring. Once contracts were agreed, he announced, "It's payback time!" Alex Sherer was equally pleased. He viewed the rematch as an opportunity to prove his own credentials and show that he had eradicated the mistakes that Hearns had made in his first fight. "I have watched that first fight against Barkley over thirty-five times," Sherer said. "Tommy clearly dominated, to the point where Richard Steele was five seconds away from stopping it. Barkley is a tough guy to fight but it will be different this time. You will see left hooks and spectacular counter-punches," he promised. "I'm sure Iran will try to jump all over Tommy at the opening bell. He'll try to wage war. So a lot of our preparation has been spent on staying cool, on basic boxing."

Sherer had no time for those who said the Hit Man was finished. He believed that much of the apparent decline in Hearns was because he had gradually departed from the basic skills that had been fundamental to his spectacular early-career success. He had to find those skills again, to revert to what Sherer called "pure boxing." Whether it would be enough to blunt The Blade remained to be seen.

Barkley was also eager for the clash and the opportunity to resurrect his own career, which had gone into reverse after his spectacular and unexpected victory over Hearns. He had been beaten by Roberto Duran, Michael Nunn and Nigel Benn in consecutive showings before he had arrested the slide and scored a quick knockout of IBF super-middleweight champion Darrin Van Horn. True to form, he dismissed Hearns' reputation as a modern-day legend. "Legends?" he spat, "I want to do away with his legend. When the history books are examined, it will clearly show that only three guys knocked out Tommy Hearns: Leonard, Hagler and Barkley. Next to my name, it will state that Iran Barkley did it twice."

Barkley entered the ring looking as determined as any fighter ever had. With his shaven head, goatee beard and fierce scowl, he cut an intense figure as he prowled in circles around the canvas, while his trainer, Eddie Mustafa Muhammad, maintained a stream of shouts, exhortations and instructions. "With his shaved head, Fu Manchu-style whiskers and eyes squeezed nearly shut in anger, he had the chilling look of a Mongol warrior," said *Sports Illustrated*. He had to be restrained from attacking Hearns during the pre-fight instructions, and at the bell he drove into Hearns like a man possessed.

It is an unwritten rule of boxing that rematches are rarely as good as the first encounter but this was turned on its head at Caesars Palace on 20 March 1992. The fight was a classic. One year after being sensationally stopped in the first round by Britain's Nigel Benn, the thirty-one-year-old Barkley made a mockery of his recent form and maintained a steady stream of pressure on the champion. They fought at lung-bursting pace, with Barkley the aggressor throughout, as his corner spurred him on with shouts of "Fort Apache!" (the nickname of a notoriously dangerous district in the South Bronx). He gained his reward by scoring the only knockdown in the fight, when he dropped Hearns with a left hook in round four. Hearns sprung back up by the count of three but the extra point advantage Barkley gained would prove crucial.

The crowd of about 4,500 remained absorbed as Barkley punched, punched and repeatedly punched the arms, shoulders and most tellingly, the jaw in a bid to weaken the Hit Man. "He's dead, his legs are gone," shouted Barkley's cornermen as he bullied Hearns around the ring, but the Detroit man, who couldn't seem to find his rhythm or range, absorbed the blows and hung in there. Barkley's superior workrate proved to be enough to impress the three judges, Chuck Giampam, Jerry Roth and Lou Tabat, who awarded him the fight by a single point, 114-113. When he reflected on his narrow victory, a jubilant Barkley, who suffered a broken jaw and ribs, said, "People said he'd got dead legs. That's a bunch of bull and I can't take nothing away from that man, he's a great champion. I knew Hearns wasn't going to quit on the night but, hopefully, he will now."

"The decision could have gone either way," rued Hearns. "I fought a bad fight. I did not use my style. I fought the way Iran wanted, he knew the inside fight. No excuses, I felt pretty good. I can't take anything away from Iran Barkley, but if I decide to come back – let's do it again, baby."

Detroit boxing writer George Puscas, a longtime admirer of Hearns, lamented his eclipse. "When last seen by his saddened following, Thomas Hearns was the embodiment of a boxing cliché. He stood on the dais, his face lumped and swollen, at Caesars Palace in Las Vegas, having lost a fight and his world light-heavyweight championship. But, as they say, you shoulda seen the other guy. Iran Barkley, the new champion, choked out a few words, and then his handlers took him to a hospital, where X-rays discovered he was suffering with a cracked jaw and several broken ribs." Puscas didn't intimate that Hearns should retire, unlike the majority of sportswriters.

And a few days later, Hearns faced the press at an arranged conference in Detroit and surprised the gathered journalists when he announced that he was *not* retiring from the sport. He now blamed his performance and defeat on his damaged right hand, which he claimed was an unfortunate legacy from his slugfest with Marvelous Marvin Hagler. "Ever since that fight," said Hearns, "I've fought with an aching right fist which felt like an electric shock going through my hand and up my arm." He believed that further opportunities to win world honours were attainable if he could fire his punches with full force. He claimed to understand the concerns about continuing but reassured his admirers, "The boxer knows best what he's got left and I want a seventh world title."

Others, however, believed that, far from the boxer knowing best, he was often the last person to make a sensible decision about his own future. "For whose benefit does Tommy Hearns fight?" asked Jon Saraceno in *USA Today*. "Has anybody told you, Tommy, that your speech has become increasingly slurred in recent years? Do you understand that concussive head blows result in cumulative brain damage? Do you realize brain tissue is not regenerative? It takes courage to step off the stage, the kind of 'want-to' you displayed in the ring." Was Hearns suffering from the condition known as pugilistica dementia? Certainly there seemed to be no medical proof and no boxing commission withdrew his licence.

IN THE SUMMER of 1992, Thomas Hearns began preparations to pump up in weight and slim down his management team. The first casualty was the controversial Harold Smith, who had been a mysterious figure in the Hearns camp following the split with Emanuel Steward. Although his duties were never publicly specified or sealed with a contract, he had acted as a go-between with promoters and had handled Hearns's training logistics. The split was attributed to a series of events that occurred before the defeat to Iran Barkley. Hearns was furious to discover that Smith had negotiated himself a fee with fight promoter Bob Arum for his help in putting the match together.

With Smith gone, trainer Alex Sherer agreed to take an expanded role in the running of Hearns's career. He handled the negotiations for an October clash with the WBA cruiserweight champion Bobby Czyz and obtained a guarantee for a purse of $1.5 million dollars. He also insisted that Hearns should box twice in tune-up bouts before meeting Czyz and follow the formula that had secured him a historic win over Virgil Hill. Sherer believed that a subsequent nine-month absence from the ring had critically blunted his edge and skewed his timing, leading to the lacklustre display against Barkley.

Just as negotiations looked close to completion, the Czyz fight suddenly collapsed. Hearns attended a charity event in California, where he told the attendees that he was expecting to return to Detroit and sign the waiting contract. Rumours emanating from his camp, however, suggested that Czyz had shocked them by demanding $5 million. This unexpected development was a huge disappointment to Hearns, who was dismayed at Sherer's inability to secure his ring return. This sparked an irreversible decline in their relationship as his absence from the ring continued. Sherer was keen to build on his profile by working with other boxers in his California base, and he and Hearns eventually agreed to part company in an amicable manner. Alex Sherer would go on to coach Michael Moorer to the IBF heavyweight championship and Jorge Paez, the former featherweight champion, before he succumbed to a lung disease and died at the tragically young age of forty-two, in 1997.

DURING A TWENTY-ONE month absence from the ring, Hearns fathered a baby boy, had an operation to repair the troublesome bones in his right hand and then stunned the boxing world by announcing that he had "made his peace" with Emanuel Steward and would be returning to his Kronk home. He was ready, he said, for his "second coming." Speaking to journalist Rebekah Brown, he said: "I have a second time around. There's not been another man to do the things I've done. I'm still King of the Block. ... I'm the king. Because God made Thomas Hearns. ... And I know that I've been blessed. Sometimes we sit back and wonder why God gave us all the gifts that we have. I did. But I knew I should use them. I'm living in my Detroit home raising my son now, and it's a blessing to see him grow every day. It's made me realize what I have." Whether he and Steward could rekindle the old magic remained to be seen, especially as Hearns still had six metal pins in his hand to hold the healing bones together.

When he finally returned to action, he faced Andrew Maynard, a former top-class amateur who had won an Olympic gold medal at the 1988 games in Seoul. Maynard had turned professional in February 1989 with Ray Leonard as his manager and racked up twelve straight wins to capture the vacant North American Boxing Federation light-heavyweight championship. This success convinced his over-ambitious management team to pitch him in against Bobby Czyz but he was cruelly exposed and flattened in seven one-sided rounds.

He then went on a six-fight winning streak, stopping shopworn legend Matthew Saad Muhammad in 1991 and setting up a fight with Frank Tate for the NABF light-heavyweight title. Tate crushed him in the eleventh round. The following year, he moved up to cruiserweight to challenge WBC title holder Anaclet Wamba, who knocked him down and won a unanimous decision. Maynard continued to fight, but gradually faded into obscurity. He saw the November bout with Hearns as an opportunity to arrest this slide against a high-profile opponent but Hearns viewed it as a safe option. His stunning first-round knockout of Maynard at Caesars Palace justified his decision. Victory was followed three months later with a bout against Dan "Pastor" Ward, from West Memphis, for the NABF cruiserweight title. Ward was dispatched in the first of a scheduled twelve rounds at the Las Vegas MGM Grand.

Three weeks later, on 19 February 1994, a galvanised Hearns went to Charlotte, North Carolina, to defend his belt against Puerto Rican Freddie "The Rock" Delgado. Hearns agreed to the fight because Bobby Czyz was on the show's undercard and he believed that it would whet the public appetite for their proposed match-up. The Hit Man scored a knockdown in the first round when he landed a right cross to the forehead, but Delgado returned the attack with interest and landed a stunning right in the next round to deck the Detroit great. This prompted Delgado to seize the initiative and assume the role of aggressor. They both traded flurries of punches and each took turns threatening to floor the other. Hearns turned the momentum in the ninth when he pressed the attack, snapping Delgado's head back on his shoulders with stiff jabs. He cut Delgado under both eyes and wrestled back control to win a unanimous points decision.

It would be another thirteen months before Hearns fought

again. This time he was due to fight Sean McClain for yet another world title, the lightly regarded World Boxing Union cruiserweight crown. But a week before their bout, scheduled for 31 March 1995, McClain pulled out, unable to make the weight. Emanuel Steward scoured his extensive boxing network to find an acceptable replacement and the name thrown up by his detective work was one Lenny "The Rage" LaPaglia, a little-known fighter from Chicago who claimed a respectable record of thirty-seven victories and eight losses. LaPaglia was on a hot streak, having knocked out nine opponents in ten victories, and was stunned but excited at the opportunity to face a boxing legend at Detroit's Fox Theatre.

The Chicago fighter talked up his credentials. "I will have the natural power advantage over Hearns because he is not a genuine cruiserweight," be said. "He's just a natural light-heavyweight and I am a very hard puncher and I don't think he can handle my punching power." Warming to his task, LaPaglia speculated that he would relish his role as a giant slayer. "He's a great fighter, but he's past his prime," he said. "It's time for him to go. I'm looking forward to having a good fight with Tommy and putting on a good show in the process."

Despite this being his first outing in a year, Hearns's drawing power was not on the wane. A clutch of celebrities took their seats at ringside, including city mayor Denis Archer, the Detroit Tigers/Red Wings owner Mike Ilitch, media heavyweight Bill Bonds, heavyweight champion Lennox Lewis and Pistons power-forward Terry Mills, as well as ten thousand local fans, who gave their thirty-six-year-old hero a rapturous ovation as he began his ring walk. They didn't seem to care much about the quality of opposition he faced and the thirty-six-year-old Hearns looked sensational as he opened up with a ripping left hook to drop the outclassed LaPaglia in the very first round. The challenger scrambled to his feet but was deposited back by a right-left combination. As he regained his equilibrium, he looked like a man about to head to the gallows. Hearns was as cool as an executioner as he calmly stepped forward and administered the final blow to record the fight's third and final knockdown after just two minutes and fifty-five seconds of the opening round. The Hit Man had claimed an unprecedented seventh "world" title.

Afterwards, Hearns beamed as he thanked the fans. "I could hear the people hollering," he said. "I could hear their support. People love me and I love them." He acknowledged that this was just one step towards the title that he claimed the fans really wanted him to pursue and he mused on the range of options opened to him, including meeting the other kings of the cruiserweight class, Alfred Cole, Orlin Norris and Anaclet Wamba, or even returning to super-middleweight to meet Roy Jones or James Toney.

Four months later, Hearns was scheduled to open the Foxwoods Casino in Connecticut by topping the bill in a ten-round contest against Uganda's Franco Wanyama. Contractual issues forced the encounter to be relocated to Detroit's Cobo Arena before it was then moved for a second time to the Joe Louis Arena, where it would be broadcast on the nationally televised *CBS Sports Show.* Just three days before the bout, Hearns pulled up during a routine sparring session and complained about a pain in his ribs. After an immediate diagnosis, it was identified as a "contusion" to the left side of his ribcage. Despite his disappointment, Hearns decided not to risk the fight and jeopardise future world title opportunities by getting beaten, looking bad or failing to attract a sizeable crowd, which would lessen his allure to the marketing men. The fight and bill were cancelled.

# 18 PROMO MAN

EVEN THOUGH HE showed no inclination to retire, Thomas Hearns knew that he was nearing the end of a long, glorious road, and had been giving some thought to what he might do when his career was over. Boxing was in his blood, and so promoting contests seemed a natural progression for him. To test the water, he decided to promote his next fight, against Earl Butler at Auburn Hills, Michigan. He included Bronco McKart, the top-ranked junior middleweight, on his first promotion, which was intended to launch what was dubbed "Thomas 'Hit Man' Hearns' Knockout Tour," a twelve-city tour where young fighters would meet other aspiring young boxers in evenly matched contests. "This is a great opportunity for young guys to get noticed and recognised," Hearns said. "If they win, they'll keep on going on the tour, which is similar to a tournament." Manager Jackie Kallen, who doubled as tour director, had four of her own fighters on the first bill. "We're hoping to develop a potential champion by the end of it," Kallen said. "The good thing is that fans will get to see top fighters from across the nation and know how good they are."

Hearns confirmed that promoting was an avenue he might pursue seriously once his own boxing career was finished. "I'm enjoying it and I like the opportunity to help young boxers," he said. "This will keep them active and it gives me an opportunity to stay in the sport I love." He also wanted to offer a decent alternative to the current batch of promoters. "I know from my own experience of dealing with promoters that I can do things differently and give the fighters something more than other promoters are giving them." He did admit, however that he found the transition harder than he had imagined. "The toughest thing is dealing with the boxers themselves," he revealed. "If they get up on the wrong side of bed, they're tough to deal with. They all have their own particular needs that need to be taken care of and it can cause you headaches."

Junior Earl Butler was a fully-fledged heavyweight from Phoenix, Arizona, who had recently slimmed down to cruiserweight to meet Michael Nunn in a fight he lost on points. Three months later, he faced Hearns in a ten-round bout at The Palace, Auburn Hills. Hearns turned from his promoting duties to discuss the fight and said that, despite losses to Nunn and to NABF cruiserweight champ Edgerton Marcus, Butler was a confident fighter who could give him trouble. "I know in my own mind though that I won't let that happen," Hearns smiled. "You guys are going to see the Thomas Hearns of the eighties."

Hearns also exchanged insults via the media with Roy Jones Jr., regarded by many as the best pound-for-pound fighter then active and someone he would have loved to cross swords with. "If he had come along in the eighties," said Hearns, "he'd have been chewed up and spit out by Ray Leonard, Marvin Hagler and Roberto Duran. He definitely was another notch in my belt." The twenty-six-year-old Jones, who was due to defend his own super-middleweight title, responded, "If he [Hearns] had come along in the nineties, he'd have been slaughtered."

Plagued by trouble with his fists for much of his career, Hearns looked as if he was continuing to suffer the effects during his contest with the bullish Butler, as he scrapped and battled his way through ten rounds to record a unanimous points victory. Hearns had already put his foe onto the canvas on three separate occasions when, in round six, he stepped forward and delivered a three-punch combination of right-left-left hook. The combo rocked Butler but, before he could press home his advantage, Hearns flinched and then beat a retreat. He had hurt his hand again and would win the rest of the contest by boxing off the back foot and keeping Butler on the end of his jab.

Afterwards, he chose to pay tribute to his durable opponent and claimed that he couldn't understand what had kept Butler upright because he had hit him harder than he had ever landed before. The media was unimpressed, with the *Chicago Sun-Times* describing Hearns as "long past his best days in the ring." More significantly for the Detroit man, his proposed series of knockout tournaments was placed in jeopardy by the disappointingly low crowd of just five thousand who came to support the initiative.

A further blow came in December when USA Network, the cable company that had vowed to show Hearns's contests, pulled the plug on his next proposed fight, in January 1996. In a withering report, the hard-hitting *New York Post* columnist Phil Mushnick wrote, "Last week, we reported that the bosses at USA Network were losing their minds because they had agreed to allow thirty-six-year-old Tommy Hearns, who is gradually losing his mind, to fight on USA on the 23rd January. Whilst it is too late for Hearns, USA's insanity proved temporary. On Wednesday, the cable network's new VP for production, Gordon Beck, announced that USA had reached a sane and charitable decision. The Hearns bout, which would have been his second in four months on their network, has been cancelled." He concluded his article with the blunt assessment, "Tommy Hearns has taken far more than one too many punches and USA no longer wishes to be party to his diminished capacity."

OPPORTUNITIES FOR THOMAS Hearns were growing scarce. The view that he should follow the lead of his peers, Sugar Ray and Marvelous Marvin, and enjoy the fruits of his labour in retirement continued to grow. Hearns refused to accede and maintained that he could and would continue to operate at world level. He kept in training but it was fourteen months before he would return to action, when he travelled to the boxing outpost of Virginia's Roanoake Civic Centre to meet Karl Willis, an uninspiring Tennessee cruiserweight. Willis had started his professional career in a promising manner by recording a one hundred per cent record in his first twenty contests, before he was brutally knocked out by Denmark's Ole Klemetson, which dented his fragile confidence and condemned him to a career on the sport's fringes, where he enjoyed sporadic success. The night he faced Hearns was not destined to be one of those bright spots. He appeared in awe of the reputation of the fabled big-punching Hit Man and the five rounds which preceded the inevitable knockout were one-way traffic, with Hearns using Willis as a punchbag.

Hearns entered 1997 with a determination to fight with a greater frequency. In January, he returned to Inglewood, California, to dismantle "Irish" Ed Dalton. Hearns rarely moved out of first gear as he opened up the outclassed Alaskan-born fighter at will and eventually forced the local referee to step in to halt the slaughter just before the end of round five. Hearns declared himself satisfied but noticed a change in the attitude of those around him, who urged him to re-consider his continued involvement in the sport. They were led by Emanuel Steward. The trainer assured him that they all had his best wishes at heart and it caused Hearns to stop training for a while and spend a long period of isolated reflection in the bosom of his family.

Nearly two years later and a month after celebrating his fortieth birthday, Hearns had resolved to embark on one final assault on the summit. He would start it back where it all began, in the Cobo Arena, Detroit, and persuaded his old team to remain loyal and back him up. His opponent was thirty-seven-year-old Toledo-based Jay Snyder, who had adopted the unmistakeable nickname of the

"Swamp Man." It would also be the first boxing tournament to be staged by Kronk 11, a new promotional venture led by Emanuel Steward. Headlining the six-bout undercard was Tom "Boom Boom" Johnson, a former IBF featherweight champion. Another feature was the International Women's Boxing Federation featherweight championship between Beverly Szymanski and Gena Davis. Steward had managed to woo Mills Lane to referee and obtain former Channel 7 news mega-star Bill Bonds as the ring announcer.

Snyder had a modest record of nineteen wins and five losses. At the pre-fight press conference, he declared his love for his opponent. "I grew up hearing the name of Tommy Hearns and his rivals Sugar Ray Leonard and Marvin Hagler. These guys, and especially Thomas, were legends to me." He said the opportunity to step into the same ring as the Hit Man was "a big honour for me, my family and the entire state of South Carolina. I am here to help Tommy on his comeback trail and he should consider me a friend." Snyder was equally accommodating when the contest began in front of 5,000 loyal fans. Hearns's first meaningful punch, a straight right hand, came eighty-eight seconds into the first round. As it connected, Hearns himself was thrown off balance and was grazed by a flailing punch from Snyder, causing them both to hit the canvas in sync. Hearns bounced up immediately while Lane knelt beside the prostrate figure of his opponent, who never looked like beating the count.

When Snyder recovered, he told ringsiders, "Power is the last thing a fighter loses and he has still got it!" Hearns smiled his thanks and was quickly swallowed up by friends and handlers, who crowded around and chanted, "Hit Man's back!" long into the night.

# 19 TWILIGHT

IN THE SPRING of 1999, Thomas Hearns brought his fading talent to Europe for the first time since his amateur days. That April, he fought on the undercard of boxing's latest rising star, Prince Naseem Hamed, in front of 18,000 fans at the MEN Arena in Manchester, many of them eager to get a live viewing of the famous Detroit Hit Man. He was boxing against another American, "Mister" Nate Miller, who hailed from Philadelphia and who had briefly risen from his status as one of the game's journeymen to stop Bert Cooper in seven rounds to capture the NABF cruiserweight championship.

The English fight fans gave him a rapturous ovation when he was called to the ring but he failed to live up to it as he plodded and laboured to a dubious points decision to capture the meaningless International Boxing Organisation cruiserweight championship. It was a sad footnote to the night that, long before the conclusion of the twelve rounds, many spectators chose to leave the arena rather than watch their memories of a once great champion being tarnished. The crowd did not heckle or boo; their respect was too sincere for that. But the contrast between the warrior who had been involved in some of the sport's greatest tussles and the pale shadow before them seemed even starker given that it was seven years since one of his fights had last been broadcast in the UK – against Iran Barkley. Few had seen how sharply he had declined and it was all the more shocking when revealed. "Maybe it is time to admit that life as a boxer does not begin at forty," acknowledged Emanuel Steward. He vowed that he would speak with Hearns about his options.

The discussions between trainer and fighter concluded with the agreement that Hearns would box at the Joe Louis Arena in Detroit for the very last time. He would, once again, feature on the October undercard of a Prince Naseem Hamed defence, against Cesar Soto; Hamed was now being tutored by Steward. But though it was announced at a press conference that Hearns would feature on the bill, it was also revealed that an opponent had not yet been secured. Eventually, Hearns had to be withdrawn after his discussions with promoter Cedric Kushner foundered. He agreed to fight English cruiserweight Crawford Ashley, but refused to accept $150,000. Hearns felt that this was around $100,000 short of his expectations. He reassured his supporters that he would bow out in style with a title fight.

In April 2000, Thomas Hearns held yet another press conference to announce that, after a swansong, he would retire from the sport he had graced for twenty-three years. The opponent for his last hurrah was to be a fellow veteran, thirty-nine-year-old Uriah Grant, at the Joe Louis Arena, Detroit. He had again been supposed to fight Crawford Ashley, but once more complications around the agreed purse (this time Ashley was unhappy with the amount offered) meant that Grant, from Jamaica, was called up as a late replacement just three weeks before the bill.

The Detroit fans flocked to buy tickets to give their prodigal son the send-off he merited, and 10,000 were sold in the week leading up to the fight. They did not anticipate the embarrassment which ensued when Hearns suffered a severe ankle sprain at the end of the second round. He limped back to his corner grimacing in pain, and Emanuel Steward was compelled to ignore his pleas to be allowed to box on and retired him on his stool. The charged, emotional crowd turned ugly and, amid a crescendo of booing and jeering, debris rained into the ring, sparking skirmishes to erupt at ringside. Hearns took the microphone and begged the fans to stop. He apologised and vowed, "This won't be my final fight."

In the sanctuary of his dressing room, he was calmer and more reflective. He told reporters that he had to discuss his future with his family before he made any more decisions. Steward was less composed and asked Hearns in an emotional conversation, "Everything has to end sometime, but does it have to end like this?" He later told Ronald Hearns, Thomas's oldest son and a promising junior at Washington University, that he wouldn't want his father's career to end the way it had, through injury. "He is a champion who deserves far better." However, he did admit, "I don't know if the public would really want to buy a second 'final' fight."

IN FEBRUARY 2001, Hearns and Steward appeared in London to launch a new transatlantic venture: the Kronk UK Gym. Situated in the Kentish Town area, it would take over the home of the well-established St Pancras boxing club and was intended to train both amateur and professional boxers. "I started at the Kronk 1969," said Steward. "I get the same feeling here as I had then. There is a lot of talent in London and Kronk UK is all about finding that talent. This is not about signing professional boxers, this is about finding Olympic champions. When I saw all the amateurs I wanted to take my jacket off and go to work. I saw a lot of effort but boxers everywhere, especially amateur boxers, need top-notch sparring. That is what makes the difference. The Kronk way is the hard way but it is my way and it makes champions."

He had that right. Steward by then had worked with around thirty world champions, from Kenty and Hearns, his first champs, to Lennox Lewis, Michael Moorer, Julio Cesar Chavez, Oscar De

La Hoya, Evander Holyfield, Mike McCallum, Aaron Pryor and Leon Spinks: all had been trained by Steward. It was an extraordinary achievement for the former electrician from Detroit Edison. Steward said the UK venture would be a long-term investment and that he planned to be in London four or five times a year to take control of the team and would also take boxers over to Detroit on exchange trips. "My dream will be to get a Kronk USA boxer and a Kronk London boxer in an Olympic final," he said. Hearns was by his side, dapper as ever in one of his numerous sharp suits, and according to one newspaper "could not resist hitting the punchbag made in the distinctive colours of the Kronk's yellow and gold." Also there was Marvin Hagler, and the two kidded around like old friends.

In 2004 a similar venture opened in Northern Ireland. Again Hearns was at Steward's side, wowing the Irish crowds and signing a slew of autographs, as they arrived to officially open the new Belfast Kronk Boxing Gym. The future looked set fair for the Kronk, described by one newspaper as "the second most recognisable name in boxing" after Muhammad Ali.

That same year, Ronald Hearns turned pro under his father's guidance after a brief amateur career. Ronald had been discouraged from boxing by his father until he had completed his college education but had always been a talented athlete, representing the American University basketball team as a junior guard. He formally adopted his father's surname in 1999, a name that obviously carried much resonance in the ring. With Thomas guiding him, he was soon putting together an impressive number of early stoppage wins, shades of the old Hit Man himself.

But Thomas Hearns had not quite hung up the gloves. The "second final fight" Steward had referred to five years earlier finally took place in July 2005. In the intervening period, Hearns had kept himself in decent shape with occasional returns to the Kronk, and during all of that time, his last engagement had been a source of constant irritation. "There's a lot of fire built up inside of me," he told the *Detroit News*. "It's the same way it was when I started boxing." He sought to extinguish that flame by stepping into the ring of the Cobo Arena to dismantle the unthreatening Missouri journeyman, John Long in nine rounds. This finally seemed to salve the ache caused by the Grant debacle and he initially declared himself content to slink away into the shadows.

That winter brought the surprising news that Hearns, a dutiful parent, had been arrested and charged with the misdemeanour assault and battery of his thirteen-year-old son. The police had arrived at Hearns's Southfield house at about 6:45 p.m. on New Year's Day after receiving a 911 call from his wife Renee, who complained that there had been a domestic dispute. Detective John Harris said the boy, who was not named because he was a juvenile, had a swollen eye and a small cut on his chin. Hearns had apparently told the boy to go to another room; when he refused, there was a scuffle. However, said, Harris, Hearns and his wife gave slightly different accounts of how the boy was injured. The police took Hearns into custody and he was arraigned before a magistrate the following day, where he was charged and released on $10,000 personal bond, on condition he would have no contact with his son. He was warned that he faced up to ninety-three days in jail and a $500 fine.

When Hearns finally appeared in court before Judge Sheila Johnson, he pleaded "no contest" to the charge and was sentenced to probation for the incident. In the courtroom, he was accompanied by Renee, who sat a few feet away, and looked humble and contrite. "The only thing I would like to say is that the last three weeks of my life, have not been the best three weeks of my life," he told Judge Johnson. "I've learned something and I will not do it again." The judge said the police report indicated that Hearns and his son had become involved in an altercation during which Hearns pushed his son and struck him once in the face with an "open-handed slap." Police reports indicated that the teenager had disobeyed his father's directive to turn up a thermostat in a cold bedroom where he was playing a computer game. "You are a dutiful parent and have always taken an interest in your children," Judge Johnson told Hearns. "This was an unfortunate, bad situation and hopefully something was learned and it would not happen again. Children have to realize there are times they have to be disciplined. And parents have to act in appropriate manner when they do and not let the heat of the moment decide it."

The incident was uncharacteristic of Hearns, who had no criminal record. After an embarrassingly public airing of his domestic life, Hearns expressed his relief at being sentenced to nine months probation, $515 in court fees and fines, two days' community service and compulsory attendance to parenting and anger management classes. Oakland County Assistant Prosecutor Keri Middleditch described the ruling as, "Just and typical, considering the circumstances of the case."

During the court case, Hearns had kept himself in good physical condition and after it was concluded, he decided to put his hard work to use for one last time. On 4 February 2006, the famed Hit Man fought his last fight. His opponent was Shannon "Sand Man" Landberg, from Indiana. The Sand Man was on a rare nine-fight winning streak in his undistinguished seventy-nine fight career. The last rites to the Hearns journey were administered at The Palace, Michigan. As expected, Hearns laboured to a plodding, pedestrian victory over ten rounds. In the tenth, Thomas Hearns jumped from his stool and for two minutes, he worked his left jab with precision, his footwork was sublime and graceful and his famed right hand worked like a missile. He created the impression that time had stood still and he was the phenomenally talented, fearsome and sublimely skilled athlete of yesteryear, as he summoned his resources to stop the hapless Landberg. But in truth it was just an illusion. After his victory had been officially declared, Thomas Hearns stepped out of the ring for good.

THERE ARE FEW happy endings in boxing. At the beginning of 2006, due to deep budget cuts, the city of Detroit threatened to close down the Kronk. Steward immediately launched a fundraising campaign to raise the estimated $500,000 a year needed to keep the centre going. He managed to draw in a large pledge from an online casino, but then the gambling site backed out. In September 2006, the gym closed temporarily after thieves stole copper pipes, cutting off the water supply, and adding to the long list of repairs needed to keep the place open. The boxers relocated to the Dearborn branch of Gold's Gym. The cost of fixing the plumbing and making other major repairs led officials to decide to make the gym's shutdown permanent, and on 28 November 2006, the unthinkable happened: the Kronk officially closed.

At the beginning of 2007, a high profile fundraiser was held at Detroit's Fisher Building in a bid to raise the cash to reopen the gym. Actor Sylvester Stallone even pledged money. Unfortunately it wasn't enough. While the Kronk team continues at another Detroit gym, the latest plan for the original building is to renovate it as part of a $50 million development offering affordable housing to senior citizens, families and retired boxers. The *Detroit Free Press* reported in October 2009 that Emanuel Steward had been joined by city officials on a walkthrough of the building to see whether it made sense to fix up the site in what was dubbed the Kronk Village project.

In February 2009, veteran trainer Walter Smith died at the age of ninety-four. The quiet, dependable stalwart had been as much a part of the Kronk as anyone. "Walt made you want to train hard," Hearns recalled at the funeral. "He'd come by the house for roadwork early in the morning. He'd blow his car horn once and if you didn't respond he'd come up and knock on the door. If you wanted to sleep in, you couldn't. Walt was always there." Just a couple of weeks later, Mickey Goodwin, one of the original Kronk stars, was found dead at his home at the age of fifty-one. It seemed he had suffered a stroke and fallen down stairs. Mickey got up, but later died from his injuries. It seemed an era was drawing to a close.

Enduring, through it all, were Hearns and Steward. Still a team, still a class act. Retirement is not a concept Hearns recognises. Always a doer, rather than a talker, he keeps active, not least with the career of his son Ronald, a 6ft 3in light-middleweight who, at the time of writing, had a 22-1 record, with seventeen inside-the-distance wins. And when he makes his numerous public appearances, it is clear that he is still not far off fighting weight, and could still fight a round or two if needed. The gleam is still in the Hit Man's eye.

Thomas Hearns was unquestionably one of the best pound-for-pound fighters of the modern era. As one of the Five Kings during an era of unprecedented talent in the welterweight and middleweight divisions – the others being Benitez, Duran, Hagler and Leonard – he featured in some of the most skilful, exciting contests of the past fifty years. For sheer drama, his primeval clash with Hagler may never be bettered. Perhaps, like many boxers, he fought on too long and in the end took too many punches, but he did what he wanted, and his legacy is secure. And for all the indelible images he has left behind, many will remember best the beanpole bomber who came out of the meanest streets of the meanest city in America and turned the boxing world on its head. As no less an authority than the late, great Joe Louis said, "I've never seen a welterweight punch like Hearns. Nobody, not even heavyweights, hit that fast or that hard."

# 20 THE LEGACY

IN ORDER TO place Thomas Hearns's career within its proper perspective, a number of seasoned boxing observers were asked to reflect upon the fighting life of the Detroit champion. Lindy Lindell, the veteran Detroit journalist, was there at the beginning of his career and followed his progress throughout:

*Thomas Hearns was a great fighter. The word "great" is all too-often used by sports journalists and commentators who, understandably, get caught up in sensational moments; one has to refrain from using the term, to quote William Wordsworth, when recording "emotion recollected in tranquillity."*

*What are the standards for greatness? My answer: to perform at an optimal level while at one's peak. Number of wins and knock-outs count for little. Championships count for little more. Hearns has won more world championships than any other man, a fact that is almost meaningless in modern-day boxing now that more than 100 world championships are available, whereas only eight classifications and champions existed until the 1960s. Henry Armstrong's accomplishment of being the featherweight, lightweight and welter-weight champion at the same time is a greater accomplishment in my estimation than Hearns winning multiple belts.*

*Hearns has put great stock in the amount of world championship belts he has won. He won a version of the cruiserweight belt in 1999 and told Emanuel Steward that he wanted to win one more world title belt before retiring. The sound of a Hearns retirement had been echoing in boxing's hallways and corridors by this time and Steward had been hearing their disconcerting noises and listening to them, but Tommy Hearns, while he may have been hearing, certainly wasn't listening. Steward's response to Hearns was, "Okay, so you win another belt. What then? At that point, you'll want to win another belt. When does it stop?" For this Hearns had no answer. In fact, to this day he still persists with telling fans he wants just "one more."*

*These depressing considerations have nothing to do with greatness or a lack thereof. Few of the greatest bowed out either not horizontal or thoroughly beaten. Fewer still have won their last fight. Fighters speak of winning their last fight, going out on a winning note. This happens so infrequently that one can say that it doesn't happen.*

*In the final accounting, Hearns should be accorded one of the greatest fighters among a handful of great fighters of the first half of the 1980s – along with Larry Holmes, Hector Camacho, Sugar Ray Leonard, and Marvin Hagler. Roberto Duran, a great fighter for much of the 1970s, decreased in effectiveness in the 1980s due to additional poundage and a certain slackness in training regimen, though he was able to give Hagler a moneysworth fight.*

*While Hearns deserves inclusion in this group, he is exceeded in greatness by Leonard and Hagler because both stopped him, albeit after mighty struggles. Hearns went on to effectively defeat Leonard in 1989, but the final round in that encounter was a demonstration that, as they rocked each other, these were two boxers beyond their prime. While there were extenuating circumstances with Hearns losing to Leonard and Hagler via the stoppage route, he was stopped in both.*

*The great fighters share the asset of courage, and in this regard Hearns was unequalled. He never took a ten count, though he was put flat on his back by both Hagler and Iran Barkley. As Pat Putnam of* Sports Illustrated *once told me, "Hearns has balls the size of schoolroom world globes." His chin, much deprecated by pundits and those jealous of his success, was very good, but not up to the level of Leonard or Hagler. Hagler was never knocked out or stopped and Leonard wasn't stopped until his final two, ill-advised comeback fights.*

*Muhammad Ali was the greatest heavyweight champion since Joe Louis because he fought and beat ten world champions, some of whom were at their peaks when he fought them. Against this standard, therefore, Tommy Hearns was great, but no one would call him "The Greatest."*

**Claude Abrams, editor of the long-established *Boxing News:***

*Those gunbarrel eyes, as Thomas Hearns set his stare so meanly on his opponent, matched the explosiveness of his weaponry. He had arms and legs like a spider and those who entered his web did so at their own peril. Hearns was a master boxer as well as a chilling puncher. He was electrifying to watch, for so few boxers have ever hurled punches with such force and accuracy and great pace whilst always retaining an extraordinary measure of composure.*

*I grew up on Hearns. He thrilled as well as dazzled. There was always excitement in the air. He brought drama to the sport during the Eighties, a magnificent time for welterweights and middleweights. Of course, he lost the really important fights – at welterweight against Sugar Ray Leonard in 1981 and the middleweight to Marvin Hagler less than four years later.*

*The Leonard match, unification for the WBC and WBA belts, was a true boxer-puncher classic between two mighty champions, whereas the intense Hagler showdown was absolute war for three rounds, the likes of which I had never seen before or witnessed since. Although Hearns eventually convinced Leonard to fight him again, at super-middleweight, Tommy was denied victory despite flooring his great nemesis twice and settling for a draw. Morally, Hearns had won. Leonard fought him only because he was convinced, like many others, the Hit Man was there for the taking. But Hagler walked away in 1987 after losing to Leonard and left Hearns with little to satisfy his craving for another bite at the Marvelous one.*

*Hearns was forced to make his mark in other ways, which he did, by winning the WBC middleweight title in another blaster, against Argentina's Juan Domingo Roldan. Then Hearns went to super-middleweight to capture another belt and twice at light-heavyweight he was crowned world champion, beating a classy boxer in Virgil Hill and Hill's opposite, the clumsy but incredibly brave and strong Dennis Andries. Winning "world" championships in six divisions is a remarkable achievement (although Hearns claims at cruiserweight are to be taken less seriously) but it's the fights Tommy was in rather than what he accomplished that left an indelible impression on his admirers.*

*Aside from the above mentioned bouts, there were three particularly destructive nights I shall never forget, two-round demolitions against Roberto Duran and Pipino Cuevas and a first-round annihilation of the then-undefeated James Shuler. Hearns's punching was faultless against Duran, who had never been knocked out. But "Hands of Stone" was sent flat on his face, out for the count, from a right to his bearded jaw that reverberated through the speakers of my television set as though someone had fired a gunshot.*

*Against Cuevas, when Hearns won his first belt, it was different. This was an announcement to the world of what Hearns was about. Cuevas was respected, fearless and a long-reigning champion. He was renowned for his durability. Hearns's telescopic right had his legs dancing frantically from a blow to the chin.*

*And then there was the Shuler dissection. Shuler was a touted former amateur, a disciple of the late great trainer Eddie Futch. This was Hearns's first fight after losing to Hagler a year earlier. Many saw Hearns as a stepping stone for Shuler. How wrong they were. I recall watching this one on the big screen via closed circuit. The cameras went to Hearns's dressing room beforehand. He'd cut off those fancy curls and looked an imposing, menacing figure – all business. That's precisely what Hearns was about. He set about Shuler with remarkable confidence and poise, giving an exhibition as to how to fight a taller man and break him down to the body before finding the eye of the needle with a straight right. The finishing shot was so perfect that Shuler crumbled on to his back and was counted out. That was 1986 and the commotion that followed, with Hagler beating John Mugabi on the same show, was for Hearns to face Hagler again. But Hagler had other ideas. Marvin talked rematch again later in 1987, after Hearns had bombed Roldan to defeat in four rounds, but I suppose Hagler couldn't get motivated. He wanted Leonard.*

*Nonetheless, Hearns, whether winning or losing, went on to feature in some classics, like the first fight against Iran Barkley, who Tommy hit with everything and busted up badly on the way to what seemed an inevitable stoppage before walking on to an amazing right that finished him. Barkley was one man Hearns just couldn't get the better of – I was ringside for their rematch in 1992, nearly four years after the first clash.*

*I also saw Hearns when he outpointed Michael Olajide at super-middleweight in 1990, though in truth the Hit Man wasn't the fighter he once was. That spark had disappeared. The moves that once flowed so effortlessly were now being forced. Still, it's evidence of his prowess and great talent that Hearns could still conquer at the highest level, though it saddened me to see him fighting on long after his best.*

*I prefer to remember him in those welterweight/light-middle/middleweight days. He was an expert marksman and craftsman. If ever a nickname fitted it was the "Hit Man," but Hearns had another side to him that was underappreciated and Tommy knew it.*

*For a short period he went back to pure boxing, which was how he established himself in the amateurs, and dropped the Hit Man moniker for the "Motor City Cobra." He wasn't as exciting, but I could watch Hearns jab and move all day. His blend of jabbing and punching against Ernie Singletary was a masterclass. There was also the ruthless manner in which he massacred Fred Hutchings in three rounds after Hutchings had knocked out Britain's Kirkland Laing, conqueror of Duran. And his classic against Wilfred Benitez, the Puerto Rican defensive master. That was the perfect clash of styles – long-armed puncher against hands-down boxer.*

*Whether Hearns is remembered as one of the greats or regarded as the best of his time is a matter of debate, but it's beyond dispute that he was hugely watchable, incredibly courageous, and thunderously hard-hitting, and featured in some of the most memorable events in history.*

**Graham Houston, former editor of *Boxing News* and *Boxing Monthly*:**

*One thing that always struck me about Thomas Hearns was the sense of drama he brought to his fights. When Hearns entered the ring, our sense of expectation was heightened and we were rarely disappointed.*

*It seems unusual in this day and age, but Hearns's early fights were not televised even though he was blowing away everyone put in the ring with him. He was much talked-about in the American boxing fraternity but only those able to attend his fights in person had actually seen him.*

*My first look at Hearns came in his fifteenth fight, when he stopped Clyde Gray, the Commonwealth champion and a three-*

*time world title challenger, in the tenth round at the old Olympia Stadium in Detroit in January 1979. Hearns had never been past four rounds but he showed he could fight at a fast pace and punch just as hard in the later rounds as at the outset of a fight. He not only outpunched the capable veteran Gray but he outboxed him. I realised that night that I had seen a special kind of fighter, and the following years were to show just how special.*

**Ted Sares, respected boxing historian and author:**

*For me, Tommy Hearns represented pure malice and danger for his opponents. With a great jab, superb body punching (see the Barkley and Shuler fights for evidence) and one-punch knockout ability in his straight right (as Pipino Cuevas will testify), he was a killing machine.*

*His unusual body structure gave him that kind of persona. His legacy should include the fact that he brought electricity into the ring every time he stepped into it, because you knew he was capable of wreaking mayhem on his foes, as in the James Shuler demolition and the Roberto Duran icing. Yet, when he needed to box, he could do that as well, as he demonstrated against Virgil Hill and Sugar Ray Leonard. His three rounds of unmitigated fury with Marvelous Marvin Hagler will always remain a part of his legacy as one of the most exciting fighters I have ever seen.*

**Hank Kaplan, American boxing historian (died December 2007):**

*Tommy Hearns was always bound for greatness. When I first saw him knocking out his early opponents, I wondered how he would perform against a higher calibre of opponent. He more than answered my early doubts in the following years. A fighter can only beat the best in the era that he is fighting and apart from his fights against Sugar Ray Leonard and Marvelous Marvin Hagler, he showed he was among the best.*

*The manner in which he won his first world championship against Pipino Cuevas is a memory I cherish. He had a few blips, but most great fighters go through those setbacks. It is how they recover and come back that sets them aside from the rest. Tommy Hearns proved his courage and belief. He was one of the great ones. His legacy is there in the record books for all to see.*

**Wayne Wilson, Canadian boxing historian:**

*Tommy Hearns is quite rightly regarded as one of the greatest punchers of his era. However, it was his stylish boxing that most impressed me. He scored only seven early wins in 163 amateur bouts and as a professional he outboxed Wilfred Benitez and Virgil Hill, two of the classiest stylists of that time. He would also have won a twelve-round decision over Sugar Ray Leonard in their first fight if it had been fought under today's rules.*

*He was a man who could box brilliantly as well as punch with terrific power. It was the textbook boxing that set up the knock-outs for Hearns. Tommy was a memorable fighter who was also one of the most exciting fighters of his time.*

**George Zeleny, former editor of *Boxing Monthly* and *Boxing Outlook*:**

*It's nearly twenty-five years since Thomas Hearns literally collided with Marvin Hagler at Ceasars Palace, Las Vegas, for three of the greatest rounds in boxing history. That fight tends to define both men, but as Hagler won, his reputation has continued to grow over the ensuing years. Perhaps the same can't be said of the loser.*

*It was the era of the Fab Four – Hearns, Hagler, Sugar Ray Leonard and Roberto Duran. They all fought each other in significant bouts. The charismatic Leonard is already regarded as an all-time great. He beat Hearns in a pulsating fight in 1981 but their rematch four years later has often been overlooked. Despite being knocked down twice, Leonard was "awarded" a draw after twelve rounds. To most observers, the Motor City Cobra looked decidedly unlucky. But the Leonard legacy is given, especially as he came out of retirement to beat the formidable Hagler. Meanwhile the brash and aggressive Duran seems to be regarded as everyone's ultimate fighting man and constantly figures in those regularly compiled lists of The Greatest Fighters Ever.*

*It is with Duran that the real Hearns legacy lies. In 1984, Tommy defended his WBC light-middleweight title against the Panamanian. Despite being thirty-three years old, Duran was still a remarkable fighter. After losing to the unheralded Kirkland Laing and slick Wilfredo Benitez, the supposedly washed up Duran had won the WBA light- middleweight title against Davey Moore in a huge upset at Madison Square Garden. He then took Hagler to a close fifteen-round decision seven months ahead of meeting Hearns.*

*But that June 15 in Las Vegas saw Hearns annihilate Duran in a chilling fashion. The final right hand that deposited Roberto onto his face in the second round was a brutal testament to Tommy's power. It was the only time in his long career that Duran was knocked clean out. Hearns had so dominated his opponent, dropping him twice in the first session, that Roberto looked headed for the knackers' yard. It is a measure of Hearns's triumph that five years later Duran was able to beat Tommy's own nemesis, Iran Barkley, for the WBC middleweight title in* Ring Magazine's *fight of 1989.*

*Both men boxed on for far too long. Only a serious car accident managed to de-rail Duran in 2001 and he retired at the age of fifty. The Hit Man followed a similar course. He managed to win rather meaningless WBU and IBO cruiserweight titles before hitting the buffers in 2006 at the age of forty-eight.*

*But to recall Thomas Hearns at his zenith, just remember that crunching right hand that rendered old Hands of Stone motionless under the clear Las Vegas sky in the summer of '84.*

# THOMAS HEARNS'S PROFESSIONAL BOXING RECORD

## 1977-2006

### 1977

| | | | |
|---|---|---|---|
| 25 November | Jerome Hill | W KO 2 | Detroit |
| 7 December | Jerry Strickland | W KO 3 | Mount Clemens |
| 16 December | Willie Wren | W KO 3 | Detroit |

### 1978

| | | | |
|---|---|---|---|
| 29 January | Anthony House | W KO 2 | Detroit |
| 10 February | Robert Adams | W KO 3 | Detroit |
| 17 February | Billy Goodwin | W RSF 2 | Detroit |
| 17 March | Ray Fields | W RSF 2 | Detroit |
| 31 March | Tyrone Phelps | W KO 3 | Saginaw, Michigan |
| 8 June | Jimmy Rothwell | W KO 1 | Detroit |
| 20 July | Raul Aguirre | W KO 3 | Detroit |
| 3 August | Eddie Marcelle | W KO 2 | Detroit |
| 7 September | Bruce Finch | W KO 3 | Detroit |
| 26 October | Pedro Rojas | W RSF 1 | Detroit |
| 9 December | Rudy Barro | W KO 4 | Detroit |

### 1979

| | | | |
|---|---|---|---|
| 13 January | Clyde Gray | W RSF 10 | Detroit |
| 31 January | Sammy Ruckard | W RSF 8 | Detroit |
| 3 March | Segundo Murillo | W RSF 8 | Detroit |
| 3 April | Alfonso Hayman | W Pts 10 | Philadelphia |
| 20 May | Harold Weston | W RSF 6 | Las Vegas |
| 28 June | Bruce Curry | W KO 3 | Detroit |

| | | | |
|---|---|---|---|
| 23 August | Mao De La Rossa | W RSF 2 | Detroit |
| 22 September | Jose Figueroa | W KO 3 | Los Angeles |
| 18 October | Saensak Muangsurin | W RSF 3 | Detroit |
| 30 November | Mike Colbert | W PTS 10 | New Orleans |

**1980**

| | | | |
|---|---|---|---|
| 3 February | Jim Richards | W KO 3 | Las Vegas |
| 2 March | Angel Espada | W RSF 4 | Detroit |
| 31 March | Santiago Valdez | W RSF 1 | Las Vegas |
| 3 May | Eddie Gazo | W KO 1 | Detroit |
| 2 August | Jose Pipino Cuevas | W RSF 2 | Detroit |
| | **(Won WBA World welterweight title)** | | |
| 6 December | Luis Primera | W KO 6 | Detroit |
| | **(Retained WBA World welterweight title)** | | |

**1981**

| | | | |
|---|---|---|---|
| 25 April | Randy Shields | W RSF 13 | Phoenix |
| | **(Retained WBA World welterweight title)** | | |
| 25 June | Pablo Baez | W RSF 4 | Houston |
| | **(Retained WBA World welterweight title)** | | |
| 16 September | Sugar Ray Leonard | L RSF 14 | Las Vegas |
| | **(Lost WBA World welterweight title)** | | |
| 11 December | Ernie Singletary | W PTS 10 | Nassau, Bahamas |

**1982**

| | | | |
|---|---|---|---|
| 27 February | Marcus Geraldo | W KO 1 | Las Vegas |
| 25 July | Jeff McCracken | W RSF 8 | Detroit |
| 3 December | Wilfred Benitez | W PTS 15 | New Orleans |
| | **(Won WBC World light-middleweight title)** | | |

**1983**

| | | | |
|---|---|---|---|
| 10 July | Murray Sutherland | W PTS 10 | Atlantic City |

**1984**

| | | | |
|---|---|---|---|
| 11 February | Luigi Minchillo | W PTS 12 | Detroit |
| | **(Retained WBC World light-middleweight title)** | | |
| 15 June | Roberto Duran | W KO 2 | Las Vegas |
| | **(Retained WBC light-middleweight title)** | | |
| 11 September | Fred Hutchings | W RSF 3 | Saginaw, Michigan |
| | **(Retained WBC World light-middleweight title)** | | |

**1985**

| | | | |
|---|---|---|---|
| 15 April | Marvelous Marvin Hagler | L RSF 3 | Las Vegas |
| | **(For WBA, WBC and IBF middleweight titles)** | | |

**1986**

| | | | |
|---|---|---|---|
| 10 March | James Shuler | W KO 1 | Las Vegas |
| 23 June | Mark Medal | W TKO 8 | Las Vegas |
| | **(Retained WBC light-middleweight title)** | | |
| 17 October | Doug Dewitt | W PTS 12 | Detroit |

**1987**

| | | | |
|---|---|---|---|
| 7 March | Dennis Andries | W TKO 10 | Detroit |
| | **(Won WBC light-heavyweight title)** | | |
| 29 October | Juan Domingo Roldan | W KO 4 | Las Vegas |
| | **(Won vacant WBC middleweight title)** | | |

**1988**

| | | | |
|---|---|---|---|
| 6 June | Iran Barkley | L TKO 3 | Las Vegas |
| | **(Lost WBC middleweight title)** | | |
| 4 November | James Kinchen | W PTS 12 | Las Vegas |
| | **(Won vacant WBO super-middleweight title)** | | |

**1989**

| | | | |
|---|---|---|---|
| 12 June | Sugar Ray Leonard | D 12 | Las Vegas |
| | **(For WBC and WBO super-middleweight title)** | | |

**1990**

| | | | |
|---|---|---|---|
| 28 April | Michael Olajide | W Pts 12 | Atlantic City |
| | **(Retained WBO super-middleweight title)** | | |

**1991**

| | | | |
|---|---|---|---|
| 11 February | Kemper Morton | W KO 2 | Inglewood, California |
| 6 April | Ken Atkins | W TKO 3 | Honolulu |
| 3 June | Virgil Hill | W Pts 12 | Las Vegas |
| | **(Won WBA light-heavyweight title)** | | |

**1992**

| | | | |
|---|---|---|---|
| 20 March | Iran Barkley | L 12 | Las Vegas |
| | **(Lost WBA light-heavyweight title)** | | |

**1993**

| | | | |
|---|---|---|---|
| 6 November | Andrew Maynard | W TKO 1 | Las Vegas |

**1994**

| | | | |
|---|---|---|---|
| 29 January | Dan Ward | W KO 1 | Las Vegas |
| 19 February | Freddie Delgado | W Pts 12 | Charlotte |

**1995**

| | | | |
|---|---|---|---|
| 31 March | Lenny LaPaglia | W TKO 1 | Detroit |
| 26 September | Earl Butler | W Pts 10 | Auburn Hills |

**1996**

| | | | |
|---|---|---|---|
| 29 November | Karl Willis | W KO 5 | Roanoke |